WRITING ACROSS TIME IN THE TWELFTH CENTURY
HISTORICAL DISTANCE AND DIFFERENCE IN THE KAISERCHRONIK

LEGENDA

LEGENDA is the Modern Humanities Research Association's book imprint for new research in the Humanities. Founded in 1995 by Malcolm Bowie and others within the University of Oxford, Legenda has always been a collaborative publishing enterprise, directly governed by scholars. The Modern Humanities Research Association (MHRA) joined this collaboration in 1998, became half-owner in 2004, in partnership with Maney Publishing and then Routledge, and has since 2016 been sole owner. Titles range from medieval texts to contemporary cinema and form a widely comparative view of the modern humanities, including works on Arabic, Catalan, English, French, German, Greek, Italian, Portuguese, Russian, Spanish, and Yiddish literature. Editorial boards and committees of more than 60 leading academic specialists work in collaboration with bodies such as the Society for French Studies, the British Comparative Literature Association and the Association of Hispanists of Great Britain & Ireland.

The MHRA encourages and promotes advanced study and research in the field of the modern humanities, especially modern European languages and literature, including English, and also cinema. It aims to break down the barriers between scholars working in different disciplines and to maintain the unity of humanistic scholarship. The Association fulfils this purpose through the publication of journals, bibliographies, monographs, critical editions, and the MHRA Style Guide, and by making grants in support of research. Membership is open to all who work in the Humanities, whether independent or in a University post, and the participation of younger colleagues entering the field is especially welcomed.

GERMANIC LITERATURES

Germanic Literatures includes monographs and essay collections on literature originally written not only in German, but also in Dutch and the Scandinavian languages. Within the German-speaking area, it seeks also to publish studies of other national literatures such as those of Austria and Switzerland. The chronological scope of the series extends from the early Middle Ages down to the present day.

Managing Editor
Dr Graham Nelson, 41 Wellington Square, Oxford OX1 2JF, UK
www.legendabooks.com

Writing Across Time
in the Twelfth Century

Historical Distance and Difference in the Kaiserchronik

❖

CHRISTOPH J. PRETZER

l

LEGENDA

Germanic Literatures 25
Modern Humanities Research Association
2022

Published by Legenda
an imprint of the Modern Humanities Research Association
Salisbury House, Station Road, Cambridge CB1 2LA

ISBN 978-1-83954-019-6 (HB)
ISBN 978-1-83954-020-2 (PB)

First published 2022

The publication of this book was generously supported by the Zeno-Karl-Schindler Foundation.

Copy-Editor: Dr Alastair Matthews

CONTENTS

❖

To
Bernadette,
Jeremias, and Helena

ACKNOWLEDGEMENTS

❖

I am greatly indebted to my supervisor, Dr Mark Chinca, whose sage advice, circumspect counsel, and constructive criticism were indispensable for finishing the thesis on which this book is based. I also wish to express my gratitude to my examiners Prof. Christopher Young, whose feedback proved very valuable, and to Dr Sarah Bowden, who has in so many ways continued to encourage and advise me much beyond her official role. My thanks also extend to Prof. Nora Behrend for her input after my first year and to Prof. Sarah Colvin for reviewing my work at the end my second and third years. Special thanks go to Ulrike Balser, secretary of the Cambridge German and Dutch Department, to Tessa Milne, graduate secretary of Corpus Christi College, and to Michael Martin and Aldona Maliszewska-Tomlin, Leckhampton site managers, all of whom made Cambridge feel like home. I am thankful to the Arts and Humanities Research Council, the Tiarks Fund, and the Master and Fellows of Corpus Christi College for providing me with the funds necessary for postgraduate study at the University of Cambridge.

For the privilege of seeing my thesis transformed into a proper book, I am indebted to the Zeno Karl Schindler Foundation, which generously supported the publication with a Walter Haug Stipend. I owe a great deal of gratitude to Prof. Ritchie Robertson, who accepted my manuscript for the Germanic Literatures series, and to Dr Graham Nelson, managing editor at Legenda, for the fruitful collaboration in difficult times of pandemic uncertainties. In particular, I wish to thank Dr Alastair Matthews, whose rigorous copy-editing greatly improved my manuscript, and Dr Anna Davies for taking on the daunting task of indexing the book.

Additional thanks go to Dr Helen Hunter, Dr Johanna Dale, and Dr Thomas Förster from the *Kaiserchronik* project, without whom working on the *Kaiserchronik* in Cambridge would have been a much lonelier experience. My way would never have led me to Cambridge in the first place had it not been for my academic teachers at the University of Bamberg. Far too many to mention them all, first of all I would like to to thank Prof. Ingrid Bennewitz and Prof. Klaus van Eickels for their support, and in particular Dr Andrea Grafetstätter and Dr Detlef Goller, who taught me everything. Many conversations with friends and colleagues over the years have helped to shape and develop this book, often without them being aware. To all of them I wish to extend my gratitude, but I am especially grateful to Prof. Nigel Palmer, Prof. Michael Stolz, Prof. Annette Volfing, Dr Ciaran McDonough, Atlanta Rae Neudorf, and Dr Ayla Lepine for proofreading my draft chapters at various stages of production.

None of this would have been possible without the unconditional love, support, and trust of my family. My parents Raimund and Edith enabled me to pursue Medieval Studies in the first place. My brothers Benedikt and Valentin dutifully fulfilled their fraternal obligations to keep me grounded with irreverent pop culture references. Finally, my wife Bernadette's part in this book cannot be overstated. Never would it have occurred to me to apply for a position at Cambridge to begin with, and never would I have brought the project to a conclusion without her in my life. It is to her and to our children, Jeremias and Helena, that this book is dedicated.

C.J.P., August 2021

ABBREVIATIONS

❖

AL	*Annolied*
AXL	*Alexanderlied*
Dt. Chron.	Deutsche Chroniken
EE	*Erec et Enide*
ER	*Eneasroman*
KC	*Kaiserchronik*
MGH	Monumenta Germaniae Historica
RUB	Reclams Universal-Bibliothek
SS	Scriptores (in Folio)
SS Rer. Germ.	Scriptores Rerum Germanicarum in Usum Scholarum Separatim Editi
SS Rer. Merov.	Scriptores Rerum Merovingicarum
TS	*Trierer Silvester*

Do not compare me unfavourably
with the pyramids of stone;
I surpass the other pyramids [...]
for I was made out of bricks,
which were formed of mud,
which was collected from a pole it had stuck to,
when the pole was plunged down into a lake.

— Inscription on the pyramid of Asychis
      (Herodotus, *Histories*, II. 136)

INTRODUCTION

❖

In April 1825, the English art connoisseur and critic Andrew Marbot finally arrived in Rome. Unlike most of his contemporaries, he maintained a somewhat reserved distance from the ancient ruins, as his biographer Wolfgang Hildesheimer reported. Subsequently, when writing about his impressions, Marbot summarizes them in the most sober manner:

> Everyone I meet here builds themselves their own city from the ruins and lives in the era of their own choosing. I too like to look at ruins, but I see them for what they really are: elements that do cast doubt on the past and thus the present, but do not elevate the past toward the absolute, let alone the ideal. For me the present is not prolonged past but a state of mind that one would sometimes wish to leave behind, if it were possible. [...] Rome lives from the past, as it attracts droves of foreigners who wish to enjoy this past and turn everything into the present.[1]

The Romantic gentleman who so succinctly captures the fascination that Rome's ancient heritage exerted for the European imagination is uniquely qualified to make this statement, as he has the advantage of being entirely fictional. Andrew Marbot is the creation of his alleged biographer Wolfgang Hildesheimer.[2] His own fictionality aptly mirrors the artifice of the image the Roman ruins conjure up. Nevertheless, his concise analysis of Rome as a ruined repository for contemporary desires and a quarry from which to construct an era of one's own choosing resonates powerfully within Western cultural history. As Hildesheimer creates Marbot, he climbs on the shoulders of generations of authors who turned to the Roman past to create meaning for their own times.

The first time this happened in German writing was nearly seven hundred years before Marbot's fictitious arrival in Rome, in the middle decades of the twelfth century, in a rather peculiar text known to twenty-first-century Medieval German Studies as the *Kaiserchronik*.[3] Probably written by one or more anonymous ecclesiastics somewhere in the south-east of the Empire — scholarship habitually

---

1   Wolfgang Hildesheimer, *Marbot: Eine Biographie* (Frankfurt a. M., 1981), pp. 243–44; my translation.

2   A creation so convincing that it fooled J. P. Stern, who reviewed Hildesheimer's book without realizing Marbot's non-existence ('Sweet Sin', *London Review of Books*, 4.14 (1982), 3–6 <https://www.lrb.co.uk/v04/n14/jp-stern/sweet-sin> [accessed 25 October 2017]).

3   *Die Kaiserchronik eines Regensburger Geistlichen*, ed. by Edward Schröder, MGH Dt. Chron., I.I (Hanover, 1895). I use *KC* to refer to the text of this edition and 'Schröder' to refer to the introduction and notes therein.

points to Regensburg — the text is the first chronicle in the German vernacular.[4]
Starting with the foundation of the Roman Empire, the *Kaiserchronik* quickly
establishes an episodic structure, with each episode dedicated to the name and
rule of an emperor. Beginning with Caesar, this sequence traces the history of the
Empire from its beginnings all the way through Constantine and Charlemagne, and
down to Conrad III and the events of the year 1147, where it stops.

As the first German vernacular text to devote itself explicitly to the task of
writing history, the *Kaiserchronik* for a long time fell between the disciplinary
demarcation lines of History and Literary Studies. The apparent clash between
the chronicle's vociferous claim to veracity, formulated in its prologue and
elsewhere in the text, and its content, which mostly covers legendary, apocryphal,
hagiographical, and mythological material, has led to a certain puzzlement among
scholars who have tackled the text. Compared to the established historiography,
both modern and medieval, of the events that the chronicle covers, much of the
Kaiserchronik's historical account is confused, muddled, and downright wrong. This
also gave rise to the notion that there must be some metastructure hidden inside
the text and some magic hermeneutical key that just has to be applied correctly in
order to unlock the *Kaiserchronik*'s historiographical programme.

Hence, the problem of the *Kaiserchronik*'s account of history has been the object of
a rich, long, and often complex scholarly discussion. Before I develop my approach,
it will be helpful first of all to retrace the scholarly discourse that has shaped the
state of the art on this topic. For the sake of both brevity and clarity, this overview
will aim to be more representative than comprehensive. This means a tight focus
on the discussion of historiography and a selection of some exemplary studies.
Chronologically, it will focus on discussion in the wake of Ohly's seminal *Sage und
Legende in der Kaiserchronik*, first published in 1940.[5]

At an early point in the discussion of the *Kaiserchronik*, the striking discrepancy
between historiographical postulate and narrative content caused Schwietering
to observe that 'es hieße den Sinn der Dichtung verkennen, wollte man hier
Geschichtliches vom Fabulistischen im modernen Sinne scheiden'. According to
him, the truth of the *Kaiserchronik* is derived from its 'Gottbezogenheit' and not its
claim to factuality. Where the text switches to the mode of episodic entertainment,

---

4   This book will not concern itself with the much-discussed question of who wrote the
Kaiserchronik when and where. For our purposes, it will suffice to assume that the chronicle was
written by a well-read, well-connected, Latinate ecclesiastical author from and in the south-eastern
parts of the Empire (largely modern-day Bavaria or Austria) some time after 1147.

5   Ernst Friedrich Ohly, *Sage und Legende in der Kaiserchronik: Untersuchungen über Quellen und
Aufbau der Dichtung* (Darmstadt, 1940; repr. 1968). A detailed overview of academic discussion of
the *Kaiserchronik*, especially its dating and conception, prior to 1939 can be found in Ralph George
Crossley, *Die Kaiserchronik: Ein literarhistorisches Problem der altdeutschen Literaturgeschichte* (Munich,
1939), pp. 9–71. A helpful overview of the more recent scholarship prior to 2004 can be found
in Monika Pohl, 'Untersuchungen zur Darstellung mittelalterlicher Herrscher in der deutschen
"Kaiserchronik" des 12. Jahrhunderts: Ein Werk im Umbruch von mündlicher und schriftlicher
Tradition' (unpublished doctoral dissertation, Ludwig-Maximilians-Universität München, 2004),
pp. 12–16. The one earlier scholar to be considered will be Schwietering, Ohly's teacher; otherwise,
earlier contributions will only be addressed where context and significance warrant it.

he suggests, this happens virtually against the will of the author, who follows a strictly eschatological scheme in the arrangement and adaptation of his material.[6]

Schwietering's perspectives had some influence on his student Ohly, who dealt with the medieval 'Geschichtsanschauung' in the first chapter of his dissertation and placed great emphasis on the concept of salvation history and the unified scheme according to which the *Kaiserchronik* was compiled. He distinguished between chronicles, which encompass 'den Gesamtraum göttlicher Heilsgeschichte' — among which he counts the *Kaiserchronik* — and 'Historien', which are mainly concerned with the genesis and development of particular peoples. In the second chapter, he then attempted to isolate the formal elements that characterize the chronicle as a genre. In his view, the German vernacular tradition that begins with the *Kaiserchronik* is to be distinguished from histories like, for example, the French, Norman, and Breton histories in the tradition of Geoffrey of Monmouth's Latin *Historia Regum Britanniae*. He argued that those texts, while they aim to root themselves in the universal historical frame of salvation-historical events, do not strive to encompass the whole of it but rather take the mythical origins of the peoples they are presenting as the starting point of their narratives. Thus, he established a dichotomy between the 'mythisch-sagenhaft-national[]' and the 'biblisch-heilsgeschichtlich-imperial[]' types of historiographical text.[7] As representatives of the latter he regarded a group of texts from around the year 1100 that go back to the birth of Christ to start their narratives, reviving the practice of older texts, like Jerome's translation and continuation of Eusebius, that seek to continue chronicles going even further back than Christ's birth.[8] He saw Frutolf of Michelsberg's and Otto of Freising's chronicles as the culmination of this development.[9]

Ohly identified the *Kaiserchronik*'s attempt to illustrate the struggle between good and evil as its fundamental 'Kompositionsgesetz'. The opposing forces, in his view, are contained within every episode, and the unfolding events enact punishment and reward according to the conduct of the historical protagonists caught between these forces. However, he argues, these processes are rarely expressed directly in the text and therefore must be made visible by an internal referential structure of typologies.[10]

Ohly went to great lengths to show how typology as an instrument of biblical exegesis could become separated from its theological roots. He differentiated between three typological relations: in addition to the established biblical typology, he postulated the existence of semi-biblical and extra-biblical typologies. Semi-biblical typologies have one of their poles in the Bible but connect it to an antitype outside the biblical corpus. As examples, Ohly referred very broadly to myths and legends, and more specifically to general natural phenomena as observed in the *Physiologus* and to certain cycles of images in which types from apocryphal traditions

6   Julius Schwietering, *Die deutsche Dichtung des Mittelalters* (Potsdam, 1932), pp. 97–98.
7   Ohly, *Sage und Legende*, pp. 10–12, 15–16.
8   See ibid., p. 13, listing Bernold of St Blase (1100), Hugo of Flavigny (1102), Lambert of St Omer (1120), and Sigebert of Gembloux (1112).
9   Ibid., p. 12.
10   Ibid., p. 238.

or pagan secular history are used to prefigure types from the New Testament or the other way round. He did not, however, offer concrete examples.[11]

But he did provide two examples of extra-biblical typologies: first, the murals of the imperial palace in Ingelheim, which do not survive to the present day but are described in a ninth-century poem by Ermoldus Nigellus; second, the early twelfth-century relief at the church of St Zeno in Verona depicting the hunt of Theoderic. Ohly did not, however, elaborate on how alleged typological patterns in these unrelated artworks might indicate the existence of similar patterns in a twelfth-century Middle High German text from Bavaria. His argument is more transparent when referring to the works of his teacher Schwietering, who interpreted the development of early Arthurian romance as a typological overcoming of classical forms and content.[12] Ohly further developed the concept as a prevalent structure within medieval literature, but characterized it so broadly that it becomes increasingly unclear how his typologies can be distinguished from other literary relations and references. He concluded by stating that the *Kaiserchronik* is especially suited to the application of an internal typological reference framework because it narrates both the historical spaces of Roman antiquity and the Christian Middle Ages.[13]

Ohly's work has been lauded as '[g]rundlegend für alle weitere Arbeit' on the *Kaiserchronik*,[14] and has served both as a stepping stone for further analysis and as a focal point for criticism of his usage of typology. Examples of the latter include the thematically linked studies of Jantsch and Jentzmik,[15] who disagree energetically with Ohly's conception of typology. Jantsch criticizes his stress on the necessity of the fulfilment of types through antitypes, rendering the former inferior when compared to the latter. According to Jantsch, this ignores the fact that typology essentially serves as an apologetic strategy to justify the Old Testament and does not have the task of illustrating the self-evidently higher degree of perfection achieved with events from the New Testament. Jantsch furthermore remarks that the terminology used by Ohly does not correspond to any kind of biblical typology.[16] Moreover, he claims that it is constitutive for typologies to make explicit the semantics of the referential relation they describe, and hence that Ohly's characterization of his findings as delineated by an unspoken connection between

---

11   Ibid., p. 27.
12   Ibid., p. 28. See also Julius Schwietering, 'Typologisches in mittelalterlichen Dichtungen', in *Philologische Schriften* (Berlin, 1925), pp. 40–55.
13   Ohly, *Sage und Legende*, p. 29.
14   Eberhard Nellmann, *Die Reichsidee in deutschen Dichtungen der Salier- und frühen Stauferzeit*, Philologische Studien und Quellen, 16 (Berlin, 1963), p. 85. Similarly, Annegret Fiebig, 'vier wilde tiere: Weltdeutung nach Daniel in der "Kaiserchronik"', in *Deutsche Literatur und Sprache von 1050–1200: Festschrift für Ursula Henning zum 65. Geburtstag*, ed. by Annegret Fiebig and Hans-Jochen Schiewer (Berlin, 1995), pp. 27–49 (p. 30).
15   Heinz Jantsch, *Studien zum Symbolischen in frühmittelhochdeutscher Literatur* (Tübingen, 1959), esp. pp. 203–26; Peter Jentzmik, *Zu Möglichkeiten und Grenzen typologischer Exegese in mittelalterlicher Predigt und Dichtung* (Göppingen, 1973), esp. pp. 222–33.
16   Jantsch, pp. 204–07.

two antithetical poles disqualifies them from the term 'typology'.[17] Additionally, he points out a distinct variation in the inner structures of Ohly's typologies and stresses the importance of discerning 'die lebendige Vielfalt des Erscheinenden' before putting it into a semantically fixed, terminological framework.[18]

Jentzmik agrees with Ohly in assigning the *Kaiserchronik* to salvation history. He believes the search for typological narratives in vernacular historiography is justified because the latter has a pivotal position when it comes to conveying 'heilsgeschichtliche[s] Gedankengut[] und theologische[] Deutung' from theological into other literature.[19] According to Jentzmik, the passages identified by Ohly have a didactic quality firmly anchoring the text 'im Dienste der Heilsgeschichte'.[20] Yet, like Jantsch, he casts doubt on the existence of a 'gemeinsame Sinnmitte' between the two constituents of Ohly's typologies, and suggests that they serve much more as moral markers that do not await their definite fulfilment by teleologically unfolding events but instead call on the audience of the text to perpetually emulate the preferred historical examples.[21]

Both Jantsch and Jentzmik mainly take issue with Ohly's identification of the structures he describes as typological, and are not convinced that these structures fulfil the rather rigid specifications of theological typology they apply. They do, however, acknowledge the existence of referential relations between the episodes of the *Kaiserchronik*.[22] But Jantsch suggests that it would be more appropriate to refer to these relations not as typologies but as a didactic reference network that employs exemplary contrasts ('exemplarische Kontrastbelege').[23] Guided by salvation-historical thinking, these relations aim to edify by their examples and create a sense of a teleological unfolding of history directed at an increasingly Christian conduct of historical protagonists.[24] With their conclusions, Jantsch and Jentzmik end up close to what Kartschoke would later characterize, when speaking about the content of the Roman part of the *Kaiserchronik*, as 'exemplary narratives in the form of tales and legends'.[25]

Ohly defended his terminology against the criticism launched against his book almost immediately after it was reprinted in 1968, but only in general terms and without providing any further insights into the typological scheme of the *Kaiserchronik*.[26] The criticism, however, did not prevent his work from continuing

---

17 Ohly, *Sage und Legende*, p. 29; Jantsch, p. 213.
18 Ibid., p. 224.
19 Jentzmik, p. 222.
20 Ibid., p. 234.
21 Jantsch, p. 205; Jentzmik, pp. 235–42.
22 Jantsch, pp. 208–10.
23 Ibid., pp. 226, 206.
24 Jentzmik, p. 254.
25 Dieter Kartschoke, *Geschichte der deutschen Literatur im frühen Mittelalter* (Munich, 2000), p. 356; translation after Alastair Matthews, *The Kaiserchronik: A Medieval Narrative* (Oxford, 2012), pp. 4–5.
26 Not only does he refute the criticism launched against his broad terminological use of 'typology'; he also provides a wealth of examples for different forms of extra-biblical typological thinking and imagery, mostly from classical and medieval Latin literature and medieval art, and traces the practice all the way down to Hölderlin's hymn 'Der Einzige'. The vernacular literature

to elicit mainly productive responses and inspiring further investigations along the lines he had laid down. For example, Annegret Fiebig uses Ohly's analysis of the *Kaiserchronik*'s idiosyncratic version of the dream interpretations of the biblical prophet Daniel to delve further into the text. Daniel 7 tells of four mythical beasts coming out of the water in short succession. In an exegetical tradition beginning with Jerome, the beasts have traditionally been interpreted as four dominant, world-spanning empires succeeding one another and culminating with the fourth, the Roman Empire. This last would, however, ultimately turn into the empire of the Antichrist and inaugurate the end times.[27] Fiebig argues convincingly that up until the twelfth century there was no singular and readily established tradition of reading the vision(s) of Daniel, and shows how the *Kaiserchronik*'s handling of the image of the four beasts and the four historical empires builds on a multitude of interpretations. Furthermore, she demonstrates that the scheme of the four beasts was regarded more as an explanatory image to justify the translation of empire in the Middle Ages, and less as a basic ordering system of history, as Ohly would have it.[28] Yet for the actual analysis of the passage she largely builds on his results.[29] He showed how the changes in the *Kaiserchronik*'s version when compared to the biblical imagery, and especially to the *Annolied* — with which it shares about 225 lines of the passage[30] — are not mere inaccuracies or clumsy insertions,[31] but instead serve a deliberate agenda of purposefully removing from the Roman Empire and its founder, Caesar, the stigma of representing the eschatologically last empire

of the twelfth century, however, remains conspicuously without any further exemplification for this kind of interpretation. Ernst Friedrich Ohly, 'Außerbiblisch Typologisches zwischen Cicero, Ambrosius und Aelred von Rievaulx' and 'Halbbiblische und außerbiblische Typologie', in *Schriften zur mittelalterlichen Bedeutungsforschung* (Darmstadt, 1983), pp. 336–60, 361–99. Ohly further substantiated his global view of typology as a 'Denkform der Geschichtsbetrachtung' in a series of essays: 'Synagoge und Ecclesia: Typologisches in mittelalterlicher Dichtung', in *Schriften zur mittelalterlichen Bedeutungsforschung* (Darmstadt, 1983), pp. 312–38; 'Typologie als Denkform der Geschichtsbetrachtung (1983)', 'Typologische Figuren aus Natur und Mythus (1979)', and 'Skizze zur Typologie im Mittelalter (1979)', in *Ernst Friedrich Ohly: Ausgewählte und neue Schriften zur Literaturgeschichte und zur Bedeutungsforschung*, ed. by Uwe Rüber and Dietmar Peil (Stuttgart, 1995), pp. 445–72, 473–508, 509–54.
27   The Daniel passage in *KC*, 526–90 is a loose adaptation and conflation of the dream interpretations by the prophet Daniel in Daniel 2, where he interprets a dream of the Babylonian King Nebuchadnezzar, and Daniel 7, where he is himself the dreamer. The *Kaiserchronik*'s version is heavily informed by the *Annolied* (1070s). The canonical interpretation of the biblical prophecies of Daniel — the *Visio Danielis* — is mainly informed by the exegesis of Jerome's early fifth-century commentary *In Danielem*, in which the Church Father offers an in-depth reading and interpretation of Daniel's visions that was later to become a cornerstone of Christian theology, especially Christology (*Commentariorum in Danielem Libri III*, ed. by F. Glorie, Corpus Christianorum: Series Latina, 75a (Turnhout, 1964)). See Régis Courtray, 'Der Danielkommentar des Hieronymus', in *Die Geschichte der Daniel-Auslegung in Judentum, Christentum und Islam*, ed. by Katharina Bracht and David du Toit, Beihefte zur Zeitschrift für die alttestamentliche Wissenschaft, 371 (Berlin, 2007), pp. 123–50 (pp. 130–31).
28   Fiebig, pp. 31–38.
29   Ibid., pp. 39–48.
30   On this problem, see Stephan Müller, *Vom Annolied zur Kaiserchronik: Zu Text- und Forschungsgeschichte einer verlorenen deutschen Reimchronik* (Heidelberg, 1999).
31   See Schröder, p. 90, n. 1.

of mankind.[32] Moreover, Fiebig shows how the *Kaiserchronik* adapts the genealogy of the German peoples to its rearranged sequence of the four empires.[33] From this new succession she infers a salvation-historical rationale for the Germans' claim to imperial power. She concludes that the more positive presentation of Caesar and his rule in the *Kaiserchronik* corresponds to the text's programmatic purpose, which is to present the history of the Empire as salvation history by shifting the soteriological turning point away from the *Pax Augusta* to Caesar and his inauguration of the Roman Empire.[34]

Karl Stackmann's examination of narrative structure in the *Kaiserchronik*, which investigates the conditions under which the text narrates history, leads us toward the methodological approach this book will employ. Stackmann states that the *Kaiserchronik*'s author does follow an established medieval understanding of historiography, but at the same time maintains an extraordinary freedom when regarding it.[35] To explain this, Stackmann employs Hanna Vollrath's theory of medieval societies structured by the mutual influence and exchange of coexisting oral and written cultures.[36] According to this concept, medieval minds modulate the past not as something necessarily concluded but as something in a direct functional connection to the present, and hence the past is not unchangeable history but an always shifting reflection of the present.[37] Stackmann argues against such an opposition between medieval oral culture on the one hand and contemporary written culture and ideas like salvation history that were predominantly cultivated by ecclesiastical authors on the other:

> Geschichte wird vorgestellt als eine gerichtete Bewegung, die von einem Anfang — der Schöpfung — her in einer geordneten Folge bedeutsamer Ereignisse bis zur Zäsur des Erscheinens Christi und von da an über die Gegenwart weiter bis zum letzten Ziel — dem jüngsten Gericht — führt. Für ein solches Denken ist eine klare Unterscheidung der Vergangenheit, des bereits zurückgelegten Weges, von der Gegenwart und der noch bevorstehenden Zukunft eine Selbstverständlichkeit.[38]

The intriguing consequence of the clash of these two simultaneously used concepts of history is the transfer of oral narrative techniques into written texts and — as Stackmann argues — even into historiographical records like the *Kaiserchronik*, which allegedly presents history as a reflected present within the framework of the Empire and its ecclesiastical institutions of salvation. To prove this, he takes a closer look at the prologue, finding 'gegenwartsbezogenes Interesse' and indicators for orality

---

32 See Ohly, *Sage und Legende*, pp. 37–38; Fiebig, p. 46.

33 See 4.2.1 in this book.

34 Fiebig, pp. 43–49.

35 Karl Stackmann, 'Erzählstrategie und Sinnvermittlung in der Deutschen "Kaiserchronik"', in *Erscheinungsformen kultureller Prozesse: Jahrbuch 1988 des Sonderforschungsbereiches 'Übergänge und Spannungsfelder zwischen Mündlichkeit und Schriftlichkeit'*, ed. by Wolfgang Raible (Tübingen, 1990), pp. 63–82 (p. 63).

36 Hanna Vollrath, 'Das Mittelalter in der Typik oraler Gesellschaft', *Historische Zeitschrift*, 233 (1981), 571–94.

37 See ibid., pp. 575–76.

38 Stackmann, p. 65.

when the text is referred to first as a *liet* (*KC*, 2) and the audience is encouraged to 'gezogenlîche vernemen' (*KC*, 3). The prologue's criticism of the 'scophelîchen worten' (*KC*, 31) that educate the coming generations with 'luge' (*KC*, 35) is key for his argument: the fact that the *Kaiserchronik* with all its fantastic and fictional content sees itself as opposed to other texts of a similar nature can, according to Stackmann, only be understood if its content is seen as an ever-shifting reflection of the present. It is considered truth by the author and his audience because it is truth by the standards of medieval 'frumichait' (*KC*, 5) and reiterates the norms and rules by which medieval society abides and which it holds to be timelessly applicable; in this way, these medieval norms are construed to be affirmed and not fabricated by their historical (re)occurrence.[39] Stackmann also identifies a further vein of 'Sinnvermittlung' in the *Kaiserchronik* based on Wolfgang Mohr's idea of symbolically opposed motifs that are presented to the audience without being explicitly linked. This is left to the listener of the text. Referring to the episode of Henry IV with its enclosed excursus about the First Crusade, led by Godfrey of Bouillon, Stackmann shows how the text opposes the bad King Henry, whose reign destroys all order within the Empire, with an ideal prince like Godfrey, who, with the extensive and frequently invoked help of God, leads the fight against the pagans to a victorious conclusion.[40] On the basis of these examples, he postulates finding meaning in the text beyond the distinction between good and evil, namely in the implementation of meaningful narrative structures.[41]

A multitude of interpretations abound, only sometimes overlapping or corresponding with and to one another. The quest for the guiding historical principle of the *Kaiserchronik* has certainly proved to be a most productive one; the proposed answers, however, have so far only brought forth a plethora of disjunct explanatory matrices that coexist largely independently of one another, without scholars finding many contact points or theories gaining momentum from synergies (with perhaps the prominent exceptions of Ohly, whose contribution is almost universally acknowledged and regularly built upon, and Stock, whose contribution has had great influence on the more recent scholarship).[42] Their variety serves as an apt illustration of the manifold narrative offerings of the text itself, but also as an admission of the still unsatisfactory solution to the problem posed. So far, no overarching theoretical system of interpretation has proved to be quite sufficient to fully understand the narrative structure of the text. The question arises as to whether it can or even should be an aim to identify a coherent and guiding historical principle that shapes the diverse and colourful textual representations that the *Kaiserchronik* finds for such a wide array of European legendary and historiographical motifs.

---

39   See ibid., pp. 65–67.
40   Ibid., pp. 71–77.
41   Ibid., p. 81.
42   Markus Stock, *Kombinationssinn: Narrative Strukturexperimente im 'Straßburger Alexander', im 'Herzog Ernst B' und im 'König Rother'*, Münchener Texte und Untersuchungen zur deutschen Literatur des Mittelalters, 123 (Tübingen, 2002).

More recent prominent attempts to turn this unruly cluster of results into a positive approach include Alastair Matthews's 2012 book on the *Kaiserchronik* as a medieval narrative, Johannes Dickhut-Bielsky's dissertation (published in 2015) examining the text's poetic and historiographical hermeneutics, and a 2017 article by Mathias Herweg on 'Kohärenzstiftung' with regard to the *Kaiserchronik*.[43] Matthews remarks that there is no all-encompassing reference to a framework of salvation history in the text, and that it has not been possible to localize the chronicle convincingly between historiographical, literary, religious, and didactic motivations.[44] By launching an array of methodologically diverse examinations of selected episodes of the text, he provides compelling close readings that excel at opening the reader's eyes to the complicated and artistic narrative structures of the episodes under consideration. However, it becomes clear at the same time that a methodologically multipronged approach trained only at selected passages neither provides the heuristic capacity to elucidate the text's narrative as a whole nor helps to clear up the question of whether the text does in fact follow a consistent narrative scheme.

Dickhut-Bielsky sets himself the rather ambitious goal of seeking out the 'Wahrheit' of the *Annolied* and *Kaiserchronik*; most of his work, however, is devoted to the latter text. While he acknowledges that the *Kaiserchronik* warrants an approach from a variety of angles, he actually follows a 'klassisches hermeneutisches Verfahren'.[45] He identifies certain clues in the chronicle's prologue that, he argues, invite the reader to undertake hermeneutical readings of the text's episodes. He emphasizes this as a 'Grundanliegen' that is expressed explicitly in the prologue:

> Dies wiederum macht deutlich, dass das vorliegende Werk einen Sinn verbirgt, der durch Ausdeutung ans Tageslicht befördert werden muss. Dieser Sinn ist das, wie wir es nennen, Grundanliegen des Werkes, welches sich sowohl in der Gesamtkonzeption als auch in den einzelnen Episoden realisiert. Der KC-Dichter macht damit deutlich, dass sich der Sinn der Erzählung erst in der Ausdeutung offenbart.[46]

His interpretations of these cues are sometimes more, sometimes less convincing, and in some cases appear rather forced.[47] In the main body of his analysis, Dickhut-Bielsky realigns established problems of *Kaiserchronik* scholarship under the lens of

---

43   Matthews; Johannes Dickhut-Bielsky, *Auf der Suche nach der Wahrheit in 'Annolied' und 'Kaiserchronik': Poetisch-historiographische Wahrheitssuche in frühmittelhochdeutschen Geschichtsdichtungen*, Beihefte zur Zeitschrift für deutsches Altertum und deutsche Literatur, 23 (Stuttgart, 2015); Mathias Herweg, 'Kohärenzstiftung auf vielen Ebenen: Narratologie und Genrefragen in der "Kaiserchronik"', *Zeitschrift für Literaturwissenschaft und Linguistik*, 47.2 (2017), 281–302 (pp. 281–82). Mathias Herweg is also to be thanked for his meritorious edition of an abridged version of the *Kaiserchronik*, which will make the text much easier to access for future generations of students (*Die Kaiserchronik: Mittelhochdeutsch/Neuhochdeutsch*, trans. by Mathias Herweg, RUB, 19,270 (Stuttgart, 2014)).

44   Matthews, pp. 4–5, 16–22.

45   Dickhut-Bielsky, pp. 51–52.

46   Ibid., p. 53.

47   Ibid., pp. 52–59. Especially his reliance on the semantics of *frumichait* seems rather overstretched. For a more detailed engagement with some of the points Dickhut-Bielsky makes concerning the prologue, see 2.2.2 in this book.

'poetische Verfahren zur Wahrheitsfindung'.[48] In the end, while Dickhut-Bielsky acknowledges the disparity of the text, he effectively only swaps one magic key for a dozen others, rather than doing away with the idea of a hermeneutically unlockable meaning in the text altogether. He still subscribes to the traditional view that the *Kaiserchronik* has an overarching and coherent meaning programmed into its idiosyncratic historiography, just waiting for the literary scholar to unlock it.

The most recent representative of this new movement within *Kaiserchronik* scholarship is Mathias Herweg. Building on Stock's idea of the generation of meaning through strategies of repetition, variation, and combination — Dickhut-Bielsky's 'sinnstiftende Bezüge' — Herweg examines the creation of coherence in the *Kaiserchronik*. He discerns three layers on which this is achieved: 'der Erzählzyklus als Ganzes', 'weitgehend autonome[] Abschnitte (die Kaiserviten) als Sammelbecken autogener Stoffe, Gattungen und Stile', and 'Binnenepisoden und -narrative innerhalb der Abschnitte'.[49] On the first and uppermost layer, 'Kohärenzstiftung' is achieved by the cyclical recurrence of patterns, terms, and motifs, which, although not interacting with each other explicitly, still create an implicit emplotment through their shared teleological trajectory. On the second layer, he identifies a multitude of strategies for establishing coherence, which he illustrates convincingly through the two specific examples of the 'Zeit-Raum-Konzept [...] und Konnex [...]' and 'abschnittsübergreifende Relektüre unter dem Vorzeichen metonymischen Erzählens'. On this level, he also identifies several plot patterns and narrative motifs, whose potential is explored in the *Kaiserchronik* for the first time, that would later become constitutive for the emerging genres of courtly literature.[50] I share many of Herweg's views on the implications of the macrostructure of the chronicle, such as the emphasis on the interchangeability of individual episodes, and often arrive at similar (but not congruent) conclusions.[51] However, much of his writing is also characterized by a great concern for questions of genre, which this book will not engage with at all.

Still, this book is very much part of this recent movement within *Kaiserchronik* scholarship, which posits that the text generates meaning on many levels and uses a wealth of strategies to inform its narrative.[52] It does not propose a magic key that might unlock the *Kaiserchronik*'s idiosyncratic historiographical account. Rather, the stories about the past that the *Kaiserchronik* offers are regarded as if through Marbot's sceptical eyes: as elements that cast doubt on the present and hence need negotiation and narrative framing for the contemporary public, who gather to look at the ruins. For Marbot's visitors to Rome to be able to construct for themselves the eras they prefer to live in, they have to draw on a powerful cultural mythology that permeates Rome, so as to find something meaningful in the relics.

---

48   Ibid., pp. 96 (quotation), 96–112 ('sinnstiftende Bezüge'), 159–76 ('[p]redigthaft-belehrendes Erzählen'), 253–55 ('Quellenberufungen').

49   Herweg, p. 286. Where Herweg uses the German term *Abschnitt* for the emperor-centric units of the chronicle, I will continue to use 'episode'.

50   Ibid., pp. 294–96.

51   It should be emphasized that most of the thesis behind this book was written before Herweg's article was published. Where I arrive at similar conclusions, this happened independently.

52   See Herweg, pp. 294–96.

Similarly, the *Kaiserchronik* — whether knowingly or not — has to bridge the gulf between the times, personalities, and places it narrates and the present for which it narrates in order for its audience to be able to derive something meaningful from its narrative offerings. This gulf has to be bridged on two levels. The first level, which I will refer to as historical *distance*, is constitutive for the very form of the *Kaiserchronik*: dozens of emperors and hundreds of years separate the time of the chronicle's stories from the twelfth century and its German vernacular audience, which probably hailed — at least in the early phase of reception — mostly from the aristocratic and monastic centres of the south-eastern reaches of the Empire. This quantifiable distance between the narrated past and the medieval present is prominently marked in the very fabric of the text: in its episodic sequencing of emperors and in the counting, at the end of each episode, of the years, months, and days for which each emperor ruled. Thus, distance will be a countable and quantifiable dimension. By contrast, historical *difference*, the second level on which the gulf has to be bridged, is a qualitative dimension. Significant religious and political alterities create a distinct difference between the narrated past and the medieval present. Initially, the Roman Empire is a pagan entity concentrated on the city of Rome and its cisalpine territories, strongly shaped by its veneration of multiple gods. But by the end of the *Kaiserchronik*, the Empire is a wholly Christian and transalpine entity. These two dimensions of distance and difference at the same time connect and separate the narrative and its audience. The analysis of the productive output of the narrative negotiation of these two dimensions will from the backbone of this book.

I believe this approach to be important because it addresses several factors that are relevant for research on the *Kaiserchronik*. First, one of the most discussed questions when studying the *Kaiserchronik* is why the part dealing with the ancient Roman past and the part dealing with the more recent Carolingian and German past receive such different narrative treatments. Applying the two dimensions outlined above to examine how the two parts are qualitatively different while they quantitatively approach the present of the twelfth century will reveal that this difference in treatment is caused by the differing historiographical premises on which the ancient and medieval emperor episodes are predicated. Second, the approach offers an opportunity for bringing together a variety of lines of enquiry concerned with the *Kaiserchronik*'s historiography from a variety of angles. This approach does not propose an all-encompassing theoretical framework for engaging with the text. Nor does it take part in the extensive discussions of the chronicle's categorization or genre classification. Rather, it aims at something much more similar to a *motivgeschichtliche* examination of two temporal structures, and their narrative furnishings, that emerge when- and wherever a text takes on the task of narrating the course of history. Several angles, from salvation history to rhetoric to concepts of nation and empire, will be organized under the concepts of historical distance and difference in order to address how the *Kaiserchronik* negotiates the historicity of its narrative.

The organizing terminology employed throughout this book — quantitative distance and qualitative difference — is of course connected to several established theoretical discourses in literary and historiographical Medieval Studies. I will mostly develop the theoretical understanding relevant for my study in chapter 1, building on Hayden White, Richard Newald, Gert Melville, and Hans-Joachim Gehrke.

I regard the episodes and emperors of the *Kaiserchronik*, both in form and in content, as organized along the two lines of distance and difference, and pose my questions accordingly. Scholarship has often focused on single, prominent episodes like the reign of Caesar, or on internally coherent narratives like those of Faustinian or Crescentia. This book, however, will follow the approach of broader studies such as Pézsa, Stock, and Dickhut-Bielsky, and draw on the full scope of the chronicle, on all the episodes from Caesar to Conrad III.[53] Thus, a conclusive picture of the *Kaiserchronik*'s historiographical negotiation of historical distance and difference will emerge.

Chapter 1 elaborates on what I call the quantitative narrative dimension and thus lays the theoretical ground for investigating the *Kaiserchronik*'s method of creating and explaining historical distance. After reconsidering the episodic structure of the chronicle, I will suggest that Hayden White's reading of form as a semanticizing structure can be productively aligned with Richard Newald's metaphor of the atomization of classical narrative traditions in the Middle Ages. From this premise, I will discuss three examples of how the episode framework makes quantitative distance available as a historiographical tool in the *Kaiserchronik*. The first of these examples focuses on the creation of continuity, the second and third on using quantified historical distance to construct examples from history, especially by narrating aetiological stories.

Chapter 2 extends the discussion of exemplarity to consider the role of the *Kaiserchronik* prologue's commitment to truthfulness. I will consider how this commitment shapes the chronicle's conception of history as an exemplary *magistra vitae* in the context of comparable texts from the second half of the twelfth century. In a discussion of a few selected lines from the prologue, I will show how the *Kaiserchronik* styles itself not as a compositional artefact but as a manifested document of history's perpetual sameness, which serves as the backbone for historical exemplarity in the *magistra vitae* tradition.

Chapters 3 and 4 turn to the qualitative dimension of history and investigate the chronicle's treatment of historical difference. In these chapters, I pursue the question of how the text narrates change in history over time, as the narrated past comes closer to the medieval present and becomes more similar to the audience's lived experience. The examination of qualitative change will focus on two areas. Chapter 3 looks at the religious composition of the Empire to show how the chronicle presents the Roman Empire's course from a polytheistic pagan entity to a monotheistic Christian one. Chapter 4 considers the same question, but in the context of the Empire's political identity, and maps its course from a cisalpine

---

53   Admittedly, there is a slant toward the ancient/Roman episodes of the chronicle. But this is well justified, as they provide the more interesting narrative material, have accumulated more scholarly literature, and make up over 80 per cent of the text.

empire centred on the city of Rome to a transalpine one under the aegis of the Germans, while always retaining its Roman quality.

CHAPTER 1

❖

The Measure of History
in the *Kaiserchronik*

1.1. Serial Form and Contingent Content

1.1.1. The Episodic Framework: A Reappraisal

The *Kaiserchronik* is composed of a string of separate episodes, usually defined as the rule of one emperor. Establishing the exact number of these episodes is not as straightforward as might be expected. Ohly counts thirty-six 'Roman' and eighteen 'German' emperor episodes.[1] Chinca and Young, in the most recent contribution, count thirty-six Roman and nineteen German episodes.[2] In order to clarify what I will be speaking of when referring to 'episodes' and what I understand as constitutive for these units of the text's macrostructure, I shall in this section undertake a reappraisal of the *Kaiserchronik*'s episode structure. Also, my approach to discussing the text's handling of historical distance will hinge on a clear and nuanced understanding of what the chronicle's building blocks are and how exactly they are delineated.

Even the most cursory overview of the episodes of the framework, their arrangement and their succession, reveals glaring deviations and obvious mistakes where the established timeline of Roman emperors is concerned.[3] The first fifteen emperors from Caesar down to Trajan (*KC*, 5840) are presented roughly in the right order, and in most cases the duration of the reign recorded in the *Kaiserchronik* is reasonably close to the actual duration. Two notable exceptions, however, stand out. The first is the inclusion of the entirely fictitious Faustinian as the elder brother of Claudius in order to allow the tale of his many family partings and reunions, based on the Pseudo-Clementine *Recognitiones*, to be told. The second is the anachronistic inclusion of the legendary King Tarquin of Roman prehistory, who has been inserted after Nero and before Galba and Piso, which is well over five hundred years out of sequence, allowing the story of Lucretia, Tarquin, and Conlatinus to be told.[4]

After Trajan's reign, the chronicle rarely presents more than two successive emperors in the right order, the notable exceptions being Philip the Arab and

---

1 Ohly, *Sage und Legende*, pp. 17–18.
2 Mark Chinca and Christopher Young, 'Uses of the Past in Twelfth-Century Germany: The Case of the Middle High German "Kaiserchronik"', *Central European History*, 49 (2016), 1–20 (p. 1).
3 See Ohly, *Sage und Legende*, pp. 17–18.
4 Tarquin's rule is usually given as 535 BCE–509 BCE. Nero died in 68 CE.

Decius, Diocletian and Severus (provided the latter is indeed Severus II and not the more famous and more likely Septimus Severus, who ruled over one hundred years earlier), and of course Constantius and Constantine. Apart from these, in this block of episodes the *Kaiserchronik* feels free to jump forward and backward in time between emperors, moving 76 years back from Helius Pertinax (d. 193 CE) to the accession of Hadrian in 117 CE, or 247 years into the future from Julian's death in 363 CE to Heraclius's accession in 610 CE. Most egregiously, after Constantine V (r. 741–75 CE) the text jumps back three hundred years to Emperor Zeno (r. 474–91 CE), only to return afterward to the eighth century with the thoroughly Byzantine Emperor Constantine VI (r. 780–97 CE).[5] The text freely includes largely or entirely fictitious emperors like Achilleus or Narcissus, or composite figures like the Emperor Galienus, who is probably a hybrid of Emperor Galerius (r. 293–311 CE) and the physician Galen.[6] It is very difficult to identify the historical counterpart of some of the emperors, for example for Severus (Septimus Severus or Severus II?), Theodosius (Theodosius I or II?), or Constantius Leo (Leo I or Constantine V?). Moreover, the *Kaiserchronik* brings together protagonists who lived years apart when, for example, Alaric kills the Emperor Commodus, although they were chronologically separated by a gulf of over two hundred years. This is especially striking as the text itself criticizes precisely this kind of historiographically confused conflation prominently in the Zeno episode, where it disparagingly comments on the impossibility of Dietrich and Etzel having met because their lifetimes were separated by forty-three years (*KC*, 14,176–87).

Especially in the time between Emperor Constantine/Pope Silvester and Charlemagne, no two emperors succeed each other or are even remotely arranged in the correct order. There are several underlying reasons for this confusion, which will be elaborated on later. One is the suppression and pejoration of 'Greekness'; another is the structural illustration of the antagonism between two clashing religious systems. Usually, there is little or no connection between the end of one episode and the opening of the next.

The episodic structure of the *Kaiserchronik* has been the object of some scholarly scrutiny. Ohly characterized it as 'sich formelhaft wiederholende[] Eingänge und Schlüsse der einzelnen Kaisergeschichten, deren locker parataktische Hinterein-anderordnung typische Chronikform ist'. While he admits that in many cases it refers to the historiographical record, he also identifies it as an 'in ihrer Formelgestalt [...] dichterisches Stilelement der Kaiserchronik, das als solches nie ohne inneres Leben ist und nie vollkommen starr wird'. Ohly calculates that the framing phrases stating the duration of each emperor's rule from Caesar to Charlemagne add up to about the same time as those from Charlemagne to Conrad III; together, they amount to precisely 1147 years, matching the year in which the *Kaiserchronik*'s record of history terminates. Considering how the chronicle takes great liberties with the individual

---

5   The years for the rules of the Western Roman emperors are taken from Fik Meijer, *Emperors Don't Die in Bed*, trans. by S. J. Leinbach (London, 2004).
6   See Ohly, *Sage und Legende*, p. 161.

emperor episodes, Ohly sees this as a clear sign of a 'besonderen Formwillen[]'.[7] While the details of Ohly's flawed calculations have been debated,[8] this overall understanding of the episode framework as a malleable structure that itself carries meaning and is at the disposal of the author of the *Kaiserchronik* will be confirmed by this chapter and in turn inform its overall argument.

1.1.1.1. Episode Markers and Episode Borders

Urbanek noted how strictly the *Kaiserchronik* adheres to its episode scheme, even compared to other contemporary texts. He shared Ohly's appreciation of the text's 'Formwillen', but went further than him to look for the cause of the seemingly deliberate composition of the number of years of the durations of reigns and the number of emperors who ruled. The calculations he provides in order to support his claim that the *Kaiserchronik* develops its own scheme of six *aetates mundi* and tries to upgrade the historical importance of the second — 'German' — part of the Empire's history will not be reproduced here, as Urbanek's calculations are of course equally flawed. He misunderstands *vierdehalp* as 'four and a half', not 'three and a half';[9] he assumes that the *Kaiserchronik* would not have taken any liberties with the duration of the reign of Conrad III; and he neglects to consider how the duration of Silvester's papacy might affect his calculations.[10] Pope Silvester is framed like an emperor and clearly envisioned as a successor to Constantine in time, holding office for twenty-four years, six months, and five days (*KC*, 10,614–18). Admittedly, it remains unclear for how many of these years he is supposed to have survived Constantine and ruled by himself. However, the puzzling compositional symmetry of this episode's arrangement, which puts Charlemagne at the threshold of a two-to-one relation between ancient and medieval kings,[11] and Constantine as twenty-seventh emperor at the centre of fifty-four emperors altogether,[12] cannot be denied.

It can be concluded from Ohly's and Urbanek's calculations that it is far from straightforward to define what actually constitutes an episode in the *Kaiserchronik*. The problem of what to make of the Silvester episode has already been mentioned,

---

7   Ibid., pp. 16–18.

8   Ferdinand Urbanek was the first to point out Ohly's various computational mistakes, such as getting the date of Lothair of Supplinburg's death wrong ('Zur Datierung der "Kaiserchronik": Entstehung — Auftraggeber — Chronologie', *Euphorion*, 53 (1959), 113–52 (p. 146)). Urbanek counts 409 years and 8 months from Caesar to the interregnum before Charlemagne takes over, a span of time filled by thirty-six emperors. From the coronation of Charlemagne to the present day of the chronicler, which in the *Kaiserchronik* encompasses eighteen emperors, he counts 394 years and 11 months. By adding the duration of the reign of Conrad III — whose rule is never concluded in the *Kaiserchronik* — Urbanek arrives, like Ohly, at 409 years and agrees with him that this annalistic symmetry cannot be an accident.

9   As pointed out by Dickhut-Bielsky, p. 60.

10   Ferdinand Urbanek, 'Herrscherzahl und Regierungszeiten in der "Kaiserchronik"', *Euphorion*, 66 (1972), 219–37 (p. 223).

11   He stands between thirty-six ancient emperors and eighteen medieval emperors.

12   Assuming that one focuses on emperors who actually ruled and does not consider the episode phrasings, which suggest a more nuanced approach, as laid out below.

but the complications go far beyond this issue. For example, in several cases one imperial rule merges with the following one, for instance when Claudius succeeds his fictitious brother Faustinian after the latter and his wife withdraw into a monastery (*KC*, 4025–38), when Piso and Galba jointly rule the Empire (*KC*, 4835–64), or when Alaric kills Lucius Accommodus and takes over as emperor from him (*KC*, 7420–25). Another problem is that the established counting of emperors as presented by Ohly and Urbanek takes the actual catalogue of Roman emperors as a reference and does not consider the structural markers the text offers for mapping out its episodes.

The first indication of the episodic framework that will later become so important to the text's structure can be found at the end of Caesar's reign:

> diu rîche er mit michelem gewalte habete
> die wîle daz er lebete,
> daz buoch saget uns vur wâr:
> niewan fiunf jâr.
> Rômâre in ingetrûwelîche sluogen,
> sîn gebaine si ûf ein irmensûl begruoben. (*KC*, 597–602)

Elements in this passage will become recurring markers of the conclusion of an episode, most prominently the reckoning of the years of the rule of an emperor and the short reference to the circumstances of his death.

The first episodic introduction of an emperor follows:

> Alse Juljus wart erslagen,
> Augustus daz rîche nâh im gewan,
> von sîner swester was er geborn.
> duo er ze rihter wart erkorn. (*KC*, 603–06)

Later, these opening formulas will become more reduced. Neither a causal connection to the events of the preceding episode nor the establishment of a genealogical or political connection to the preceding emperor (which would legitimize the following emperor's ascent to the throne) figure prominently in the Roman part of the *Kaiserchronik*. Here, these episodes are usually introduced with a short tripartite formula of the following pattern:

> Das buoch kundet uns sus,
> daz rîche besaz dô Tybêrîus,
> der gewan Rômæren michel êre. (*KC*, 671–73)

Quite similarly, when Nero is introduced as the successor of Claudius:

> Daz buoch kundet uns mêre:
> daz rîche besaz duo Nêre;
> der was der aller wirste man
> der von muoter in dise welt ie bekom. (*KC*, 4083–86)

And much later, when Helius Pertinax succeeds Severus:

> Daz buoch chundet uns daz:
> Hêlîus Pertinax
> der besaz dô dâz rîche. (*KC*, 7136–38)

The tripartite formula is simple. It often starts with a reference to the authoritative book, which reports the rule, then introduces the name of the emperor who ascends to the throne, and concludes with an often prefigurative phrase that points to what the audience can expect from the content of the episode to come.

Most of the time, the connection between the emperor and his empire is contained in the word 'besaz', the third-person singular preterite of the strong verb *besitzen*. One of its idiomatic meanings is 'to ascend the throne', but it also carries connotations of 'to sit in judgement' and 'to conquer'.[13] Three aspects are communicated by this simple, recurring lexeme at the beginning of episodes: the inaugural, the successive, and the judicial.[14] Interestingly, there is a marked decline in the interest of this phrase in the medieval part of the *Kaiserchronik*, where only three of the eighteen emperors are introduced in this way.

In terms of content, there is usually very little intratextual correspondence or explicit relation between the episodes. It comes almost as a surprise when at the beginning of the otherwise rather inconspicuous Achilleus episode, the destruction of Rome by Alaric in the preceding episode is acknowledged and the new emperor has to do a fair amount of reconstruction (*KC*, 7426–35). This extensive report on the construction and ornamentation carried out in Rome under Achilleus is not directly related to the remainder of the episode (which deals mostly with the emperor's assassination by Posthumus; *KC*, 7436–51) and is only required because in the episode before, Alaric thoroughly devastated the city and decimated its population (*KC*, 7404–11, 7417–19). At the same time, this narrative treatment of the destruction and rebuilding of Rome illustrates the clear conceptual cut marked by each episode boundary. Events that are actually parts of a single historical sequence, like the devastation and subsequent reconstruction of Rome in this example, are not presented as such if they run across the boundary between reigns. This is corroborated by the role of the temple of Jupiter in the Gaius episode. Despite being extensively introduced in the review of the pagan week at the very beginning of the *Kaiserchronik* (*KC*, 139–56), when the temple next features it is treated to a fully fledged reintroduction: the sacrifice is carried to 'ainem betehûs' (*KC*, 1128) and both the god's name and his domain as the god of weather are stated again as if they had never featured in the narrative before (*KC*, 1127–32).

The content of each episode is self-contained and exists unaffected by previous references to the same material. This raises the question of whether the text is at all interested in creating a coherent diegetic idea of Jupiter within its narrative or

13   See Matthias Lexer, *Mittelhochdeutsches Handwörterbuch*, 3 vols (Leipzig, 1872), s.vv. *besitzen* (I (1872), cols 217–18), *sitzen* (II (1876), cols 944–45).

14   'Besaz' recurs at the beginning of most episodes: Tiberius (*KC*, 672), Caligula (*KC*, 1116), Faustinian (*KC*, 1220), Claudius (*KC*, 4036), Nero (*KC*, 4084), Tarquin (*KC*, 4302), Galba and Piso (*KC*, 4835), Otho (*KC*, 4847), Vitellius (*KC*, 4851), Vespasian (*KC*, 5100), Domitian (*KC*, 5558), Nerva (*KC*, 5684), Trajan (*KC*, 5840), Philip (*KC*, 6098), Decius (*KC*, 6157), Diocletian and Maximian (*KC*, 6451), Severus (*KC*, 6623), Helius Pertinax (*KC*, 7138), Achilleus (*KC*, 7427), Galienus (*KC*, 7453), Constantius (*KC*, 7605), Julian (*KC*, 10,635), Heraclius (*KC*, 11,139), Narcissus (*KC*, 11,353), Justinian (*KC*, 12,814), Theodosius (*KC*, 13,068), Constantius Leo (*KC*, 13,671), Zeno (*KC*, 13,825), Ludewic (*KC*, 15,318), Karl (*KC*, 15,400), and Otto II (*KC*, 15,977).

whether the two Jupiter temples exist in entirely disjointed story worlds mostly influenced by the source tradition and not by the paradigmatic narrative axis of the *Kaiserchronik*.

1.1.1.2. From Historiography to Genealogy

Alongside the confused historical account, a further quality of the *Kaiserchronik* has attracted scholarly scrutiny and sometimes provoked bewilderment. The chronicle seems to fall into two clearly divided parts, one dealing with the Roman emperors of antiquity and one dealing with the 'German' emperors of the Middle Ages. Indeed, the qualitative differences between the two parts are striking.[15] As early as Ernst Scheunemann, who wrote the article on the *Kaiserchronik* in the original *Verfasserlexikon*, scholars have remarked on the conceptual difference that seems to separate the two parts. Scheunemann contrasted the 'Wirklichkeitsbericht' of the German part with the 'geformte Wirklichkeit' (aspiring to 'epische Darstellung') of the Roman part.[16] Ohly argues that with the beginning of the German emperor episodes, the larger legendary and mythological traditions fade out and give way to smaller, sometimes still legendary or mythological but increasingly also historical reports. Ohly goes on to contend that the time of the ancient Roman emperors was more open to free narrative reshaping by the *Kaiserchronik*'s author and therefore became the main focus of the author's literary attention.[17]

More recently, Christoph Petersen has taken an inverted stance on the question. Initially stating that the German part of the chronicle was written according to totally different premises from the Roman one, he sets out to look for a categorical differentiation to explain why more expansive legendary, hagiographical, or mythological narratives are produced only in the ancient part of the chronicle. Finally, he attributes to the Roman part a negative meaning such that the history of the Empire was semanticized retrospectively from the perspective of the twelfth century and through this lens the ancient Roman part could only be read as an 'Aufschub des im Anfang der Geschichte schon angelegten Zieles'. The ancient history of the Empire, he suggests, had to be artificially injected with meaning, through narrativization and abundant mythopoiesis, while the history of the Empire

---

15   There is a helpful summary of the four most obvious categories of differences between the two parts in Christoph Petersen, 'Zeit, Vorzeit und Narrativierung von Geschichte in der "Kaiserchronik"', *Zeitschrift für deutsche Philologie*, 126 (2007), 321–53 (p. 323): 'Die Traditionsbindung: Vor Karl d. Gr. zeigt der Text Eingriffe in die überlieferte Kaiserfolge (Umstellungen, Auslassungen, Hinzufügungen), die dem Standardwissen mittelalterlicher Chronistik Hohn sprechen, danach nicht. Die Materie: Legenden-, Sagen-, Mirakel- und Mirabilienstoffe werden bis Karl d. Gr. breit entfaltet, danach nicht. Die Quellenheuristik: Im antiken Teil sind höchst heterogene, kaum aber chronikalische Überlieferungen aufwändig kompiliert, danach beruht die Erzählung weitgehend auf der chronikalischen Tradition. Schließlich die Erzählweise: Personale Rede (Gespräche, Dispute, Ansprachen, Berichte) bestimmt im antiken Teil weithin die Erzählung, ist nach Karl d. Gr. aber nur sporadisch eingestreut; Schlachten sind unter Vespasian, Commodus oder Heraclius mit heldenepischer Topik ausgemalt, unter den deutschen Kaisern nur summarisch abgehandelt.'
16   Ernst Scheunemann, 'Kaiserchronik', in *Verfasserlexikon*, ed. by Wolfgang Stammler and Karl Langosch, 5 vols (Berlin, 1933–55), II (1936), 732–46.
17   Ohly, *Sage und Legende*, p. 7.

since Charlemagne shared a 'konzeptuelles Kontinuum' with the twelfth-century present and therefore did not require such treatment.[18] His analyses offer very satisfactory results on specific points, but they suffer strongly from very selective argumentation and also have the rather surprising consequence of rendering 83 per cent of the content of the text, the entire ancient Roman part, void of any inherent meaning. As Petersen remains vague about the implications and the borders of this conceptual continuum, the examination of its limits and extents will be an important task of the following sections.

Explanations like those offered by Ohly or Petersen share the focus on the content and its differing development in the two parts of the chronicle. They overlook, however, that the phraseology and form of the episode framework itself provide a useful conceptual distinction between the two parts that enables a definition of the dichotomy without speculating about the author's intentions or resorting to ascribing a negative meaning to 80 per cent of the text. It is striking that the introductory phrases of the medieval emperor episodes after Charlemagne no longer refer to a *buoch* as the authoritative source for the presentation of the incipient imperial reign, but shift to a genealogical model.

During the ancient part of the *Kaiserchronik*, genealogical connections between emperors are rarely mentioned. We find only Augustus introduced as Caesar's nephew ('von sîner swester was er geborn'; *KC*, 605); Domitian as Titus's brother (*KC*, 5558); and Constantine as the son of his paternal predecessor, Constantius, and Helena (*KC*, 7610–13, 7806–09). After the death of Charlemagne, the *Kaiserchronik* focuses on the genealogical ties that connect the subsequent emperors much more consistently. Most of the emperors ascending to the throne are introduced in relation to their imperial predecessors. Louis the Pious is presented as Charlemagne's rightful heir: 'Do der mære kaiser versciet, | ain guoten erben er verliez' (*KC*, 15,092–93).

Lothair, Louis's son and successor, is introduced in a similar pattern: temporal and causal connection to the death of his predecessor, explication of the family ties connecting the two men, then proclamation and affirmation by the princes of the Empire. The election by the princes is an element that is also new, as a factor of political succession asserts itself at this point (*KC*, 15,236–41).

Ludewic has been introduced as the son of Lothair (*KC*, 15,304–15) before succeeding him, and the struggle for mastery between Lothair's 'edelre sune viere' (*KC*, 15,305) drives the narrative of the episode. The transition from Ludewic to his elder son, Karl (*KC*, 15,394–99), is constructed analogously, only in this case without the strife between the brothers.

Arnulf of Carinthia is the first Carolingian king in the *Kaiserchronik* not to succeed to the throne in direct patrilinear descent; he is introduced as son of Karelmann (probably Carloman of Bavaria; *KC*, 15,522), Karl's younger brother (*KC*, 15,398), and so the genealogical model remains unperturbed. When Arnulf dies, he is succeeded by his son, the young Louis IV, who is commonly singled out by scholarship — and the *Kaiserchronik* — for becoming king while still a child (*KC*, 15,582–87).

---

18   Petersen, pp. 352–53.

With the strengthening of the genealogical model in the establishment of the Carolingian dynasty at the beginning of the medieval part, the 'besaz' phrase, which was characteristic of the ancient emperors, fades into the background. It does not disappear altogether, but rather loses its sense of taking up office and finds its way into different contexts. More generally, the refrain with the pattern 'daz buoch chundet uns sus | das rîche besaz dô [name of emperor]'[19] of the ancient episode openings is replaced with the phrase 'alse chaiser [name] verschiet | einen guten sun/erben er liez'.[20] For both formulas, the phrasing varies quite significantly from case to case, but the logic of this new pattern is the same: the death of the father triggers the election and succession of his heir, usually his son. The *Kaiserchronik* no longer harks back to the authority of knowledge transmission via written tradition ('das buoch chundet uns sus'), but now deploys a straightforward genealogical model of succession. This marks a conceptual break in the episodic paradigm of the *Kaiserchronik*, not between Roman and German emperors, but rather between historiographically and genealogically legitimized ancient and medieval emperors.

The first break in the genealogical model is negotiated with the death of Louis the Child. The bishops and princes of the Empire elect Conrad I at a diet in Mainz. The text provides some context, such as the name of Conrad's father and the lands he owns, but does not tie him to the Carolingians or elaborate on his qualifications as king (*KC*, 15,652–63). However, the phrase that introduces the process of his succession is quite similar to the established scheme: 'Also der chunich Ludewîch erstarp | unt âne erben vur wart' (*KC*, 15,652–53). Conrad I also dies without issue, whereupon the princes elect Henry I, the first of the Saxon Ottonians, to be the next king (*KC*, 15,760–66).

Here again, the election by a college of princes is mentioned and a genealogical background at least hinted at, though no connection to previous incumbents is established. Additionally, the chronicle stresses Henry's resistance to becoming king (*KC*, 15,768–71). His reluctance to have his rank exalted is a classical trope of modesty that will feature again when Lothair of Supplinburg, another extra-dynastic king, is proclaimed. The following three generations of Ottos are all clearly marked as a patrilinear genealogy going back to Henry I, passing rule down from generation to generation. Otto I succeeds his father (*KC*, 15,850–53), and his father's excellence as a ruler further qualifies the son in the eyes of the princes, who elect Otto as their new king: 'want der vater alsô biderbe was | sô lobeten si den sun deste baz' (*KC*, 15,856–66).

The mechanism is already automatic when his 'tiurlîche[r] sun' (*KC*, 15,975),

19   In this or similar form, it opens the episodes of Tiberius (*KC*, 671), Gaius (*KC*, 1115), Faustinian (*KC*, 1219), Nero (*KC*, 4083), Tarquin (*KC*, 4301), Vitellius (*KC*, 4862), Vespasian (*KC*, 5099), Domitian (*KC*, 5557), Nerva (*KC*, 5683), Trajan (*KC*, 5839), Philip (*KC*, 6097), Severus (*KC*, 6622), Helius Pertinax (*KC*, 7136), Achilleus (*KC*, 7426), Galienus (*KC*, 7452), Constantius (*KC*, 7604), Julian (*KC*, 10,634), Heraclius (*KC*, 11,138), Narcissus (*KC*, 11,352), Justinian (*KC*, 12,813), Theodosius (*KC*, 13,067), and the second Constantius (*KC*, 14,194).
20   In this or similar form, it opens the episodes of Ludewic (*KC*, 15,582), Lothair I (*KC*, 15,236–37), Charles II (*KC*, 15,394–95), Louis the Child (*KC*, 15,582–83), Otto I (*KC*, 15,850–51), Otto II (*KC*, 15,974–75), Otto III (*KC*, 16,064–65), and Henry III (*KC*, 16,376–77).

Otto II, follows him onto the throne, and the *Kaiserchronik* quickly falls back to only pointing out that he 'besaz' the Empire, without mentioning an election by the princes (*KC*, 15,974–78). When the third Otto succeeds his father of the same name, the diet that elects him is again mentioned at length, together with the fact that he 'newas niht alt, | wan ze zwelf jâren gezalt' (*KC*, 16,066–67). When, finally, the last Ottonian is elected by the princes, the *Kaiserchronik* only mentions that he is 'der Baier herzoge' (*KC*, 16,146); Henry's II dynastic relation to the main line of the Ottonians is not mentioned at all. As if to compensate for this, the prefigurative praise, which concludes the opening of his episode, extols him all the louder (*KC*, 16,147–49).

Henry's II successor, Conrad II, the first Salian on the throne, is elected by the 'vursten in dem rîche' (*KC*, 16,255) without any further comment, and the following Salian emperors are clearly introduced as a patrilinear dynasty. Henry III is Conrad II's son (*KC*, 16,377), and he is in turn succeeded by his own son, Henry IV (*KC*, 16,534). The latter's accession is accompanied by a remark that mirrors the introduction of Otto I in relation to his father:

> durch den michelen ruom
> den der vater hête gewunnen
> sô gunden si iz dem jungen. (*KC*, 16,535–37)

But unlike Otto I, Henry IV will not prove worthy of the advance in trust granted to him by the princes, as the *Kaiserchronik* turns him into the paradigmatic bad emperor among the German rulers.

The *Kaiserchronik* reduces Henry V to an antagonist of his father completely contained within the Henry IV episode (*KC*, 16,804–16,920), and goes from Henry IV directly to the tumultuous election of the dynastically unconnected Lothair of Supplinburg (*KC*, 16,942–71). Apart from being tied to Saxony, he is not part of the genealogical lines established previously. As in the case of Henry I, Lothair is at first very apprehensive and seeks counsel about how to avoid this elevation of his rank, before the princes manage to persuade him (*KC*, 16,957–68). Lothair is greatly praised and lamented by the *Kaiserchronik* when he dies (*KC*, 17,165–81), and the audience of his story is explicitly asked to pray for his soul in a way reminiscent only of the conclusion of the Silvester episode (*KC*, 10,619–33). Lothair is succeeded by Conrad III, 'der ê wider dem rîche was' (*KC*, 17,184). This is a reference to Conrad becoming counter-king (in 1127) to Lothair in the Lothair episode (*KC*, 17,039–69) but only succeeding Lothair after his death. The *Kaiserchronik* finally terminates mid-sentence as Conrad III is making preparations to go on crusade (*KC*, 17,270–83).

These observations point toward several complex questions. Does the switch from a historiographical to a genealogical model of imperial authority and succession merely reflect the different traditions of knowledge about the ancient and medieval Roman Empire that were available to medieval authors? Do the two different models correspond to a change in the author's modus operandi from compiling several written traditions into one account to building his writing on a more cohesive authority system that allowed him to draw on knowledge more easily available to him? Certainly, the conceptual implications for the *Kaiserchronik* are clear: while the ancient Empire emerges as an entity of historiographical knowledge and tradition, the medieval Empire takes on the shape of a genealogically organized polity. They are united by their shared Romanness and transpersonal or even transpolitical existence.

1.1.2. Modified Episode Framework

Building on the results of this new appraisal of the episode framework of the *Kaiserchronik*, I would like to propose the following episodic breakdown of the work's content.

Episode number	Emperor	Non-Episodic Content	Lines	Corresponding Figure*
		Prologue		
		Invocatio	1–14	
		Narratio	15–26	
		Polemic	27–42	
		Pre-Imperial Rome		
		Romulus and Remus	43–62	
		Review of the Pagan Week	63–185	
		Conversion of the Pantheon	186–208	
		Salvatio Romae	209–46	
1	Juljus Cêsar		247–602	Julius Caesar
2	Augustus		603–70	Augustus
3	Tybêrius		671–1115	Tiberius
4	Gâjus		1116–1218	Gaius
5	Faustinjânus		1219–4037	Faustinian
			4038–82	Claudius
6	Nêre		4083–4300	Nero
7	Tarquînius		4301–4834	Tarquin
8	Galbâ and Pîsô		4835–46	Galba and Piso
9	Ottô		4847–57	Otho
10	Vitellus		4858–5098	Vitellus
11	Vespasjânus		5099–5364	Vespasian

* The corresponding figure will in most cases be a historical Roman emperor but sometimes also an entirely literary or mythological figure. The identification of the Carolingian kings between Lothair and Arnulf of Carinthia is not straightforward. To indicate this uncertainty, the names used in the *Kaiserchronik* are retained for them.

12	Tîtus		5365–5556	Titus
13	Domîciânus		5557–5682	Domitian
14	Nervâ		5683–5838	Nerva
15	Traianus		5839–6096	Trajan
16	Philippus		6097–6150	Philip the Arab
17	Dêcîus		6151–6450	Decius
18	Dioclêtîânus		6451–6621	Diocletian
19	Sevêrus		6622–7135	Severus
20	Hêlîus Pertinax		7136–7211	Helius Pertinax
21	Hêlîus Adrîânus		7212–43	Hadrian
22	Lûcîus Accommodus		7344–7419	Commodus?
			7420–25	Alaric
23	Achillêus		7426–51	Fictitious
24	Gallîênus		7452–7603	Galerius and Galen?
25	Constantîus		7604–7805	Constantius
26	Constantînus		7806–10,510	Constantine
27	Sancte Silvester		10,511–632	Pope Silvester
28	Juljânus		10,633–11,137	Julian the Apostate
29	Herâclîus		11,138–11,351	Heraclius
30	Narcissus		11,352–72	Fictitious
			11,373–12,812	
31	Justinjânus		12,813–13,067	Justinian
32	Theodôsîus		13,068–13,650	Theodosius I and/or Theodosius II?
		Interregnum	13,651–67	
33	Constantînus Lêô		13,668–13,824	Leo I and/or Constantine V?
34	Zênô		13,825–14,193	Zeno
35	Constantîus		14,194–14,281	Constantine VI
		Interregnum	14,282–95	
36	Karl		14,296–15,091	Charlemagne
37	Ludewîch		15,092–15,235	Louis the Pious
38	Liuther		15,236–15,317	Lothair I

39	Ludewic		15,318–93	Probably an amalgamation of Louis the German and Louis II of Italy
40	Karl		15,394–15,517	Probably Charles the Fat
41	Arnolt		15,518–81	Arnulf of Carinthia
42	Ludewîch		15,582–15,651	Louis the Child
43	Chuonrât		15,652–15,760	Conrad I
44	Hainrîch		15,761–15,849	Henry I the Fowler
45	Ottô		15,850–15,973	Otto I the Great
46	Ottô		15,974–16,063	Otto II
47	Ottô		16,064–16,141	Otto III
48	Hainrîch		16,142–16,253	Henry II
49	Chuonrât		16,254–16,375	Conrad II
50	Hainrîch		16,376–16,531	Henry III
51	Hainrîch		16,532–16,941	Henry IV
52	Liuther		16,942–17,181	Lothair of Supplinburg
53	Chuonrât		17,182–83	Conrad III

This new scheme leaves the work with fifty-three emperor episodes altogether, thirty-five of them from Caesar to the second Constantius/Constantine VI, and eighteen of them from Charlemagne to Conrad III. It also singles out a block at the beginning of the *Kaiserchronik*, from the prologue to the *salvatio Romae*, that precedes the episode structure. At a later point in this book, I will show that this pre-episodic part plays an important role in setting up the constitution of the qualitatively largely stable Roman Empire, which provides the axis for the episodic part of the chronicle.[21] Moreover, it will become clear that the conventional distinction between Roman and German emperors cannot be maintained. Where there are important conceptual distinctions to be made between the two groups, in what follows the first thirty-five will be referred to as the ancient emperors and the subsequent eighteen as the medieval emperors.

According to this reckoning, Philip and Decius have each discrete episodes, while Claudius and Alaric become codas to Faustinian and Commodus respectively. Piso and Galba are given a joint episode, and Maximian features only as the antagonist of Diocletian in the latter's episode. The scheme allows for an independent episode for Pope Silvester, who gets a similar episodic framing to the emperors of the *Kaiserchronik*, but leaves the reign of the two Dietrichs firmly confined to the Narcissus episode. Through this lens the two periods of interregnum, which frame

21   See 4.1.2 in this book.

the time of the problematic Greek emperors, become more pronounced and point toward the pivotal structural importance of this block of episodes.

This new format is of course not without its flaws. It does little to mitigate the fact that the Caesar episode is rather organically intertwined with the preceding pre-episodic *salvatio Romae* passage. This passage ends up lumped together with the prologue and the other pre-imperial and pre-episodic material.

1.1.3. *Atomized Antiquity as the Quantitative Continuum of History*

Despite its idiosyncrasies, a great deal of insight can be derived from the episodic structure of the *Kaiserchronik* if it is not regarded merely as a silent framework but more as a running commentary in its own right that contributes to the generation of meaning as much as to the content of the episodes.

It is, after all, the form that was regarded as the appropriate one by the author of the *Kaiserchronik* for realizing the programmatic statements of the prologue. The *rîche* is presented as a succession of rules — a horizontal, linear, progressive, and continuous paradigm. It builds on long-established and authoritative forms of imperial historiography, going back all the way to Suetonius and still informing Latin historiography at the time of the *Kaiserchronik*, as is evident from the examples of Otto's *Chronica* or Godfrey of Viterbo's *Pantheon*. The principle is applied coherently and observed consistently, providing the narrative with regularity and reliability. Continuity lies at the heart of this form of presentation: the history of the Empire as a continuum. Consequently, the Empire remains Roman, even after the transalpine Carolingian and German kings or emperors take over its reign. The epithet *tiutsch* is only used together with *lant* or *rîche* in a transalpine-geographical sense, to localize a group of people (*KC*, 464, 6811, 14,819, 16,495) or to define a destination (*KC*, 253, 263, 462, 684, 15,554, 16,804, 16,816). It is never used to describe the political quality of the Empire; even under the rule of Charlemagne (*KC*, 15,085), Otto II (*KC*, 15,995), or Henry III (*KC*, 16,504), the Empire stays Roman. This remains true in the thirteenth-century continuations of the *Kaiserchronik*, where *roemisch* is now exclusively used in conjunction with *rîche* (*KC*, 'Erste (baierische) Fortsetzung', 157, 388, 'Zweite (schwäbische) Fortsetzung', 29, 69, 80, 146, 156). Thus, as the emperors change, and even as their ethnic and political background shifts from the Romans to the Greeks and on to the Carolingians and Germans, the Empire remains qualitatively unchanged.

Hayden White has provided a useful methodological approach that can be used to read the imperial continuum of the *Kaiserchronik*'s episode framework as a semanticizing structure. Adapting the ideas of his 1982 book *The Content of the Form* allows us to take the semantic achievement of non-narrative framing structures of medieval historiographical texts into account. White developed this approach with reference to a tripartite model according to which medieval narrative historiographies are classified as either annals, chronicles, or histories. According to White's criteria of differentiation, the *Kaiserchronik* would clearly be a chronicle due to its 'higher' form of historical conceptualization, its greater comprehensiveness and narrative coherence, the organization of its material by topics and reigns, and its focus on a central subject.[22] However, the theoretical principles applied here are mainly derived from White's work on annals. It will be argued that the episodic framing structures of the *Kaiserchronik* function analogously to the non-narrative enumerative lists that synchronize years and events in annals.

Building on Hegel, who wrote that 'it is only the state which first presents subject-matter that is not only adapted to the prose of History, but involves the production of such history in the very progress of its own being',[23] White states that a central requirement for historiography to happen is the existence of a legal and social system 'against which or on behalf of which the typical agents of a narrative account militate'.[24] In the case of the *Kaiserchronik*, the episodic framing structures can be read as constituting this system, and the agents that militate against it are the disjunctive, self-contained, and often contingent stories that are framed by the episodic structural markers fleshed out above.

In relation to this system, the stories that the *Kaiserchronik* contains in its episodes are largely interchangeable, especially when dealing with the ancient history of the Empire. Antiquity in the *Kaiserchronik* is treated — to borrow a concept introduced by Richard Newald — in atomizing terms.[25] The process of atomizing narratives detaches them from their historical meaning and frees them of their context, turning them into a highly fluid cloud of freely floating schemata readily available for insertion and rearrangement. The atomized narrative material in the *Kaiserchronik* is composed as sets of two elements: an authoritative label and a malleable and fluid pool of narrative material. The label — usually the name of a prominent protagonist, like Lucretia or Alaric, which serves as a shorthand — attached to a story gives it authority and ensures instant recognizability. The fluid pool of narrative material surrounds the authoritative label and is actualized when- and wherever the label is introduced into a new narrative context. Audience expectations would be disappointed if a story introduced with the 'Lucretia' label did not also tell of Conlatinus and Tarquin and did not end with Lucretia's suicide. In the *Kaiserchronik*, the mobility and availability of these story atoms affects both the order and succession of emperors and the narrative material contained in the frames labelled with the name of an emperor.

Prominent examples of these atomized narrative elements abound in the *Kaiserchronik*. First of all, there is the Cyclops, who features in the *origo gentis* of the Franks (*KC*, 346–60). In its version, the *Kaiserchronik* connects the Trojan origin story of the Franks to the Aeneas material, which was well familiar to writers of the twelfth century through Virgil but is triggered here by the reference to Troy and the Greeks.[26] It also inserts a short excursus on the Homeric story of Ulysses'

22   Hayden White, *The Content of the Form* (Baltimore, 1987), pp. 1–25.
23   Georg Wilhelm Friedrich Hegel, *Lectures on the Philosophy of History*, trans. by J. Sibree (New York, 1956), p. 63.
24   White, p. 13.
25   Richard Newald, *Nachleben des antiken Geistes im Abendland bis zum Beginn des Humanismus: Eine Überschau* (Tübingen, 1960), pp. 192–93.
26   See Charles Homer Haskins, *The Renaissance of the Twelfth Century* (Cleveland, 1967), pp. 105–07; also Paul Klopsch, 'Vergil im Mittelalter, I: Lateinische Literatur', in *Lexikon des Mittelalters*,

fight against the Cyclops, who remains nameless in this case. Here, Ulysses serves as the authoritative label and the Cyclops as the core of the story material that label evokes. The passage appears as if entirely disconnected from the rest of the Frankish *origo gentis*. The place where it is inserted, however, reads like an attempt to transfer the mythical authority of the Homeric tale onto the Franks. Homer was largely unknown in the Middle Ages, and his work was mostly accessible through later Latin reworkings like the fifth-century *Historia de Excidio Troiae* by Dares Phrygius, the fourth-century *Ephemeris Belli Troiani* by Dictys Cretensis, or the anonymous and entirely independent tradition of the *Excidium Troie*, first conceived between the fourth and the sixth century.[27] But the narrative atom of Ulysses and the Cyclops still seemed to contain enough authority from deep ancient history to be deemed valuable for insertion at this point in the narrative.

A similar case occurs in the Tarquin episode, when Lucretia is introduced: 'si stât in Ovîdîô gescriben dâ' (*KC*, 4337). To be able to tell the story of Lucretia, the text needed to insert Tarquin, whose Latin epithet 'Superbus' is contained in the introductory phrases the *Kaiserchronik* devotes to him: 'der was der ubermuotigeste man | der ie von muoter in dise werlt bekom' (*KC*, 4303–04).

Interestingly, Ovid is not invoked with the introduction of Tarquin, but only when the story turns to Lucretia. She is introduced as the chosen Roman wife of the episode's male main protagonist, Conlatinus: 'Ain furste bi den ziten ze Triere' (*KC*, 4305). Conlatinus, nephew of King Tarquin and husband of Lucretia, figures both in Livy's and Ovid's version of the story. It is his boasting about the virtue of his wife that sets the whole chain of events in motion.[28] In the *Kaiserchronik*'s version, he has to flee from Trier because he killed another prince there (*KC*, 4310–13), and is honourably received in Rome, where the Senate ponders how to adequately welcome such a great guest.

> duo gevuoct iz sih alsus,
> daz im gebôt der senâtus,
> daz er aine frowen von Rôme næme,
> diu sîner edelkait wol gezæme.
> Ainer frowen er duo bat:
> wie schiere man im sie gap!
> diu hiez Lucrêtîâ. (*KC*, 4331–37)

Ohly reads the reference to Ovid — who is the only ancient poet to be mentioned by name in the *Kaiserchronik* — as a sign of the emerging *aetas ovidiana* in the middle of the twelfth century.[29] More importantly, he turns the *Kaiserchronik*'s explicit

ed. by Robert-Henri Bautier, Gloria Avella-Widhalm, and Robert Auty, 10 vols (1980–99), VIII (Munich, 1997), cols 1522–26 (esp. cols 1525–26).

27   See Elisabeth Heyse, 'Homer, I: Lateinisches Mittelalter', in *Lexikon des Mittelalters*, ed. by Bautier, Avella-Widhalm, and Auty, V (Munich, 1991), cols 109–10.

28   Livy, *Ab Urbe Condita*, ed. by Robert Seymour Conway and Charles Flamstead Walters (Oxford, 1914), I. 57–59, pp. 1085–88.

29   Ohly, *Sage und Legende*, p. 89. In French florilegia of the twelfth century, about twelve times as much space is devoted to Ovid than it is to Virgil. See Ernst Robert Curtius, 'Zur Literaturästhetik des Mittelalters', *Zeitschrift für romanische Philologie*, 59 (1938), 1–50, 129–232, 433–79 (p. 134).

reference to Ovid into an argument for his typological system by arguing that medieval calendars employed aetiological stories in the same way as Ovid's *Fasti*, where Lucretia figures,[30] and that both the choice and the mentioning of Ovid as a source indicated medieval typological thinking.[31] However, it seems much more likely to be just another marker for an atomized piece of antiquity, required because the Lucretia story has been detached from its chronological context and inserted into a new historical setting.

Other examples of the atomized used of ancient narremes inform many of the *Kaiserchronik*'s more idiosyncratic narrative decisions. It does not matter if Caesar initially conquers the Gauls or the Germans, as long as his conquests lead to him becoming the first emperor.[32] Faustinian could be introduced as the brother of any other emperor, as long as St Peter could still be reasonably imagined to have been alive, thus allowing the insertion of material from the fourth-century Pseudo-Clementine *Recognitiones*. Tarquin can be inserted anachronistically between Nero and Galba without inflicting any harm on the chronicle's narrative cohesion. The goal is not to present a causally integrated account of the chaotic circumstances of Nero's death and the following 'Year of the Four Emperors' (69 CE) spanning the episodes of Nero, Galba and Piso, Vitellus, and Vespasian, but to insert the story atom of Lucretia. Thus, the story of Lucretia, with its associated figures (like Tarquin and Conlatinus) and established plot elements (like Lucretia's rape and subsequent suicide), can be anachronistically implanted without disrupting the narrative fabric or the paradigmatic structure of the chronicle. The only limitation to this mobility is that the narrative environment into which her story gets inserted still has to be dominated by pagan religious beliefs. The Christian discourse on her moral exemplarity, which goes back to Augustine, is too closely linked to her being a pagan.[33] And creating meaning by contrasting her behaviour as a woman who has been unjustly condemned with Crescentia's behaviour from the Narcissus episode, as Ohly suggests, only works if Crescentia is read as a Christian antipode to the pagan Lucretia.[34]

The mobility of those story atoms also explains why the sack of Jerusalem and the diaspora of the people of Israel — the salvation-historical watershed chiefly associated with Vespasian and Titus[35] — can be told entirely independently of the episodes that are actually dedicated to the rule of Vespasian and Titus. The authority of the ancient tradition of the Veronica story ties — as part of the *Vindicta*

---

30   *Ovid's Fasti*, ed. by Sir James Frazer (London, 1931), II, pp. 111–14.

31   Ohly, *Sage und Legende*, p. 91.

32   Needless to say, this also happens in the source texts and in other chronicles of the time, like Godfrey of Viterbo's *Pantheon*; once more, the structure of the *Kaiserchronik* is mostly informed by its sources. This points to a more widespread treatment of the ancient past as atomized, which the *Kaiserchronik* shared with other texts, both older and contemporary, and made those materials all the more attractive for narrative inclusion.

33   Augustine, *De Civitate Dei*, ed. by B. Dombart and A. Kalb, Corpus Christianorum: Series Latina, 47–48, 2 vols (Turnhout, 1955), I. 19.

34   Ohly, *Sage und Legende*, pp. 194–98.

35   See Manfred Kern, 'Titus' and 'Vespasian', in *Lexikon der antiken Gestalten in den deutschen Texten des Mittelalters*, ed. by Manfred Kern and Alfred Ebenbauer (Berlin, 2003), pp. 620, 669–71.

Salvatoris tradition[36] — the destruction of Jerusalem to the Jews' killing of Jesus in a retributive logic. From the viewpoint of chronology and historiographical tradition, the sack of Jerusalem (70 CE) would be expected to take place during the reign of Vespasian. But by connecting the sack of the city to a command given by Tiberius in order to punish the Jews, the *Kaiserchronik*'s adaptation of the Veronica legend separates the story from its traditional place in history.

In the *Kaiserchronik*, antiquity becomes visible and readable in sign and tradition, by being inserted by means of story nuclei that bring with them associated material from their narrative traditions. Antiquity gains a transtemporal and transspatial semantics.[37] The *Kaiserchronik* displays all the traits that Richard Newald singled out as characteristic for medieval adaptation of ancient material: '[m]osaikartiges Zusammensetzen, Weiterspinnen oder naives Umdeuten des durch die Autorität Gesicherten, durch den Glauben Geheiligten und durch die Gewohnheit Gestärkten'.[38]

1.1.4. Dimensions of Qualitative Change: Political and Religious Identity of the Empire

As the example of the Lucretia story shows, there are limits to the mobility of story atoms. The principles that determine these limits are in turn shaped by the two main dimensions of qualitative difference that the chronicle must modulate for its twelfth-century audience: the political and religious identities of the Empire, and the changes within those identities. While the Empire remains a precisely measured and quantitatively anchored framework, essential change in these two dimensions has to be modulated, negotiated, and communicated. How did the cisalpine polytheist pagan Roman Empire become a transalpine Christian one? Frank Shaw already hinted at these two dimensions when he characterized the trajectory of the *Kaiserchronik*, whose poet saw the history of the Roman Empire 'as proceeding in two massive steps toward a God-ordained perfection and permanence. The first step is the embracing of Christianity by Constantine the Great; the second is the *translatio imperii* from the "Romans" to the "Germans"'.[39] Shaw's 'massive steps' correspond to the two dimensions of qualitative change that the chronicle has to negotiate; but, as will become apparent in the later chapters of this book, the result of this change is neither definitive nor permanent.[40]

---

36   *Vindicta Salvatoris*, in *Two Old English Apocrypha and their Manuscript Source: The Gospel of Nichodemus and the Avenging of the Saviour*, ed. by E. J. Cross, Cambridge Studies in Anglo-Saxon England, 19 (Cambridge, 1996), pp. 248–93.

37   Curtius, 'Literaturästhetik', p. 139.

38   Newald, p. 285. How 'naive' the reinterpretation of ancient tradition in the *Kaiserchronik* and in medieval texts in general actually was would be a matter of some debate. Ernst Robert Curtius, *European Literature and the Latin Middle Ages* (Princeton, 1953; repr. 2013), p. 19, also sees medieval reception of antiquity as shaped by 'misunderstandings', but in a productive way.

39   Frank Shaw, '"Kaiserchronik" and "Enide"', *German Life and Letters*, 24.4 (1971), 295–303 (p. 296).

40   The underlying premise of these observations — that the form carries continuity while the content negotiates change — has recently been described by Dickhut-Bielsky, p. 62, but obviously with a slightly different focus: 'Aus der kompositorischen Perspektive ist die bewusste Prägung einer Makrostruktur auch nicht notwendig, geht es doch vor allem um die Zeichnung der Kontinuität des

Both dimensions of change are simultaneously marked by diegetic insertions in the narrative and by the more redactional decisions of episode arrangement and textual composition. At the very beginning of the chronicle, the text establishes a pagan order of the world:

> Hie bevor bi der haiden zîten
> duo anbette man wîten
> abgot die unrainen.
> die haiden algemaine
> muosen si êren unt anebeten
> al nâch der chunige gebote. (*KC*, 43–48)

When, after Caesar, Augustus is the first emperor to be presented in a fully fledged episode frame, his paganness is stressed by the text (*KC*, 607). Philip is explicitly singled out as the first Christian emperor:

> der was der aller êrste hêrre
> der den gewalt und die êre
> in dirre christenhait ie gewan. (*KC*, 6099–6101)

This new and heightened diegetic presence of Christianity in the *Kaiserchronik* is used by the author to present, in short and anachronistic succession, the rules of the two most infamous persecutors of Christians: Decius and Diocletian (*KC*, 6151, 6451). If the episodic framework before Philip largely adhered to the historical order of emperors, the mobility of emperors as points of orientation in the episode framework now appears much increased as the extratextual historical context of the *Kaiserchronik* enters a time of opposition between paganism and Christianity. The great confusion in this part of the chronicle could in itself be seen as a commentary on the confusion of the struggle between emergent Christianity and defensive paganism. The content of the episodes contained in this block does not foreground this struggle often, but it is certainly the defining element in the first episodes, which focus on Philip, Decius, and Diocletian, and again in the last episodes, which focus on Constantine and Theodosius. Constantine introduces the official Christianization of the Empire. The narrative uses Constantine's conversion and his seven days of Christian legislating side-by-side with Pope Silvester (*KC*, 7986–8199), and the lengthy disputations of Silvester against the Jewish scholars — whom the *Kaiserchronik* sets up as representatives of a universal heathendom — to introduce some of the dogmatic underpinnings of conversion and to present a string of mass-conversion events (*KC*, 8574–10,372).

The programmatic framing of this block of episodes is corroborated by the striking conception of time and space in the Seven Sleepers passage, which concludes the Theodosius episode. In it, seven Christian princes from Ephesus go into hiding to escape Decius's persecution of the Christians, only to be found again under the reign of the exemplarily Christian Emperor Theodosius (*KC*, 6421–42). At that

Römischen Reiches von Caesar bis in die Gegenwart [...]. Diese Kontinuität wird durch das additive Erzählen erzähltechnisch umgesetzt. Die Entwicklung (*translatio fidei, translatio imperii*) vollzieht sich auf der Inhaltsebene; kompositorisch bestimmend stellen sich die immer wiederkehrenden Einleitungs- und Ausgangsformeln dar.'

point, they have slept through not only 248 years but also several thousand lines of narrative (*KC*, 13,496–13,503). The 248 years the author claims they have been sleeping (*KC*, 6425–27) does not correspond to the *Kaiserchronik*'s own reckoning of time passed between Decius and Theodosius (around 110 years)[41] or to the actual historical distance between the two (128 years).[42] When Serapion, the first of the sleepers to awake, realizes that he, after going to sleep to evade persecution by the pagan Roman authorities, is now surrounded by Christians, his confusion is registered not in temporal but in spatial terms:

> 'ich enwaiz, wannen ich her bin komen',
> sprah der hailige man.
> 'dô wir wærlîchen hôrten sagen,
> daz diu æhte geboten wart
> z'Effesô uber die stat,
> duo fluhe wir hin —
> ich enwaiz aver in der werlte, wâ ich pin —
> ad celeum montem.
> [...]
> hêrre, wi haizet diz lant?
> oder wi bin ich her komen?
> der berg haizet Cêlêôn.
> ist er hie iht nahen bî?
> ist hie iemen dem dar kunt sî?' (*KC*, 13,550–68)

Even though Serapion has just come down from the mountain, where he believes he has spent only four days, to get food and now expects to be martyred for it (*KC*, 13,508–20), the spatial environment of Ephesus and Mount Celeon, which should be immediately familiar to him, loses all meaning when he realizes that times have changed and he has come back to a Christian world. His confusion about historical change over time is expressed as a total loss of spatial orientation. He does not know where he is any more, what the country he is in is called, or how he got there. He does remember Ephesus and the mountain to which he and his companions fled, but with the times having changed so dramatically, he is no longer capable of reconciling the topography he remembers with the spatially unchanged but religiously differently semanticized topography he finds now. Therefore he has to ask whether the mountain to which he fled is anywhere nearby and whether anyone knows the way there.

41   The reigns of Diocletian and Maximian (20 years, 6 weeks), Severus (6 years, 6 months), Helius Pertinax (7 months, 5 days), Helius Adrianus (11 months), Lucius Accommodus (not specified), Alaric (4 years, 6 months), Achilleus (9 months), Galienus (4 years), Constantinus (17 years, 5 months), and Constantine (30 years, 6 months) add up to 85 years, 3 months, and 2 weeks. The final total is obscured by the unspecified duration of Lucius Accommodus's rule before he is slain and succeeded by Alaric, and complicated by the duration of the rule of Silvester (24 years, 6 months, 5 days), where it remains unclear how much overlap has to be assumed with the duration of Constantine's rule. Adding the entire rule of Silvester brings the final sum to 109 years, 9 months, 2 weeks, and 5 days (assuming for simplicity's sake that one month breaks down into four weeks).
42   Decius died in 251 CE, and Theodosius came into power in 379 CE. As the Theodosius of the *Kaiserchronik* seems to be an amalgamation of the historical Theodosius I and II, the time would increase to 151 years, as Theodosius II came into power in 402 CE.

The meanings of time and space are inseparably linked here. Meaning is mainly bestowed by religion. As religion as a temporal structure changes over time, it renders space unrecognizable. As Serapion is asking for spatial orientation, it becomes clear that it would also work the other way round: if he knew where the mountain is, he would be able to make sense of the time again.

The specific configurations of time, space, and meaning that Serapion and the Seven Sleepers transcend can be clarified by adapting Mikhail Bakhtin's concept of the chronotope:

> We will give the name chronotope (literally, 'time space') to the intrinsic connectedness of temporal and spatial relationships that are artistically expressed in literature. [...] it expresses the inseparability of space and time (time as the fourth dimension of space). [...] In the literary artistic chronotope, spatial and temporal indicators are fused into one carefully thought out, concrete whole. Time, as it were, thickens, takes on flesh, becomes artistically visible, likewise, space becomes charged and responsive to the movements of time, plot and history.[43]

If it is to be understood as the fourth dimension of the three-dimensional coordinate system of Serapion's movement through space, time has now been inexorably altered by the qualitative change in its religious composition. The space Serapion inhabits, which is now no longer semanticized by Serapion's permanence in it but has been 'charged' by the altered time, responds to the temporal change by rendering itself unrecognizable. As the *Kaiserchronik* moves through its episodes, the passing of time is mainly registered quantitatively, but between the Decius and Theodosius episodes one qualitative shift has also transpired, namely the establishment of Christianity as the dominant religion in the Empire. Serapion and the Seven Sleepers, however, have been suspended from any qualitative change over time; they have remained out of time and have now, as they return to the reshaped temporal continuum of the Theodosius episode, passed from a pagan chronotope into a Christian one.

The chronotopical change foregrounds the qualitative change, which the *Kaiserchronik*'s episode framework usually works hard to suppress. It also marks the preliminary end of the process of Christianization. Neither the time nor the place of the sleepers' awakening are an accident. Emperor Theodosius is only in the vicinity because just before the return of the sleepers, there was a synod in Ephesus to debate the Arian heresy, which in the narrative of the *Kaiserchronik* is about the truth of the bodily resurrection (*KC*, 13,377–88) and not about the Christological debate between homoiousians and homoousians.[44] Now, after Arius has died by

43   Mikhail Bakhtin, 'Forms of Time and of the Chronotope in the Novel: Notes toward a Historical Poetics', in *The Dialogic Imagination: Four Essays by M. M. Bakhtin*, ed. by Michael Holquist, trans. by Caryl Emerson and Michael Holquist (Austin, 1998), pp. 84–110 (p. 84).

44   The Christological debate of the fourth century circled around the question of whether Jesus was of the same (*homo-ousios*/ὁμοούσιος) or of similar (*homoi-ousios*/ὁμοιούσιος) substantial essence as God his Father. The Council of Nicaea in 325 ruled that Jesus was of the same substance as God. Arian's contrary Christology was strongly coloured by, but not completely congruent with homoiousianism. He stressed the divinity of the Father over that of the Son and implied that the Son was created, meaning that there was a time when Christ did not exist and that he is not coeternal with the Father. Later ecumenical councils, however, confirmed homoousianism as orthodoxy, and

divine decree ('dâ rach got sîne cristenhait'; *KC*, 13,475) just before the disputation could actually begin, the miraculous return of the sleepers proves the theological truth of the orthodox position represented by the emperor (*KC*, 13,484–90). The events at the end of the Theodosius episode correspond to the prophetic passage after the sleepers have gone into hiding during Decius's rule (*KC*, 6437–42). When Theodosius first hears of Serapion's wondrous condition, he echoes the prophetic words from the Decius episode, filled with hope of finding the divine truth — 'urkunde | der jungisten urstende!' (*KC*, 13,538–39) — revealed in them. Theodosius immediately leads a procession back to Mount Celeon (*KC*, 13,569–78). As the narrative's representative of the Christian chronotope, he knows the way. There, the rocks hiding the other sleepers have been miraculously destroyed and they find the other sleepers in a quasi-angelic state

> [...] âne wandel
> in hâre unt in gewande.
> an in newas mail nehain. (*KC*, 13,588–90)

The scene with the removed stone and the angel-like figures inside is sure to be modelled on the biblical record of the discovery of the empty tomb (Mark 16. 1–8, Luke 24. 1–12, Matthew 28, John 20. 1–10), which signifies the resurrection of Christ. So, this mirror scene can be used as a signifier of the truth of the bodily resurrection. Only now does Serapion regain his spatial orientation when he exclaims: 'hie ist der berg Cêlêôn!' (*KC*, 13,594). Moreover, he announces that the revelation that Theodosius and his people were hoping to witness will indeed prove the truth of his word (*KC*, 13,595–97). One of the sleepers confirms to Theodosius: 'die wâren urstende ich dir kunde: | da disem lîbe wis gesunde' (*KC*, 13,603–04).

The sleepers have crossed a gulf of centuries into a time space without meaning for them, to bring meaning to it themselves: their miraculous crossing over from the pagan chronotope signifies the final and conclusive proof of a debate contemporary with the Christian chronotope. It also finalizes the process of Christianization, which is all but concluded in the *Kaiserchronik*'s narrative after the last attacks from the outside (Astrolabe) and from the inside (Arius) have been thwarted by the end of the Theodosius episode. However, as will be demonstrated later, this does not mean a clear teleological fulfilment of a programmatic trajectory in the *Kaiserchronik*; it is rather the case that Christianity and the Christians remain fragile and their religious identity can easily be threatened so as to generate narrative potential.

With the aetiological religious question of Christianization for now resolved by the events of the Theodosius episode, the focus can turn to the second dimension of qualitative change: the political identity of the Empire. The *Kaiserchronik* deploys a deliberate and programmatic pejoration of Greekness in order to manage the transition from the ancient to the medieval Empire. The foundation of Constantinople as the second Rome in the fourth century is only briefly mentioned

---

Arian and his Christology were considered anathema after his death. See Hermengild Biedermann, 'Homoiousios, Homoiousianer' and 'Homoousios', in *Lexikon des Mittelalters*, ed. by Bautier, Avella-Widhalm, and Auty, v, cols 112, 112–13; Günther Binding, 'Arius, Arianismus, Arianer', in *Lexikon des Mittelalters*, ed. by Bautier, Avella-Widhalm, and Auty, i (Munich, 1980), cols 949–51.

in the Constantine episode, and then without great consequence: to escape a looming food crisis, Constantine leads the Roman citizens to Greece, where he, after an angelic vision points out a specific site, founds Constantinople as the new Troy (*KC*, 10,401–38). Originally, the move was intended as a temporary measure of one year only to attenuate the stresses of famine in Rome, but Constantine resolves to stay there for longer and has to trick the Romans who came with him into staying and not returning to Rome. He does this by transporting their wives and Roman soil to Constantinople, where they subsequently start building their new homes (*KC*, 10,449–10,504). The founding of Constantinople is presented as a divine decree (*KC*, 10,438, 10,441) and as a monument to Constantine surviving into the twelfth-century present day (*KC*, 10,447–48) and even further until Judgement Day (*KC*, 10,436–38). Nevertheless, the historical impact of the event in the *Kaiserchronik* falls flat. The foundation ultimately appears just as one of several cities that the emperor founded, and after his death the focus of the chronicle moves seamlessly back to Rome (*KC*, 10,511). After Constantine, the chronicle returns to Constantinople only six times: as the place where Julian's soul languishes in fire and sulphur until Judgement Day (*KC*, 11,108–13); three times as Greek antipole to Rome in the Constantius Leo episode (*KC*, 13,712–16, 13,718–38, 13,739–68); and two times in the Zeno episode, first as the place that Zeno prefers to rule from instead of Rome (*KC*, 13,825–38), and second as the place where he is finally put to rest (*KC*, 14,188–93). All these cases frame Constantinople as a problematic place that creates or amplifies the internal tensions within the Empire between Romans and Greeks that are negotiated in the episodes of Constantius Leo and Zeno.

The two famous Eastern Roman emperors Justinian and Heraclius, who both feature prominently in the *Kaiserchronik* directly after the Silvester episode, are neither explicitly labelled as Greek nor surrounded by circumstances that would indicate any amount of Greekness. To maintain their positive position in the framework of the *Kaiserchronik*, they had to be expelled from the phase of Greek emperors and their Greekness had to be entirely suppressed. Uta Goerlitz argues that the suppression of any Greekness in these emperors is part of a programmatic strategy in the *Kaiserchronik* to play down the Greek imperial phase between Constantine and Charlemagne, not only because of the text's negative view of anything Greek, but in particular to marginalize the historical timeframe of the great migrations and the reign of the Merovingians, which, as the 'heroic age', serves as the historical background to most of the heroic epics against which the *Kaiserchronik* seems to agitate in several instances.[45]

Theodosius is the first emperor whom the text introduces as 'von Criechen geborn' (*KC*, 13,069), but he nevertheless remains an entirely positive figure who fears God, does good deeds, adores Christ, and is rewarded with great glory for it (*KC*,13,067–75).

---

45   Uta Goerlitz, '(Un-)Wahrheit und (Nicht-)Erinnern: Erzählen *ze diute* in der frühmittelhochdeutschen "Kaiserchronik"', in *Damnatio in Memoria: Deformation und Gegenkonstruktionen in der Geschichte*, ed. by Sebastian Scholz, Gerald Schwedler, and Kai-Michael Sprenger, Zürcher Beiträge zur Geschichtswissenschaft, 4 (Berlin, 2014), pp. 225–42 (pp. 238–42).

Constantius Leo, who could be an amalgamation of the fifth-century Thracian Eastern Roman Emperor Leo I and the eighth-century Eastern Roman Emperor Constantine V, seems to be a hybrid figure with shared Roman and Greek roots. On the one hand, the Greeks rejoice when he starts ailing, 'wande si daz rîche von rehte wolten hân' (*KC*, 13,687), and the Romans promptly call for a 'hervart' (*KC*, 13,689) to defend him. On the other hand, the Greeks send a delegation to Constantius Leo, trying to dissuade him from this military campaign against Constantinople by appealing to his ancestral or family ties to the city: 'dîn geslæhte ist ze Constenobile, | iz gezimet dir, hêrre, ubele' (*KC*, 13,715–16).

When Zeno succeeds Constantius Leo, his Greekness is explicitly fleshed out as something divisive:

> want er von Criechen geborn was.
> dô minnet er sîn geslähte baz
> danne Rômære;
> daz wart in harte swære. (*KC*, 13,827–30)

The last emperor to be identified as Greek is another Constantius, who can be read as an approximation to Constantine VI, a contemporary of Charlemagne who ruled the Eastern Roman Empire from 780 to 797 CE. The *Kaiserchronik* relates of him that he was 'von den Criechen geborn; | di hêten in ouch ze rihtære rekorn' (*KC*, 14,196–97). The emphasis on 'di' who have elected him ruler, in the last line, contrasts the Greeks once more with the Romans and widens the gap between the two groups. This ruler has been installed exclusively by the Greeks and without any Roman participation.

All in all, only three emperors are clearly identified as Greek: Theodosius, Zeno, and Constantine VI. Theodosius's positive position in the *Kaiserchronik* remains unblemished by this designation. He is succeeded by the ambiguously framed, but ultimately Roman Constantius Leo, whose episode mainly deals with war between the Romans and the Greeks. Constantius Leo is in turn succeeded by the two other Greek emperors, Zeno and Constantine VI, but in both cases their Greekness is portrayed as something divisive. This indicates that the episode centred on the fictitious Constantius Leo was mainly interpolated to mark the pejoration of Greekness in the intradiegetic continuum of the *Kaiserchronik*.

The murder of Constantine VI by personal rivals finally leads to the Romans separating their empire from the Greeks: 'Von dannen wart Rômisc rîche | gesceiden von den Criechen' (*KC*, 14,278–79). This separation creates a void in imperial power. However, the *rîche* continues to exist; it even features as the subject of the line in which *sede vacante* is declared: 'Daz rîche stuont dô lære' (*KC*, 14,282). Under circumstances to be examined in a later chapter of this book, it is at this point that Charlemagne takes power. His accession marks an essential shift of perspective on the Roman Empire, from an ancient cisalpine Roman Empire to a medieval transalpine German Empire.

But initially, Charlemagne is a figure whom the *Kaiserchronik* is reluctant to pin down clearly. His father, Pippin, is king 'von Karlingen' (*KC*, 14,309), and Charlemagne himself is initially introduced as one of his sons who stays at home with him, while his other son, Leo, is pope and away in Rome (*KC*, 14,308–15). Later, after he has become Roman king, he resides in 'den Riflanden' (*KC*, 14,423). When he returns to Rome and finally takes on the imperial dignity, he is presented to the audience as 'der êrste kaiser [...] ze Rôme | von Diutisken landen' (*KC*, 14,818–19). 'Karlingen'/'Kerlingen' features primarily as the kingdom of Pippin in the *Kaiserchronik*, and is replaced by 'Franckrich' for line 14,309 in the fifteenth-century Zeil manuscript of recension C.[46] 'Riflan[t]' features only as a place that Charlemagne moves to or away from. In the Zeil manuscript, it is in one case replaced with 'Rinlan[t]'.[47] The convergence of these three terminologically distinct geographies or polities in Charlemagne will be examined at a later point.[48] For the time being, it suffices to say that after Charlemagne all the emperors, including the later Carolingians, are unequivocally characterized as German.

To summarize: the story of continuous imperial rule is told on the linear axis of the episodic framework markers, the mobility of atomized narratives of antiquity is limited, and the causal integration of the plot is organized in terms of the two aspects in which qualitative change has to be acknowledged and subsequently negotiated. This allows the maintenance of qualitative equivalence between the content of the episodes, which is necessary in order to keep the content available as didactic or exemplary reference points, and at the same time to explain the main lines of qualitative historical change to the contemporary audience, which looks to the text for orientation regarding its own past and the historical role and responsibility that derives from it.

If the content of the episodes is (within the limitations sketched out above) contingent and therefore interchangeable, and the correct succession of episodes is at the author's disposition, this indicates that all episodes belong to the same qualitative order of meaning. According to White, a 'metaphysical principle' is required to translate difference into similarity and thus to be able to group a set of events together. He circumscribes such a principle as a '"subject" common to all of the referents of the various sentences that register events as having occurred'.[49] In the case of the *Kaiserchronik*, this principle, which translates the difference of the content of the episodes into qualitative similarity, is the registering of all the atomized events of the *Kaiserchronik* as having happened under the rule of a specific emperor. The reigns of the emperors emerge as White's 'common subject'. They are manifestations of the linear and continuous existence of the Empire. Untied from their historical causation, the events are completely contained by the temporal unfolding of the Empire. They are no longer random events that happen to occur at the time of one emperor or another; instead, from this perspective they are occasioned by the rule of the emperor in any given case. Not because his politics propel the action on a diegetic level, but because the time in which events happen is merely a function of imperial rule and each historical event of the *Kaiserchronik* is thus existentially conditioned by the presence of a linear, imperial continuum.

---

46   Schloss Zeil, ZAMs 30, fol. 290[r].
47   Ibid., fol. 292[v].
48   See 4.2.2 in this book.
49   White, p. 16.

Generally, only the initial and concluding formulas of the episodes, which introduce and conclude the rule of emperors and count the years of their reign, provide a sense of historical difference between the content of the episodes, of quantifiable progress in history through time. They are also the signifiers of qualitative change over time in history. The impression of an orderly progression in the course of history suggested by the form of the enumerative episodic frames, each tied to a particular name, is not, however, mirrored in their diverse content. The bewildering diegetic phenomenology of the narrative material enclosed between the episode markers does not speak as historical narrative itself: this material is only semanticized as history by the framing phrases.

1.2. Functions of Quantity: Exemplarity, Aetiology, and Continuity in the *Kaiserchronik*

How does the *Kaiserchronik* make use of the historiographical technique of mostly semanticizing its episodic content as history through its macrostructure on the level of form and less through its microstructure on the level of content? To understand this, the workings of historiography have to be examined more closely. Historiography is the constructive organization of historical matter by the historiographer for the purpose of his argument: 'Geschichte [...] ist nicht einfach "da", sondern wird erst durch das deutende, ordnende, auswählende Tun des Geschichtsschreibers geschaffen.'[50] The writing of historical narrative creates perspectives and brings order to the chaos of historical occurrences. Neither the perspective created in this way nor the plot that shapes the resultant narrative are rooted in factuality; they are shaped by the linguistic parameters of narration as the historian submits the past to a literary structure.[51] This means that the text of the chronicle is always at least to some extent 'intentional history',[52] as the historian

---

50   Hartwin Brandt, 'Historia magistra vitae? Orosius und die spätantike Historiographie', in *Jenseits der Grenzen: Beiträge zur spätantiken und frühmittelalterlichen Geschichtsschreibung*, ed. by Andreas Goltz, Millennium-Studien zu Kultur und Geschichte des ersten Jahrtausends n. Chr., 25 (Berlin, 2009), pp. 121–33 (p. 129).

51   See Chris Lorenz, 'Kann Geschichte wahr sein? Zu den narrativen Geschichtsphilosophien von Hayden White und Frank Ankersmit', in *Konstruktion von Wirklichkeit: Beiträge aus geschichtstheoretischer, philosophischer und theologischer Perspektive*, ed. by Jens Schröter and Antje Eddelbüttel (Berlin, 2004), pp. 33–63 (pp. 36–37). Lorenz is summarizing the implications of the historical philosophies of Hayden White and Frank Ankersmit. I am aware of the criticism levelled at their ideas, which Lorenz, e.g. pp. 41–44, goes on to express, like others before him.

52   Hans-Joachim Gehrke, 'Die Bedeutung der (antiken) Historiographie für die Entwicklung des Geschichtsbewußtseins', in *Die antike Historiographie und die Anfänge der christlichen Geschichtsschreibung*, ed. by Eve-Marie Becker (Berlin, 2005), pp. 29–51 (p. 30). Much ink has been spilt over the question of the extent to which any author is in control of his narrative since Derrida wrote: 'We should begin by taking rigorous account of this *being held within* [*prise*] or this *surprise*: the writer writes in a language and in a logic whose proper system, laws, and life his discourse by definition cannot dominate absolutely. He uses them only by letting himself, after a fashion and up to a point, be governed by the system. And the reading must always aim at a certain relationship, unperceived by the writer, between what he commands and what he does not command of the patterns of the language that he uses. This relationship is not a certain quantitative distribution of shadow and light, of weakness or of force, but a signifying structure that critical reading should *produce*' (*Of*

Hans-Joachim Gehrke puts it. He laid out the basic principles of this intentional process of historiographical composition, which I paraphrase and summarize here.[53] Intentional historiography

1. anchors the group whose past it represents in the depths of time and explains its origins;

2. connects to the group's present, often (metaphorically) with genealogical models;

3. does not distinguish between 'fact' and 'fiction', which fall together;

4. draws past and present together, knowing only quantitative, not qualitative differences;

5. collects and conveys through socialization 'recipe knowledge' for cultural orientation; and

6. catalyses the sociocultural reification of history.

The traits Gehrke identifies for ancient Greek historiography are not only applicable to medieval historiography but also provide a useful umbrella for the various historiographical concepts discussed in this chapter. The sentiment expressed in point 4 resonates in particular with the findings of the previous section.

> Das Verhältnis von Vergangenheit und Gegenwart war sehr eng, gleichsam distanzlos. Gerade was die moderne Geschichtswissenschaft betont und sichtbar zu machen sucht, das Differente, fehlte. Die Entfernung war eine zeitliche, aber keine qualitative. Es wurde immer nach den gleichen Regeln gespielt. Im Grunde war alles statisch und ließ für die Zukunft Ähnliches erwarten [...].[54]

In the context of medieval texts, this caters to the institutional desire for great age shared by most medieval audiences. To be considered as worthy or legitimate in the eyes of medieval audiences, things had to possess as long a pedigree as possible, ideally all the way back to the earliest possible point beyond which there was no other point to connect back to. Melville calls such points 'unvordenkliche Anfänge'.[55] The demand for a pedigree reaching back to these beginnings coloured medieval discourses of history and legitimacy. In the *Kaiserchronik*, it is most clearly displayed in the self-evident continuity that connects the ancient Roman Empire with the medieval German one. Only through the confirmation of age could the

---

Grammatology, trans. by Gayatri Chakravorty Spivak (Baltimore, 1967), p. 158). To counter the 'massive dehistoricization' inflicted on historiographical texts by Derrida and the deconstructivists following in his wake, Gabrielle Spiegel suggested understanding texts as 'sites of linguistic usage, as lived events, [which] are essentially local in origin and therefore possess a determinate social logic of much greater density and particularity than can be extracted from totalizing constructs like "language" and "society"' ('History, Historicism, and the Social Logic of the Text in the Middle Ages', *Speculum*, 65.1 (1990), 59–86 (p. 77)).

53   Gehrke, pp. 30–31, 50–51.
54   Ibid., p. 50.
55   Gert Melville, 'Durch Fiktionen von der Wirklichkeit zur Wahrheit: Zum mittelalterlichen Umgang mit Widersprüchen zwischen Empirie und kultureller Axiomatik', in *Fiktion und Fiktionalität in den Literaturen des Mittelalters: Jan-Dirk Müller zum 65. Geburtstag*, ed. by Ursula Peters and Rainer Warning (Paderborn, 2009), pp. 83–104 (p. 100).

Empire's rank and status be ascertained. The problem with this powerful mentality was that proof of great antiquity was hard to demonstrate for any entity, both because these continuities often simply did not exist and, even if they had, because of the low degree of reliable record-keeping throughout the Middle Ages. The requirement that one's own present should be legitimated by great age collided with the empirical reality in which this great age was either not there or not conclusively demonstrable.[56] This renders the present different from the past: 'Dem Eigenen zeigte sich die Vergangenheit fern, sie vermochte anhand empirischer Gegebenheiten eben nicht zu legitimieren, sie konnte keine Rangerhöhung fördern, obgleich es von ihr fortwährend axiomatisch gefordert wurde.'[57] Thus, it falls to historiography to reconcile Melville's axiomatic cultural demand with the empirical fact. In short, one of the core tasks of historiography was to translate empirical historical difference into cultural similarity, or at least acceptability. The *Kaiserchronik* confronts this task through its episode framework, which registers all historical occurrences within qualitatively equalizing parameters expressed in the introductory and concluding phrases of the emperor episodes. Historical difference is thus translated through similarity into countable distance. The alienation between the present and the past is reduced, and the axiomatic cultural demand for opening up the past as an anchor-point for the discursive creation of legitimacy is met.

With the quantitative framework that the episodic paradigm of the *Kaiserchronik* provides, the qualitative difference between the content of the individual episodes collapses. As all the historical narratives in the text are organized according to the same ordering principles, their paradigmatic similarity suppresses their contextual and traditional diegetic differences. This process of conflating difference and distance in a narrative paradigm makes the individual links of the episode chain available for diachronous exemplary reference.

Gehrke's paraphrase echoes Aristotle's reflections on historiographical exemplarity in his *Rhetoric*. Aristotle grounds the oratorical authority of examples based on 'actual past facts' (πράγματα προγενομένα/*pragmata progenomena*)[58] in the unchanging nature of patterns of events and motivations, which remain the same for all times, past, present, and future. To illustrate, Aristotle devises an example:

---

56 See ibid., pp. 100–01.

57 Ibid., p. 101.

58 Aristotle, *Opera Omnia: Volumen Alterum*, ed. by Immanuel Bekker and Georg Reimer (Berlin, 1831), p. 1393, quoted following *Perseus Digital Library*, ed. by Gregory Crane <http://www.perseus. tufts.edu/hopper/text?doc=Perseus%3Atext%3A1999.01.0059%3Abook%3D2%3Achapter%3D20> [accessed 13 July 2017]. Aristotle provides the theoretical underpinnings for this in the preceding chapter, where he muses on the possibility and impossibility of future facts. Aristotle, *Rhetoric*, trans. by William Rhys (New York, 1954): 'How questions of Future Fact should be argued is clear from the same considerations: That a thing will be done if there is both the power and the wish to do it; or if along with the power to do it there is a craving for the result, or anger, or calculation, prompting it. That the thing will be done, in these cases, if the man is actually setting about it, or even if he means to do it later — for usually what we mean to do happens rather than what we do not mean to do. That a thing will happen if another thing which naturally happens before it has already happened; thus, if it is clouding over, it is likely to rain. That if the means to an end have occurred, then the end is likely to occur; thus, if there is a foundation, there will be a house' (II. 19, p. 109).

if the king of Persia conquered Egypt before he attacked Greece in the past, then this means for the present that if the king of Persia conquers Egypt, Greece must ready for war. The difference is merely a quantitative one: if the first Persian king to attempt conquering Greece after having conquered Egypt was Darius, and the second one was Xerxes, the third king who conquers Egypt will undoubtedly proceed identically. The quality of the pattern and the results remain unchanged, and thus the past can endow rhetorical examples with persuasive power for the present:

> But while it is easier to supply parallels by inventing fables, it is more valuable for the political speaker to supply them by quoting what has actually happened, since in most respects the future will be like [ὅμοιος/*homoios*] what the past has been.[59]

This means that a quantitative axis is required along which temporally discrete but similar stages of history can be plotted. In Aristotle's example, this quantitative axis is the political situation of Greece and Persia from the sixth to fourth century BCE. The group identities for both sides necessarily have to be assumed to remain unchanged for the example to hold any validity as an argument. In the case of the *Kaiserchronik*, the quantitative axis is provided by projecting the group identity that the author shares with his presumed audience back from its contemporary environment to the past extension of the Roman Empire. This identity finds textual expression in the episodic compartmentalization of the Roman Empire and the narrating of its history. After naming kings and popes, both good and bad (*KC*, 19), as the object of the *crônicâ*'s account, the text goes on to qualify their relation to the present, the text and its audience

> die vor uns wâren
> und Rômisces rîches phlâgen
> unze an disen hiutegen tac. (*KC*, 20–22)

The axis allows projection in both directions. Not only can exemplarity of the past be projected onto the present; the present shapes expectations about the historical universe within which the past operates. Vollrath characterizes this quality of medieval historiography as 'rückprojizierte Gegenwart'.[60] The past is qualitatively similar enough to the present to allow the forward and backward movement of mental patterns that create meaning.

Custodianship of the Roman Empire is the unifying historical role that connects the present *uns* containing both the *Kaiserchronik*'s author and audience with the past. The protagonists of this past — popes and kings — are removed from the present only in a quantifiable dimension of easily countable years and emperor episodes. This quantitative dimension forms the backbone of the *Kaiserchronik*'s compositional structure and its emperor-centric episodes. However, there is no awareness of or interest in qualitative change along this axis of imperial continuity. The historical obligation to *phlêgen* the Roman Empire, which anchors the group identity of the

---

59   Ibid., II. 20, p. 110.
60   Vollrath, p. 575.

present in the past, remains unchanged 'unze an dîsen hiutegen tac'. To emphasize this qualitatively constant responsibility, the *Kaiserchronik* introduces the presence of the Germans in sometimes surprising places, and most prominently in the Caesar episode.[61] Consequently, the changes in governance as the *Kaiserchronik* modulates from the Romans, to the Greeks, and to the Carolingians and Germans could be read as mere quantitative change framing a qualitatively unchanged historical mission at its core: the rule and stewardship of the consistently Roman Empire. The old man from the *wîlsælde* disputation in the Faustinian episode puts it bluntly:

> die werlt ienoh hiute stât
> sô si von allerêrste wart.
> si newirt niemer wirs noh paz,
> wan sô si ze allerêrste was. (*KC*, 3659–62)

However, the purpose of this book is not to argue that the *Kaiserchronik* is not interested in qualitative change. It is, and one of its essential tasks is to negotiate qualitative change in the context of historical premises that leave only limited space for it. Besides, the twelfth century displayed a keen awareness of its temporal alterity from the past. For example, the author of the anonymous *Central Franconian Rhyming Bible*, written in the earlier twelfth century, comments on Elisabeth's childlessness in old age: '{Elisabet} vil ofte wart verwizzen, {thaz sie so lange a} ne kint havede gesezen. | <w>{ande man tho ein} wif bose sagede, thie bi iren <jaren kint ne hav>ede' (*Central Franconian Rhyming Bible*, 21. 107–08).[62] The fact that Elisabeth's lack of children warranted societal scorn clearly needed at least some sort of comment and explanation, which the text provides by anchoring it in the past. In the twelfth century, female childlessness was not necessarily a reason for social marginalization, at least not within the normative frameworks of matrimony or monasticism, where women could demonstrate their virtue by remaining chaste despite being married or aspire to even higher forms of female social validity by maintaining their virginity.[63]

Building on these preliminary observations, further examination will show to what extent the *Kaiserchronik* utilizes its paradigmatic, quantitative axis to manipulate its historical record, making its temporality visible to develop historical continuity, to exploit the exemplary potential of the past, or as a background for explanatory aetiological models.

---

61   See Chinca and Young, p. 13.

62   *The Central Franconian Rhyming Bible ('Mittelfränkische Reimbibel'): An Early Twelfth-Century German Verse Homiliary: A Thematic and Exegetical Commentary with the Text and a Translation into English*, ed. and trans. by David Wells, Amsterdamer Publikationen zur Sprache und Literatur, 155 (Amsterdam, 2004), pp. 6–7.

63   See Georges Duby, *The Knight, the Lady and the Priest: The Making of Modern Marriage in Medieval France* (London, 1984), pp. 4–8, 29; Christopher Brooke, *The Medieval Idea of Marriage* (Oxford, 1989; repr. 2002), pp. 126–28; Klaus van Eickels, 'Ehe und Familie im Mittelalter', in *Geisteswissenschaften im Profil: Reden zum Dies Academicus 2000–2007*, ed. by Godehard Ruppert, Schriften der Otto-Friedrich-Universität Bamberg, 1 (Bamberg, 2008), pp. 43–65.

1.2.1. Continuity

The first function of quantity I wish to examine is continuity. How does the episode framework accommodate a complex concept like religion over the course of several episodes? How is the pagan religion imagined on a trajectory that purposefully leads the text from a pagan past to a Christian present? Is it subject to change, or does it retain a consistent core of traits that the episode framework transports throughout the text? Is the influence of the differing source traditions problematic, or does the *Kaiserchronik* endeavour to harmonize the different strands that informed its account?

As a good starting point for this examination, we can take the 'sûl' featuring at the end of the Astrolabe legend in the Theodosius episode (*KC*, 13,086–13,375). This 'sûl' is also connected to the present by the word 'hiute' (*KC*, 13,364). After the spell of the idol of Venus has been lifted from the boy Astrolabe, Emperor Theodosius decrees the erection of 'in der gottes minne | ain ander hûs' (*KC*, 13,351–52) at the same site. The new church is to be built around the column, which is going to be rededicated to St Michael. The chronicle adds that 'si ubertriffet ze Rôme alle di stat, | alse man hiute wol kiesen mach' (*KC*, 13,363–64). The text remains vague as to what exactly the 'sûl' is supposed to be. The idol with the miraculous 'wurze' (*KC*, 13,335–46) buried under it — which caused Astrolabe's sufferings to begin with — has previously been introduced as a 'pilde lussam' (*KC*, 13,109), and has since usually been referred to as 'pilde' (*KC*, 13,116, 13,122, 13,123, 13,128, 13,152, 13,344) or as 'aine statuam' (*KC*, 13,336), and sometimes further qualified as 'in honore Veneris' (*KC*, 13,124, 13,337), but it is never described as a 'sûl'. Presumably, the text assumes some sort of column on which the 'pilde' stood and which is now, after the idol's removal, being repurposed. This column is still present in Rome, towering over the rest of the city, as anyone who goes there today can see for themselves, as line 13,363 implies. The story is not aetiological but memorial in purpose, and introduces a topographical element that ensures the visual commemoration of an apparently important event and at the same time invites the audience to go there themselves to verify the truthfulness of the *Kaiserchronik*'s account. But the memory of what exactly is being projected into the present time of the twelfth century? Two crucial things pertaining to the question of qualitative change on a quantitative time axis happen immediately before and after the rededication of the column to St Michael.

At the beginning of the episode, Astrolabe was introduced as one of two obdurately pagan brothers who had little regard for their own salvation, actively strove to honour the pagan gods, and were deaf to the emperor's personal pleas to renounce their erroneous faith (*KC*, 13,086–13,100). Now that — thanks to the cunning of the priest Eusebius, who is also well versed in the dark arts (*KC*, 13,218) — Astrolabe has been saved from the clutches of the 'valânt' that took control of him with the cursed 'vingerlîn' (*KC*, 13,125–26), the youth becomes Christian and with him all the other pagans who are present (*KC*, 13,365–68).

Situated in the Theodosius episode, the conversion of Astrolabe marks the final occasion in the *Kaiserchronik* where Roman pagans become Christian. It thus concludes one of the main strands running through the text: the transformation of the Empire from a pagan into a Christian entity. The ultimate victory of orthodox Christianity is further cemented in the second part of the Theodosius episode, in which the Arian heresy is ended by Arius's ignominious death in a privy (*KC*, 13,475–83) and by the return of Serapion and the Seven Sleepers (*KC*, 13,496–13,642).[64] Both pagans, as external assailants, and heretics, as internal enemies of Christianity, have been assimilated into or repelled from the Empire. Christianity's introduction into the Empire, which started with Philip the Arab and culminated with Constantine and Silvester, is now complete. But this of course raises the question of how the process of Christianization relates to the problems of qualitative historical change and quantitative historical distance. How does the *Kaiserchronik*'s episodic paradigm react when faced with a clear qualitative change in the religious make-up of the Empire? After all, the episode structure quantifies temporal historical distance and does not show the qualitative changes that separate the chronicle's present time from its narrated time. The beginning of a possible answer can be found at the heart of the Astrolabe legend, directly before the rededication of the column by Pope Ignatius. In order to save Astrolabe from his predicament, Eusebius conjures up a devil and follows him into a distant hellscape ('in aines tiefen moses grunt'; *KC*, 13,303) where other devils guard Astrolabe's ring. There, Eusebius extorts the devils into releasing the ring and disclosing information crucial for redeeming Astrolabe (*KC*, 13,225–13,346). To Eusebius's question

> [...] von welhen dingen
> daz aller êrist kôme,
> daz dem jungelinge missescæhe (*KC*, 13,332–34)

the distraught devil — much to his chagrin — has little choice but to answer, as Eusebius is addressing him 'in verbo domini' (*KC*, 13,314): as the devil admits, Astrolabe's initial enthralment was not due to the statue itself having any kind of godly or magical powers, but was solely due to a miraculous root buried underneath it:

> di wîle di wurze dar under ligent.
> swer daz pilde oben an sihet,
> der muoz iemer minnen. (*KC*, 13,343–45)

Everything that happened after was arranged by the devil using Astrolabe's cursed ring. In a radical euhemeristic reduction, the entire religious service of the pagans is reduced to a root's bewitching qualities, in respect of which the text gives no further indication as to whether they are natural or magical. The result remains the same: paganism is exposed as a fraud, a prestidigitation, that never related to any true gods. The cosmological forces in the background have always been the same and remain unchanged: God and the devils, who in Astrolabe's case deployed one of the pagan illusions he was so drawn to in order to corrupt his soul.

The pattern is corroborated by other episodes where devils act through or are associated with pagan edifices and gods. In the Julian episode, the graven image of

---

64   See 1.1.4 in this book.

a pagan god is hidden in a river when a woman betrayed by Julian, her adoptive son, happens upon it (*KC*, 10,688–97). At first, she gives the pagan idol a good thrashing with her laundry, which prompts the image to plead with the woman to stop. It is, however, not the image itself that speaks, but a devil camouflaged as a deity speaking out of — 'ûz' (*KC*, 10,701) — the image. When challenged by the woman, the devil identifies itself more specifically: 'wîp, ungebâre dû niht sô! | ich pinz, der got Mercûrîus' (*KC*, 10,731–32). In what follows, the image is only referred to as a god in direct speech, for example when the woman orders the image to be raised from the waters (*KC*, 10,771) or when Julian begs it to relinquish its hold on him (*KC*, 10,790). The narrator consistently calls the entity inhabiting it a 'tievel' (*KC*, 10,721, 10,730, 10,801, 10,817, 10,823, 10,844) or 'vâlant' (*KC*, 10,782, 10,813). When the idol is later actually recovered from the river on Julian's orders to be reinstated as a cult object, it is called an 'abgot' (*KC*, 10,839). The Christian martyrs Paul and John, who are killed for their refusal to worship the idol (*KC*, 10,848–10,935), naturally refer to it as 'vâlant' (*KC*, 10,902). The text does not specify whether a devil has possessed the image and is now feigning an animate version of the pagan deity Mercurius, or whether the deity venerated by the pagan Romans as Mercurius was a demon all along. Both possibilities are present and converge in the idol's and the demon's shared name, Mercurius, by which they are referred to both by the narrator (*KC*, 10,856) and by the protagonists of the episode (*KC*, 10,896).

A look at the explanation of the days of the pagan week provides additional insights into the quality of pagan gods and devils as the *Kaiserchronik* conceives of them (*KC*, 63–208). When the pagan gods are introduced together with the days dedicated to them, they are often referred to as *got*: the nameless sun god in lines 77 and 82, the nameless god of war ('wîchgote') in line 117, Jupiter in line 150, or Saturn in line 174. When the text is more interested in the materiality of the idols representing these gods, they are called 'abgot' (e.g. *KC*, 45, 65, 130). Interestingly, these gods are always qualified by an article like 'den got' (*KC*, 77, 82), 'der got' (*KC*, 119), or 'ein got' (*KC*, 150). In contrast, the Christian God is always set apart with great care from them and referred to as the 'wâren' (*KC*, 64, 74, 205) or 'almehtigen' (*KC*, 190) God. However, in the Pantheon passage at the end of the review of the week, directly after the introduction of the 'got' Saturn, the relationship between the pagan gods and the devils receives some elaboration:

> An dem sameztage sâ:
> einez haizzet Rotundâ,
> daz was ein hêres petehûs.
> der got hiez Saturnus,
> dar nach was iz aller tievel êre. (*KC*, 171–75)

The Pantheon, primarily dedicated to Saturn, also serves in a subordinate function as a temple for all the devils. While the lines do not specifically group Saturn and the gods named before among the devils, it is strongly implied that Saturn is seen only as the first among the devils. When Boniface later rededicates the building, this has a dramatic effect on the devils, who are imagined to inhabit the Pantheon physically: 'die tievel brâsten oben ûz, | sumelîche in daz abgrunde' (*KC*, 206–07).

The pagan gods are revealed to have been devils all along, who tricked the humans into venerating them as pagan deities.

The persistent cosmological stability this implies is heavily utilized as a foundation for the argument during the *wîlsælde* disputation when the unrecognized Faustinian makes the case for an unchanging universe to his likewise unrecognized son Clement. He argues that the twenty-four hours of the day have always been and will always be 'gelîch lanch' (*KC*, 3523) and 'neverwandelent sich nie mêre' (*KC*, 3522); thus, they remain beyond the reach of human manipulation (*KC*, 3525–30). Ancient authorities like Pythagoras are invoked to vouch for the perpetual validity of the cosmic laws that govern time: what was an hour a thousand years ago, will also be an hour in the present and retains its temporally structuring authority unassailable by human agency. The same notion of time is prevalent in both the Astrolabe and Titus passages analysed below. It is certainly no accident that both examples operate with columns to suggest the continuity of Roman exemplarity and history into the twelfth-century present. Neither the column in the Titus episode nor the column in the Astrolabe episode are taken from the source material. The Titus column seems to be entirely without precedent in the source material, and if the author of the *Kaiserchronik*, as Ohly claims,[65] really took the conversion of the Venus image into an image of St Michael from Cassiodorus's *Historia Ecclesiastica Tripartita*, he would not have found a column there *expressis verbis* either.[66] Instead, both columns seem to have been wilfully introduced by the compiler of the *Kaiserchronik*, who must have found something useful in the imagery of the ancient column. As Dale Kinney points out, the discourse on columns brings one to the heart of 'the medieval discourse of "Romanness"'.[67] After columns had ceased to be produced in the Carolingian era, Rome was perceived to be the only possible point of origin for all columns. Their connection to foreign geographies, which had made their erection in Rome a veritable map of the Empire, had been all but forgotten.[68] The *Kaiserchronik*'s quantitative paradigm of unchanging Romanness capitalizes on this special meaning of columns to assert itself in passages that actualize the historical difference between pagan past and Christian present.

Whether the examples discussed so far are modelling exemplarity, developing aetiology, or negotiating continuity, they all use the quantitative dimension of history that the episode framework of the *Kaiserchronik* maps out in different ways and to different effect.

Exemplarity has to be projected forward from the past to become available as a

---

65   Ohly, *Sage und Legende*, p. 208.

66   Cassiodorus Senator, *Historia Ecclesiastica Tripartita*, ed. by Walter Jakob and Rudolf Hanslik, Corpus Scriptorum Ecclesiasticorum Latinorum, 71 (Vienna, 1952): 'Insignis itaque locus ex illo tempore claruit peregrinis et urbicis, ubi olim quidem Vesta colebatur, postea vero ecclesia facta est. Qui locus nunc Michahelium nuncupatur in dextra positus parte navigantium a Ponto ad Constantinopolim, distans ab ea navigio quidem stadiis fere triginta et quinque, per terram vero circueuntibus omnem sinum usque ad septuaginta et amplius tenditur' (II. 19).

67   Dale Kinney, 'The Discourse of Columns', in *Rome Across Time and Space: Cultural Transmission and the Exchange of Ideas c. 500–1400*, ed. by Claudia Borgia and others (Cambridge, 2011), pp. 182–99 (p. 183).

68   Ibid., pp. 192–93, 198–99.

template for decisions based on historical analogies. For this to work, it is necessary that the episode structure suppresses or at least significantly reduces the qualitative difference between the episodic past and the historical present. Only thus can the similarity that is required for historical analogies to work be maintained.

Aetiology takes the puzzlement of the present audience as a starting point from which to look back at historical phenomenology and create meaning by bringing order to apparently chaotic phenomena with an explanatory model. Aetiologies have to translate difference, which triggered the audience's puzzlement in the first place, into similarity and give the present's question a tangible anchor-point both in the present physical reality and in the text. Whether these anchor-points correspond to actual physical spaces or places is secondary.

Finally, continuity transports content and meaning in a linear fashion through time to the present to cause an effect of recognition and familiarity on the part of the medieval audience. It preserves the temporal quality of the content it conveys.

All three strategies are intentionally implemented functions of the episode framework of the *Kaiserchronik*, and preserve the semantic qualities of their content and bypass the qualitative dimension of historical change, which separates the diegetic generation of meaning from its target audience. At the same time, all three functions are aimed at the present and the audience of the text, and they all operate on the basis of translating historical difference, which suddenly actualizes itself in the text, into similarity. They achieve this by quantifying it into distance and thus mitigating difference for an audience that would use the *Kaiserchronik* as a discourse space to learn about its historical identity.

1.2.2. Exemplarity: Heraclius

There is a strong tradition in criticism of reading the *Kaiserchronik* as a collection of historical tales aimed to inform, educate, and entertain a German-speaking lay audience. John of Salisbury provides a very illuminating tract on the value of exemplarity in one of his letters, written in 1167, quite close in time to the presumed writing of the *Kaiserchronik*:

> But if my advice is asked in the meantime, then before God, whom I call as witness of what I say at the last judgement, in full liberty of the spirit and in good faith promised and owed to him as to a father I reply that in all cases of stubborn doubt one should act as follows. First let us enquire and follow the prescriptions of the divine law on the matter; if this gives no certain solution, one should go back to the canons and examples of the saints; if nothing sure meets one there, one should finally investigate the mind and counsel of wise men in the fear of the Lord; and those should be preferred (be they few or many) who place God's honour before any personal convenience.[69]

John of Salisbury assigns exemplary value both to law and to ethical role models

69   *The Letters of John of Salisbury*, ed. and trans. by H. E. Butler and W. J. Millor, rev. by Christopher Brooke, 2 vols (Oxford, 1979), II, 364–67. See Peter von Moos, *Geschichte als Topik: Das rhetorische Exemplum von der Antike zur Neuzeit und die Historiae im 'Policraticus' Johanns von Salisbury* (Hildesheim, 1988), pp. 1–2.

and personalities with a particular focus on their generalizability. People take on the function of tropes as carriers of plausibility for an argument. At the core of these personalized examples lies an analogy that allows one to examine, affirm, or reject a practical decision in the present based on historical data.[70] John extols the general value of personalized historical exemplarity in his *Historia Pontificalis* when he writes that, except for the law and grace of God, no knowledge is more beneficial for the living than the deeds of their ancestors.[71]

In the context of scholarly discourse, the more exemplary and didactic elements of the *Kaiserchronik* have typically been emphasized by those who resist Ohly's influential typological reading of the text. Jantsch developed a nuanced model of the chronicle's exemplarity when criticizing Ohly's approach:

> Die Kaiserchronik hat zum tragenden Gerüst den Gedanken des geschichtlich sich gründenden und sich durchsetzenden Gottesreiches auf Erden. Dies ist die Linie, die die einzelnen Herrscher und Epochen aneinanderreiht. Die Geschichte selbst also — wie man sie auffaßte — , nicht ein Kompositionsprinzip, 'macht' die Struktur des Werkes. Gestalten und Episoden weisen sich dabei jeweils aus als pro oder contra, 'gut' oder 'böse', als Organe oder Gegenspieler Gottes in diesem Prozeß. Sie sind repräsentierende 'Muster' des Erfülltseins oder Nichterfülltseins vom göttlichen geschichtlichen Auftrag: im positiven Falle verkörpern sie 'das Wahre', das sich durchsetzen will und durchsetzt. [...] In der Linie des sich gründenden Gottesreiches sind Gestalten und Episoden exemplarisch und werden allenthalben als solche, z.T. moralisch didaktisch wertend, angesprochen und charakterisiert, jedoch nirgends als Exponenten einer 'Unvollkommenheit' oder 'Erfüllung' gegen- oder miteinander ins System gebracht.[72]

In order to explain his notion of exemplarity, Jantsch states that an example by definition contains in itself a higher degree of fulfilment than can be expected of those to whom it appeals. Jantsch continues to make a point of differentiating between a prefigurative use of examples (presumably the way Ohly reads them in order to categorize them as typologies) and a moral use that precludes typology 'weil nämlich "der Antitypus" nicht gegeben, sondern erst noch zu leisten ist'. Thus, he understands many of the cases Ohly treated as poles of a typological pairing simply as 'Berufung auf Instanzen'.[73]

Jentzmik, who follows Jantsch in much of his approach, emphasizes 'Exemplarik' in contrast to typology, as he finds that most factors constituting biblical typology are not present in the *Kaiserchronik*.[74] Instead, he characterizes the *Kaiserchronik* as

---

70 See ibid., pp. 3–4.
71 John of Salisbury, *Historia Pontificalis*, ed. by Reginald Poole (Oxford, 1927): 'nichilque post gratiam et legem Dei uiuentes rectius et ualidius instruit quam si gesta cognouerint decessorum' (p. 4).
72 Jantsch, pp. 210–11.
73 Ibid., pp. 210–23.
74 Jentzmik, p. 244, lists as these factors: 'Die gemeinsame Gottbezogenheit als Sinnmitte historischen Geschehens, der eschatologisch-geschichtliche Charakter des Antitypus, die Christozentrik, die jede biblische Typologie ausmacht, Vorausweis- und Verheißungsfunktion des Typus, die ausdrückliche Bezugnahme des Antitypus auf eine Präfiguration, das antitypische Selbstverständnis.'

exemplary in its approach toward its historical figures and events. They serve as either exemplary or deterrent patterns or anticipations of salvation-historical ideas. And while this means their exemplary framework is '[u]nzeitlich-jederzeitlich[]', it does not necessarily imply a typological system at its core. By pointing this out, Jentzmik shifts the perspective on Ohly's extra-biblical typologies and characterizes them as 'Heilsgeschichtliche Exemplarik'. By employing this terminology, he hopes to get around the problematic lack of Christocentricity in the *Kaiserchronik* while maintaining the salvation-historical trajectory in the interpretation of the chronicle.[75]

Stressing the exemplarity of the *Kaiserchronik*'s episodes has since become a staple of scholarship on the work's historiographical agenda. Otto Neudeck sees 'Exemplarität' as the benchmark for the historical truth of the *Kaiserchronik* and identifies a concept of history that utilizes history as *magistra vitae*.[76] Pézsa summarizes the presentation of history in the *Kaiserchronik* as targeted at the present and motivated by didactic and pedagogical concerns. The text's 'Wirkungsabsicht' is to present certain prominent events and figures as exemplary value statements.[77]

Markus Stock likewise took the text's exemplarity as the basis for his examination of 'korrelativer Sinnstiftung'.[78] Using Lotman's 'Sinngenerator' terminology,[79] Stock identifies a duality in the text's arrangement of figures and events in three stories (Julian, Jovinus, and Crescentia). Through the use of 'Äquivalenzrelationen', these dualities supplement and expand the paradigmatically linear narrative of the chronicle to a point where the dualities concentrate the essential messages of each story.[80]

Most recently, Udo Friedrich has elaborated on 'Topik und Narration' in the *Kaiserchronik* to point out the range of functions exemplary narratives can fulfil. He shows how the author of the chronicle develops his exemplary themes by forming arguments with rhetorical tropes that draw their authority from many different registers, like catalogues of vices and virtues, moral philosophy, and common sense, or from their correspondence to conventional narrative patterns. For Friedrich, the *Kaiserchronik* presents its examples by drawing on both salvation history and collective historical experience.[81]

How can exemplarity be generated across historical distance and difference? On the basis of the observations made above, a group of structures in the text of the

75   Ibid., pp. 244–46.
76   Otto Neudeck, 'Karl der Große — Der beste aller werltkunige: Zur Verbindung von exegetischen Deutungsmustern und heldenepischem Erzählen in der Kaiserchronik', *Germanisch-Romanische Monatsschrift*, 53 (2003), 273–94 (p. 277).
77   Tibor Friedrich Pézsa, *Studien zu Erzähltechnik und Figurenzeichnung in der deutschen 'Kaiserchronik'*, Europäische Hochschulschriften: Reihe I, 1378 (Frankfurt a. M., 1993), p. 19.
78   Stock, p. 37.
79   See Jurij Michailowitsch Lotman, 'Vorwort zur deutschen Ausgabe', in *Kunst als Sprache: Untersuchungen zum Zeichencharakter von Literatur und Kunst*, ed. by Klaus Städtke (Leipzig, 1981), pp. 7–19 (p. 15).
80   See Stock, p. 71.
81   See Udo Friedrich, 'Topik und Narration: Zur rhetorischen und poetischen Funktion exemplarischen Erzählens in der "Kaiserchronik"', *Poetica*, 47.1–2 (2016), 1–24 (pp. 1–8).

Kaiserchronik can be identified as anchor-points for the implementation of literary exemplarity. First, there are the instances where the use of language explicitly signals exemplarity, by means of words such as *bîspel* or *bilde*. The only relevant instance of *bîspel* occurs in lines 11,206–51, when Emperor Heraclius addresses his men before battle against Cosdras and the pagans who have sacked Jerusalem and stolen the relic of the Holy Cross (*KC*, 11,156–71):[82]

> owol ir helde snelle,
> ich sage iu ze aim bîspelle:
> ain liut haizet Hebrêî,
> dâ sult ir nemen pilde bî. (*KC*, 11,208–11)

The language here explicitly foregrounds the exemplarity of the passage. The Old Testament story from Numbers 13–14, where the Israelites are led by God into the land of the Canaanites, is introduced as a *bîspel*, and Heraclius's audience is called on to follow its *bilde* (*KC*, 11,211). The tale is utilized as an example to spur Heraclius's soldiers on to greater courage in the impending battle. For the example of Heraclius, the author of the chronicle reaches back into the past, into imagery presented in the Old Testament. The carriers of the historical analogy are the Hebrew people and the specific situation for which their example is meant to provide a strategy for managing reality in the diegetic tension in the run-up to a battle.[83] The addressees are Heraclius's 'helde snelle', whom he addresses at the end of his exemplary tale as 'helede Rômære' (*KC*, 11,247) and who are at this point fully synonymous with the 'cristen' (*KC*, 11,258) who rush to storm the enemy lines on the field of battle. The incentive offered in Heraclius's example is eschatological. Whoever joins him in shedding his blood that day will be saved, no matter how sinful they may be. The promised land of Canaan, to which God commanded his people to move, signifies the Christian paradise; the Israelites who are cowed by the exaggerated reports of the hostile inhabitants of Canaan and refuse to carry out God's decree signify those who do not follow Heraclius's order to follow him into battle at the risk of death. The analogy is immediately understood by his troops, as their collective response shows: they swear that those who will not fight will not win the land they are about to conquer (*KC*, 11,252–56).

   After the explicit command by the voice of God to go out and recapture the Holy Cross (*KC*, 11,176–86), the Old Testament analogy conveys the divinely decreed quality of Heraclius's campaign in the lands of the pagans to the collective he is addressing. As this collective is marked as Roman and Christian, in the conceptual logic of the *Kaiserchronik* his exemplary appeal can be read as aiming far beyond the historical Roman army and at the German audience of the twelfth century. The text returns to this extension of its exemplary impact beyond its own diegesis at the end of the episode. Heraclius, having defeated Cosdras and recaptured the Holy Cross, approaches Jerusalem in triumph, but is stopped by an angel who admonishes him to approach the Holy City in a more humble manner. Upon hearing this, the

---

82   The other instance can be found in *KC*, 10,011, where Pope Silvester during the disputations refutes one of Zambri's rhetorical suggestions as a 'pôse bîspel'.
83   von Moos, *Geschichte als Topik*, p. 7.

emperor carries the Cross barefoot and in woollen clothes through the gate of the city. At this point, the narrator of the *Kaiserchronik* steps into the foreground and winds up the Heraclius story by explicitly unlocking the exemplarity of the story and elaborating on its moral:

> daz ist uns armen gesaget ad exemplum:
> von diu suln wir unsern hêrren
> vurhten und flêgen
> mit zuhten unt mit guote
> mit grôzer deumuote. (*KC*, 11,339–43)

From retrospectively characterizing the Heraclius material as an *exemplum* targeted at the contemporary community of author and audience, the narrator moves on to provide explicit instructions on religious observance and concludes with an almost sententia-like couplet: 'ubermuot ist sô getân: | die gescendet ie den man' (*KC*, 11,344–45).

The intradiegetic *bîspel* Heraclius devises for his men is mirrored by the final *exemplum*, which now addresses the extradiegetic audience and author of the text: 'uns armen'. The exemplarity of the Heraclius episode is generated by drawing on three temporal levels: the twelfth-century present, the imperial past, and the even more distant biblical past. The exemplary value for the twelfth-century present is the sum of the exemplary analogy of the biblical past and the imperial past, which is generated by Heraclius's reference to and interaction with the analogical potential of the biblical material. To enable the transposition of exemplarity from one historical diegetic collective to another present and extradiegetic one, the *übermuot* for which Heraclius is reprimanded is clearly developed as a collective transgression, for it is the entire Roman army that meets with 'micheln nôten' (*KC*, 11,313) because of 'grôzer ubermuote' (*KC*, 11,312).[84]

Smits suggested we should read the Heraclius episode as an example of the fourfold exegetical sense of the Bible.[85] As the monk and mystic John Cassian demonstrated in his *Conferences* in the early fifth century to illustrate the fourfold sense of the Bible, Jerusalem can take on four dimensions of meaning:

> And so these four previously mentioned figures coalesce, if we desire, in one subject, so that one and the same Jerusalem can be taken in four senses:

84   See Kathryn Smits, 'Zweimal Heraclius: Zu Sprache und Erzählstil der Heraclius-Episode in der "Kaiserchronik" und im "Buoch der künige niuwer ê"', in *Deutsche Sprache: Geschichte und Gegenwart: Festschrift für Friedrich Maurer zum 80. Geburtstag*, ed. by Hugo Moser and Heinz Wupp (Berne, 1978), pp. 155–67 (p. 159).

85   Smits, pp. 159–60: 'Jerusalem ist zunächst die historische Stadt, die im Jahre 614 von den Sassaniden verwüstet wurde und zu der Heraclius 629 das geraubte Kreuz zurückführte. Allegorisch ist sie aber die Kirche, die Christenheit, für die Heraclius im Auftrag Gottes kämpft und deren Ehre er durch die Wiedergewinnung des Kreuzes rettet. Tropologisch ist sie die Seele des gläubigen Lesers, der vom Erzähler immer wieder dazu aufgefordert wird, das Geschehen auf sich zu beziehen. Anagogisch ist das himmlische Jerusalem gemeint: Heraclius' *ubermuot* gefährdet ja gerade seinen Eingang in das Himmelreich.' See Hans-Jürgen Horn, 'Origenes, Cassian, der vierfache Schriftsinn und seine Beziehung zu ontologischen Vorstellungen des Platonismus', in *Platonismus im Orient und Okzident*, ed. by Ralf Georges Khoury and Jens Halfwassen (Heidelberg, 2005), pp. 49–60 (pp. 50–51).

historically as the city of the Jews; allegorically as Church of Christ, anagogically as the heavenly city of God 'which is the mother of us all,' tropologically, as the soul of man, which is frequently subject to praise or blame from the Lord under this title.[86]

Applied to the Heraclius example of the *Kaiserchronik*, this results in the following layers of interpretation: in the literal sense, Heraclius and his men's *superbia* imperils their service to the historical place Jerusalem; on the typological-allegorical level of the spiritual sense, it imperils their service to the temporal Church; on the tropological and moral level of the spiritual sense, it imperils their own souls; and ultimately, on the anagogical-eschatological level of the spiritual sense, it imperils their entry into the Kingdom of Heaven. The exemplary historical analogy, with biblical authority, to Heraclius and his men are the craven Israelites from Heraclius's example, who would not fight and to whom entry into the promised lands would therefore be forbidden (Numbers 14. 27–35).

The Heraclius episode employs all the registers of exemplary writing available to a medieval author. It draws on biblical and historical authority, modulates the two, comments explicitly on them, and addresses the target audience. This strategy is not unusual in the *Kaiserchronik*, but it is by no means consistently applied throughout the text. Other examples, like Titus and Trajan, employ similar strategies, as will be shown below, but the author does not display any programmatic strategy of turning all or even most possible episodes with exemplary potential into explicit examples. The stern justice Nerva displays in his treatment of the artisan who forged the moving horse, fuelled by the life energy of a living soul locked into it (*KC*, 5779–5810), would have been a fitting place to implement an exemplary tale, but the text is conspicuously void of any commentary or analogical pattern, and simply does not seem interested in turning Nerva into an example analogous to Heraclius.

1.2.3. Aetiology: Etymology, Toponyms, and the Pantheon

Other possible functions of quantity identifiable in the *Kaiserchronik* have received much less scholarly attention than exemplarity. In the following, the chronicle's aetiological episodes will be examined more closely.

Aetiologies are narratives that aim to explain why something has come to be and how it became the way it is. These explanatory models often operate in detachment from the actual historical or etymological origins of the phenomenon they aim to explain. In some cases, a historical occurrence might be turned into an aetiological narrative, but generally the relationship between aetiology and factuality remains tenuous and has to be critically examined on a

---

86 *The Conferences of John Cassian*, trans. by Edgar C. S. Gibson, Select Library of Nicene and Post-Nicene Fathers of the Christian Church, 2nd ser., 11 (New York, 1894), p. 222. John Cassian, *Conlationes XXIIII*, ed. by Michael Petschenig (Vienna, 1886): 'Igitur praedictae quatuor figurae in unum ita si volumus confluunt, ut una atque eadem Jerusalem quadrifariam possit intelligi: secundum historiam civitas Judaeorum, secundum allegoriam Esslesia Christi, secundum anagogen civitatis Dei illa coelestis quae est mater omnium nostrum; secundum tropologiam anima hominis, quae frequenter hoc nomine aut increpatur, aut laudatur a Domino' (XIV. 8).

case-by-case basis.[87] Westermann defines aetiologies as narratives in which the answer to the question that the aetiology sets out to explain coincides with the general resolution of dramatic tension in a genuine narrative.[88]

A particularly striking example for an aetiology of the etymological variety can be found in the *Annolied* (*AL*), when the Romans send Caesar out to fight the rebellious Germans: 'duo santin si den edelin Cêsarem, | dannin noch hiude kuninge heizzint keisere' (*AL*, 18. 9–10).[89] These lines showcase the narrator's erudition, connect the German present to the Roman past, and prefigure the close association Caesar and the Germans are going to have in the *Annolied*. In this case, the etymological derivation happens to be correct, but this is by no means necessary for explanatory models like this one to take full effect, as later examples will illustrate.[90]

When looking at the *Kaiserchronik*, a natural connection from exemplarity to aetiology opens up when — given the scarcity of language that explicitly indicates exemplarity — one starts to look for more subtle structures that create narrative effect by negotiating the temporal gulf between the past and the present and thus mark a quantifiable connection between the diegetic past of the *Kaiserchronik* and the present of its audience. A worthwhile place to start looking is in temporal adverbs like *hiute* or *nû*. For our purposes, we are not concerned with the prominent use of these words by intradiegetic figures to denote their diegetic present time. An example of this is King Nerva's condemnation of the craftsman who created the iron horse only to suffer death in his own creation:

> mit dir wirt ouh verendet der list.
> in gelirnet hinnen vur niemer nehain man:
> er muoz hiute disses tages ende hân. (*KC*, 5760–62)

The adverb marks an effect that is clearly confined to the diegetic present time of Nerva's punishment of the presumptuous artisan, which anchors the event in the past for the extradiegetic audience. Similarly, *nû* is overwhelmingly used in the sense of 'now' or 'in this moment' to indicate the present or a consecutive action.[91] But there are examples more relevant for our purposes, for example when Agrippa and Tiberius go about founding cities in the German lands.[92]

> er hiez si Agrippînâ,
> Colonjâ ist si nû genant,
> si zieret elliu frenkiskiu lant.
> [...]

87 Burke Long, *The Problem of Etiological Narrative in the Old Testament*, Beihefte zur Zeitschrift für die alttestamentliche Wissenschaft, 108 (Berlin, 1968), pp. 1–4.

88 Claus Westermann, *Forschung am Alten Testament*, Theologische Bücherei, 24 (Munich, 1964), pp. 18–20.

89 *Annolied*, in *Deutsche Dichtung des Mittelalters*, ed. by Michael Curschmann and Ingeborg Glier (Munich, 1980–81), I: *Von den Anfängen bis zum hohen Mittelalter* (1980), pp. 92–147.

90 See *Kluge: Etymologisches Wörterbuch der deutschen Sprache*, 25th edn, ed. by Elmar Seebold (Berlin, 2011), s.v. *Kaiser* (p. 464).

91 W. F. Tulasiewicz, *Index Verborum zur deutschen Kaiserchronik* (Berlin, 1972), pp. 228–29.

92 The lands north of the Alps have at this point already been mapped out by Caesar's forays as inhabited by various German peoples.

ain stat worht er dâ
geheizen Tyburnîâ.
nû haizet si aver Ratispônâ. (*KC*, 648–89)

In both cases, *nû* links the ancient past of the founding of the city with the medieval present by contrasting its past Latin with its present German name. The 'now' is not a diegetically consecutive 'now' but the present of the twelfth-century text, audience, and author.

The same gulf is often straddled by the temporal adverb *hiute*, and narratives that connect both sides of this temporal divide with an aetiological purpose are quite common in the *Kaiserchronik*. Establishing an enduring connection with the present day has been singled out as the key identifier of aetiological narratives.[93] Examples of these aetiologies are often tied to toponyms or topographical features that could theoretically still be witnessed by the text's twelfth-century audience. A straightforward example is Constantine's renaming of 'Bisantîâ' (*KC*, 10,445) after him, such that it is still known 'hiute' as 'Constantînobele' (*KC*, 10,448). In a slightly varied example in the Helius Adrianus episode, the eponymous emperor rebuilds Jerusalem and is led by his hubris to rename the city after himself:

er begunde di stat ze lieben,
harte wol zieren,
er verte wider die stat,
alse man hiute wol chiesen mach,
er verwandelt ir den namen,
er wolte si vur aigen haben:
si solte dô haizen Hêlîâ. (*KC*, 7222–28)

In this case, the aetiology does not pertain to the present-day name of the city. Adrianus's display of hubris to rename the Holy City after himself is immediately punished by God when Adrianus is slain in Damascus, and Jerusalem retains its name 'also si dâ vor gehaizen was' (*KC*, 7232). Instead, the aetiological explanation of the *Kaiserchronik* makes the topography of Jerusalem accessible to the *Kaiserchronik*'s present (*KC*, 7225).

Other short aetiological remarks focus on specific landmarks in Rome. The most entertaining is certainly the etymological derivation of the toponym 'Lateran'. Nero's alchemically induced attempts to bear a child occasion unforeseen results when he vomits out a massive toad. Upon this sight, the Romans present call out 'lâtâ rânâ' (*KC*, 4152), literally 'wide toad', from which the site of the event draws its name: 'daz si hiute haizzet Lâterân' (*KC*, 4154).

This example introduces a different function of aetiologies, which was already present in the earlier examples but is now focused on more strongly: the *Kaiserchronik*'s aetiologies not only serve as explanatory models for imparting meaning to the phenomenological chaos of the past from the vantage point of the present; they also operate as strategies for verifying the truth of the *Kaiserchronik*'s

---

93 Martin Noth, 'Der Beitrag der Archäologie zur Geschichte Israels', in *Congress Volume: Oxford 1959*, ed. by G. W. Anderson and others, Vetus Testamentum: Supplements, 7 (Leiden, 1960), pp. 262–82 (p. 287).

historical narratives. Line 4150 is seemingly inserted to intervene in a passage that challenges the audience's credulity: a toad bursts out of Nero's throat after he is made pregnant by imbibing several alchemical concoctions. The narrator of the *Kaiserchronik* actualizes himself, his audience, and their communicative relationship to stress the truth — 'zewâre' — of what he conveys. Paradoxically, insertions like these, which interrupt the diegesis and bring the relational divide between narrator and audience into the foreground, can heighten awareness of the artificiality of the reception situation. In this context, the etymological aetiology of explaining the name 'Lateran' by linking it to Latin *lata rana* for 'wide toad' not only works backward by anchoring the origins for a well-known toponym in the historical record. It also works forward by assuring the audience of the historical veracity of the *Kaiserchronik*'s narrative.

A more complex example can be found early in the chronicle, at the end of the establishment of the days of the pagan week and the introduction of the pagan gods. Here, the text inserts a short excursus on events that from the perspective of the diegesis lie in the future, but from the perspective of the audience still lie in the past. Both perspectives are meaningfully connected by the phrase 'noch hiute' (*KC*, 208). The object of the excursus is the exorcism and Christianization of the Roman Pantheon, identified by the chronicle as a temple of Saturn (*KC*, 171–75). The Pantheon passage develops a complicated temporal structure in order to link various historical stages of past occurrences to the present. While this passage is still part of the review of the pagan week, the text now gets ahead of itself to give a preview of Pope Boniface's exorcism and rededication of the temple as a church to Mary and all saints:

> daz buoch saget uns daz;
> der guote sancte Bonifâtîus
> der wîhete sît daz selbe hûs. (*KC*, 186–88)

The temporal adverb 'sît' clearly points to future events. Having just established a pagan system for ordering time,[94] the text invalidates that order and feeds in a temporal fragment from a future yet to come. To add at least some context to this passage, the text situates Boniface in time as the fourth pope after St Gregory (*KC*, 193–95). While the popes as a structuring feature of the *Kaiserchronik* quickly fade into the background (with the notable exceptions of Silvester and a few other popes, like Peter, Clement, and Leo, who feature prominently in the content), at this point the line from the prologue where the text states that it will tell 'von den bâbesen unt von den chunigen' (*KC*, 19) still resonates. The historiographical principle is abandoned in favour of a systematic one, the future to come, and the Christianization of the Rotunda is mentioned before the event itself occurs in the historical trajectory of the text. It does not recur at what would be the relevant chronological point in the textual narrative for this event, which happened under

---

94   Thus creating a second stage of order, following the incipient 'promiscuous idolatry' of 'polluted idols' and predating the imperial order of the Empire established by Caesar. See Chinca and Young, p. 11.

the Eastern Roman Emperor Phocas in 609 CE.[95] As Phocas does not feature in the *Kaiserchronik*, from a chronological point of view the 'correct' place for it would have been in one of the three Greek emperor episodes.

Boniface decides to convert the Pantheon because he is worried that immorality might still persist in his own time:

> do besante sich der heilige man
> nâch allen den guoten christen
> die er ze Rome weste. (*KC*, 198–200)

Within the textual excursus reaching into the historical future, Boniface's knowledge of many good Christians in Rome is well legitimated, but in the course of the *Kaiserchronik* this knowledge serves as a further glance into the future: Rome, which has just been presented as a place filled with pagan temples and inhabited by pagans who worship idols and celebrate pagan rites and feasts, will in future be a city inhabited by Christians who will overturn those pagan sites and customs. The conversion of the Pantheon had been a staple of Christian historiography since Bede's *Historia Ecclesiastica Gentis Anglorum*.[96] It marks the first occasion on which a pagan temple was turned into a Christian church: 'multitudo ibi sanctorum memoriam haberet'.[97] Its intrusion into the pagan calendar in the *Kaiserchronik* signifies a programmatic theme of the text: in the future, the incipient pagan order will be overcome by a Christian one. The belief that pagan places of worship were inhabited by demons[98] finds strong expression in the *Kaiserchronik* when, as soon as Boniface consecrates the temple to the Christian God, 'die tievel brâsten oben ûz, | sumelîche in das abgrunde' (*KC*, 206–07).

The Rotunda excursus concludes with a passage that reconnects it to the chronicle's main historical trajectory:

> des ist ze Rôme noch hiute urchunde.
> Nû sculen wir wider grîfen
> dâ wir die rede liezen. (*KC*, 208–10)

95   *Liber Pontificalis*, ed. by Theodor Mommsen, MGH Gesta Pontificum Romanorum, 1 (Berlin, 1895): 'Bonifativs IIII. [...] Eodem tempore petiit a Focate principe templum qui appellatur Pantheum, in quo fecit ecclesiam beatae Mariae semper virginis et omnium martyrum' (life 69, p. 165). Bede dates the synod that Bishop Mellitus of London attended in Rome in *The Complete Works of Venerable Bede*, ed. by J. A. Giles, 8 vols (London, 1843–44), II–III: *Historia Ecclesiastica Gentis Anglorum* (1843): '[...] et ipse Mellitus inter eos adsedit anno VIII imperii Focatis principis, indictione XIIIa, tertio die Kalendarum Martiarum' (II. 4, vol. 2, p. 186).

96   See Ohly, *Sage und Legende*, p. 39. Bede, *Historia Ecclesiastica*: 'Hic est Bonifatius, quartus a beato Gregorio Romanae urbis episcopo, qui inpetrauit a Focate principe donari ecclesiae Christi templum Romae, quod Pantheon uocabatur ab antiquis, quasi simulacrum esset omnium deorum; in quo ipse, eliminata omni spurcitia, fecit ecclesiam sanctae Dei genetricis atque omnium martyrum Christi; ut, exclusa multitudine daemonum, multitudo ibi sanctorum memoriam haberet' (II. 4, vol. 2, p. 186).

97   Ibid.

98   See Friedrich Wilhelm Deichmann, 'Frühchristliche Kirchen in antiken Heiligtümern', in *Rom, Ravenna, Konstantinopel, Naher Osten: Gesammelte Studien zur spätantiken Architektur, Kunst und Geschichte* (Wiesbaden, 1982), pp. 56–94 (pp. 56–59); Max Wehrli, 'Antike Mythologie im christlichen Mittelalter', in *Max Wehrli: Gegenwart und Erinnerung: Gesammelte Aufsätze*, ed. by Fritz Wagner and Wolfgang Maas, Spolia Berolinensia, 12 (Hildesheim, 1998), pp. 90–104 (pp. 93–97).

While 'des' refers clearly to the story of the conversion of the Pantheon, 'hiute' refers to the time of the *Kaiserchronik*'s compiler and the text's audience. The text gives an assurance of the historical persistence of an event that is still one step away in the future from the point of view of the diegesis, but still in the past of the twelfth-century historical present. Knowledge still available in the present time of the audience is causally linked back to the historical record of the *Kaiserchronik*. And only now can the record allow itself to revert to the diegetic present of the first century BCE and begin the Caesar episode.

1.2.4. Aetiological Exemplarity: Titus and Trajan

Another remarkable toponymical aetiology centres on a fictitious column situated in the city of Rome that was imagined as still being visible to the *Kaiserchronik*'s contemporaries. Unlike the previous examples of aetiologies, this account uses the transtemporal structure of aetiological narratives to intertwine them with a moral and didactic example more closely related to the previously examined Heraclius episode. After the Emperor Titus has thwarted a plot against his life, through personal cunning and a display of great civic justice, he has the twelve conspirators executed (*KC*, 5377–5530). The structural marker for historical continuity is *ienoch* in the sense of 'still' and not 'anyway'.[99]

> er hiez die aitgenôzze vâhen
> unt alle di an dem râte mit in wâren,
> er hiez si vuoren ûf den hof —
> daz urkunde ist ze Rôme ienoh — ,
> mit rehter urtaile
> Rômære algemaine
> hiez er in diu houbet abslahen. (*KC*, 5521–27)

The bridge between the present and the past marked by *ienoch* is *urkunde*, a word spanning a broad semantic field from 'sign' or 'proof', via 'argument', to 'testimony' and even 'testament'.[100] The place where this testimony is available is Rome. The matter that the testimony conveys from the past to the present is the way Titus punishes his assailants 'mit rehter urtaile' (*KC*, 5525). It is not explicitly stated, but the context suggests that after this the text aims to further illustrate the specific form in which the *urkunde* of Titus's justice is secured: the emperor orders a 'sûl êrîn' (*KC*, 5533) to be built to memorialize his just verdict. The text claims that this atectonic column is still to be seen in Rome 'hiute' (*KC*, 5534), although it corresponds to no actual topographical landmark in the city and is not part of a broader legendary tradition. Instead, its introduction is down to the *Kaiserchronik*'s author, but it remains unclear whether he perceived the column as a real monument or intentionally fabricated it. In either case, within the *Kaiserchronik*, the monument's purpose is decidedly public and civic: the statue on top of the column shows Titus as a just ruler, with the sword as the sign of his *imperium*, which entails the judicial

---

99   See Lexer, s.v. *ie-noch* (III (1878), cols 1415–16).
100 See Lexer, s.v. *ur-künde, -kunde* (II (1876), col. 2006).

authority to condemn the perpetrators to death. As a deterrent, he has the names of the twelve conspirators whose executions exemplify his justice engraved on the column 'sô man hiute dâ lesen mac | ze ainem urkunde unz an den jungisten tac' (*KC*, 5537–38).[101]

Not only is the column temporally still present; it is also visible over a wide spatial distance, as the column 'scînet verre in di lant' (*KC*, 5542). Indeed, it is assumed to be still visible, as the present-tense 'scînet' suggests. The column is imagined as permanent in time and space, and at least theoretically accessible to the audience of the text in the same way as Constantinople, Jerusalem, or the Lateran are.

The implications of this passage are complex. The fact that the column does not actually exist does not mean that the passage loses its main qualifier as an aetiology. The author and the audience of the *Kaiserchronik* might well have thought it to be an actual Roman site. However, it becomes clear that the launching point for this particular enquiry into the Roman past is not puzzlement at present physical phenomenology but the wish to reify the continual historical exemplarity of the event the monument memorializes: the justice of Titus. It shines through the centuries not as an actual monument but as a textual anchor of the absoluteness of Titus's exemplarity. It becomes unchangeable in its validity. The text constructs it not with an interest in explaining a phenomenon of the past but to imbue a historical example with authority for the present.

> daz wart umbe daz getân —
> sô wir das buoch hôren sagen —
> swer das zaichen iemer dâ ersæhe,
> daz er bilde der bî næme. (*KC*, 5543–46)

Now the *Kaiserchronik* switches into explanatory mode, not, however, looking back from the present, but the other way round: looking forward from the diegetic past toward the present of the author and the audience. Everyone in the future — 'wir' — should 'iemer' benefit from the 'zaichen' of Titus's justice, from which they might *bilde nemen*.

The scene lends itself to comparison with the end of the Trajan episode, another case of exemplarity persisting through time, but without the disguised aetiology of the Titus episode and instead through the insertion of another fragment from the diegetic future (*KC*, 6013–95). Trajan lends himself to comparison because he is, like Titus, singled out for his good judgements (*KC*, 5969–84, 6007–18). Because of this, 'uber zwai hundert jâr' later (*KC*, 6024), Pope Gregory the Great takes pity on the pagan emperor, who is apparently languishing in hell. The two hundred years mark the distance between the pagan empire Trajan used to rule and a future Christian empire, not yet actualized but heavily foreshadowed in the *Kaiserchronik*, in which Pope Gregory presides over the Church. Gregory's concern echoes medieval considerations about the virtue of the gentiles who had not known God and yet displayed exemplary virtuousness, as expressed for example by John of Salisbury, a contemporary of the *Kaiserchronik*.[102]

---

101 See Ohly, *Sage und Legende*, p. 109.
102 'For who is there that can embrace the very self of virtue? Who now clothes himself in even

Thinking of Trajan's 'guot gerihte' (*KC*, 6033), Pope Gregory wonders whether he 'iemer erlôset solte werden' (*KC*, 6036). Thereupon, an angel descends to grant Gregory the power over Trajan's salvation: Gregory can either let the soul of Trajan suffer as he has deserved, or the pope can vouch for the pagan emperor's soul personally. Should Gregory wish to preserve Trajan's soul until Judgement Day, he will in return have to suffer seven ailments and ultimately die from them (*KC*, 6052–61). It is implied, but not explicitly stated, that Gregory agrees to the terms, as the narrator suddenly materializes and, speaking in the first-person plural pronoun 'wir', includes his audience in an expression of hope for the redemption of Trajan's soul when the Last Judgement comes (*KC*, 6080–82). The change of tone is significant because it shifts the text from a narrative to a more exhortative style in which the narrator continues to elaborate on the exemplarity of Trajan's administration of justice:

> Nû suln alle werltkunige
> dâ bî nemen pilede,
> wi der edel kaiser Trajân
> diese genâde umbe got gewan,
> want er rehtes gerihtes phlegete
> di wîl er an dirre werlte lebete.
> der selben genâden suln si gewis sîn,
> behaltent si an ir gerihte mînen trähtîn. (*KC*, 6083–90)

Trajan's historical justice gains him a chance of salvation in an eschatological future even though he had the soteriological bad luck to live and die a pagan. If the 'werltkunige' of the narrator's present take up his example — the phrase 'nemen pilede' in line 6084 links Trajan to Titus (*KC*, 5546) — and dispense justice with Jesus in their minds, they too can hope for the same divine clemency. Trajan's good performance as a ruler has made him eligible for salvation and transports the question of his soteriological fate from a pagan into a Christian horizon. However, the final decision on Trajan's salvation remains open until the Last Judgement. Gregory's sacrifice does not actually redeem Trajan's soul — that would be dogmatically highly problematic — and does not mark any real qualitative change either; it merely enables a divine reconsideration of his fate. Again, qualitative change in time is not thematized or problematized but in this case postponed for the eschatological future. Nevertheless, papal and angelic intervention ensures the continuity of Trajan's example and thus the availability of his beneficial exemplarity for a Christian audience. Interestingly, the text speaks about the 'werltkunige' in the third person plural (*KC*, 6083) and does not directly invite the audience to emulate

the shadow of the virtues in which we see that gentiles excelled, albeit having no Christ they did not attain the fruit of true blessedness? Who imitates the diligence of Themistocles, the gravity of Fronto, the continence of Socrates, the honor of Fabricius, the innocence of Numa, the modesty of Scipio, the patience of Ulysses, the frugality of Cato, or the pity of Titus? Who does not admire and venerate, since Honesty is praised but shivers in the cold?' (*Frivolities of Courtiers and Footprints of Philosophers: Being a Translation of the First, Second, and Third Books and Selections from the Seventh and Eighth Books of the Policraticus of John of Salisbury*, trans. by Joseph Pike (New York, 1972), pp. 197–98). John of Salisbury, *Policraticus*, ed. by Clement Webb (London, 1909), III. 9, pp. 197–98.

the pagan emperor's example: here, the *Kaiserchronik* truly becomes a mirror of princes and creates an opposition between the 'wir' of the author and his audience, and the 'si', the temporal rulers of God's creation.

As a closing remark, the parallel with Boniface's conversion of the Pantheon is striking. Both passages are inserted toward the end of their episodic units. Both employ the figure of a virtuous pope who features anachronistically as a visitor from a safely Christian future. In the Pantheon passage, Boniface foreshadows a Christian future for the pagan city of Rome and affirms the validity of the twelfth-century religious axioms that would have governed the worldview of the chronicle's audience by temporarily levelling the chronological distance yet to be covered. In comparison, Gregory in the Trajan episode also collapses chronological distance, but in order to respond to questions about Trajan's salvation. Both respond to immediate concerns the *Kaiserchronik*'s audience would have had regarding the religious quality of the present it inhabited and its connection to the past. Crucially, both figure only in their anachronistic spaces in the episode framework and are not narrated later in their proper chronological places. This shows how the episode paradigm creates quantitative distance and not qualitative difference, which makes it possible to collapse the distance and to suppress the difference between the past and the present. As the past is made similar enough to the present, and only removed by quantities of time and not by qualities of composition, it is not necessary to repeat the stories of the good Christian popes where they chronologically belong.

CHAPTER 2

❖

The Poeticity and Historicity of the *Kaiserchronik*

The prominence of exemplary narratives in the *Kaiserchronik* warrants examination in a broader context than the one adopted by the previous chapter, which considered exemplarity as a function of the text's episode framework. But the relevance of exemplary narrative in the chronicle goes beyond this; after all, the idea that history should provide a lesson to posteriority and that it is the historian's task to frame this lesson is a central topos of medieval historiography and is also emphasized in the *Kaiserchronik*'s prologue.

After contextualizing the *Kaiserchronik* in the broader tradition of exemplary historiography, I will examine how the chronicle's prologue articulates a programme of historical veracity and how the key claims of this programme help to model the text's poeticity as a chronographical account of historical truth. To achieve this, I will undertake close readings of some core passages of the prologue, considering how they are linked to previous and contemporary medieval literature, and what can be gleaned from them.

While this may seem like an excursus — if not a digression — away from the main line of my argument, I will ultimately show how the results of this examination corroborate the findings obtained so far and relate to the chronicle's negotiation of historical distance and difference.

2.1. The *Kaiserchronik* and the *Historia Magistra Vitae* Tradition

Cicero's famous dictum of history as a *magistra vitae* has become a label for a didactic and rhetorical tradition of historiography that employs recurring historical patterns and contrasting examples to educate and edify. In Cicero's treatise *De Oratore*, his character Antonius asks (rhetorically): 'By what other voice, too, than that of the orator, is history, the witness of time, the light of truth, the life of memory, the directress of life [*magistra vitae*], the herald of antiquity, committed to immortality?'[1] The various aspects of history, which are presented as a string of metaphors, can only be imbued with immortality by the orator. Cicero draws on Hellenistic

---

1   Cicero, *Rhetorica*, ed. by A. S. Wilkins, 2 vols (Oxford, 1963), I: *De Oratore*: 'Historia vero testis temporum, lux veritatis, vita memoriae, magistra vitae, nuntia vetustatis, qua voce alia, nisi oratoris, immortalitati commendatur?' (II. 36); my translation.

rhetorical principles[2] to demonstrate how knowledge of history is mainly deployed for rhetorical ends,[3] providing many examples for instructive employment: 'Plena exemplorum est historia'.[4]

In order to be conveyed from the first century BCE to the time of the compilation of the *Kaiserchronik* in the mid-twelfth century CE, the ancient notion of history as *magistra vitae* had to negotiate the Christian scrutiny of much of the pagan writing from antiquity, which was categorized in opposition to the Bible's authority.[5] But history came to be cultivated for educative Christian purposes by Augustine in his *De Civitate Dei*, an approach which his student Orosius was the first to apply consistently in a historiographical context in his *Historiae adversum Paganos*, and not despite but because of history's pagan connotations. The exemplary and comparative retrospective on the horrors of events from a pagan past lends itself naturally to Orosius's agenda of presenting contemporary events in a more favourable light and educating his contemporaries about an appropriate understanding of their time. According to Orosius, whether or not one can draw the right conclusions from history depends on the inner attitude with which it is reflected upon.[6] 'O, the suffering that we see here! Do the men who grumble about recent events, read about the past? Indeed, they do, and draw their conclusions from jaundice not judgement.'[7] This is where Orosius can apply the didactic lever of *historia magistra vitae* to demonstrate the beneficial influence of the temporal presence of Christianity on historical occurrences, for example when he comments on an earthquake that was prophesied for his day and age: 'But modesty dictates that I note, rather than discuss, these matters, so that he who knows of them may remember them and he who does not may make enquiries about them.'[8]

Over two hundred years later, another Spaniard, Isidore of Seville, would acknowledge the concept, albeit somewhat 'furtively',[9] in his *Etymologiae*, and in

---

2   See e.g. Polybius, *The Histories: Books 9–15*, trans. by W. R. Paton, Loeb Classical Library, 159, 6 vols (Cambridge, MA, 2011): 'The peculiar function of history is to discover, in the first place, the words actually spoken, whatever they were, and next to ascertain the reason why what was done or spoken led to failure or success. 2 For the mere statement of a fact may interest us but is of no benefit to us: but when we add the cause of it, study of history becomes fruitful. 3 For it is the mental transference of similar circumstances to our own times that gives us the means of forming presentiments of what is about to happen, and enables us at certain times to take precautions and at others by reproducing former conditions to face with more confidence the difficulties that menace us' (XII. 25b).

3   Reinhart Koselleck, *Futures Past: On the Semantics of Historical Time* (Cambridge, MA, 1985), p. 23.

4   Cicero, *Über die Weissagung: De Divinatione*, ed. and trans. by Christoph Schäublin (Berlin, 2013), I. 50, p. 56.

5   See Koselleck, p. 24.

6   See Brandt, pp. 127–31.

7   Orosius, *Seven Books of History against the Pagans*, trans. by Andrew T. Fear, Translated Texts for Historians, 54 (Liverpool, 2015), p. 168. Orosius, *Historiarum adversum Paganos Libri VII*, ed. by Karl Zangmeister (Vienna, 1882): 'Pro dolor, leguntne ista de veteribus, qui de recentibus conqueruntur? Immo legunt et ea non aequitate sed aemulatione coniciunt' (IV. 6. 34).

8   Orosius, *Seven Books of History*, p. 116. Orosius, *Historiae*: 'Sed haec ut commemorata sint magis quam explicita uerecundiae concesserim ut et qui scit relocat at qui nescit inquirat' (III. 3. 3).

9   Koselleck, p. 24.

doing so turn it into 'august and useful clichés'[10] readily accessible to Christian writers of the Middle Ages:

> Histories of peoples are no impediment to those who wish to read useful works, for many wise people have imparted the past deeds of humankind in histories for the instruction of the living. Through history they handle a final reckoning back through seasons and years, and they investigate many indispensable matters through the succession of consuls and kings.[11]

The *Kaiserchronik* prologue's announcement that the chronicle will report the deeds 'von den bâbesen unt von den chunigen | baidiu guoten unt ubelen' (*KC*, 19–20) fits into the moral extensions of this approach to history, implementing the presentation of didactic content in the tradition established in the preface of Bede's *Historia Ecclesiastica*:

> For if history relates good things of good men, the attentive hearer is excited to imitate that which is good; or if it mentions evil things of wicked persons, nevertheless the religious and pious hearer or reader, shunning that which is hurtful and perverse, is the more earnestly excited to perform those things which he knows to be good, and worthy of God.[12]

About four hundred years later, and at the same time as the compilation of the *Kaiserchronik*, Otto of Freising, in his *Chronica*'s dedicatory epistle to Emperor Frederick I, emphasized the immediate political usefulness of a knowledge of history for the present-day ruler:

> I have therefore obeyed your command willingly and gladly, so much more devotedly as I regard it as thoroughly in accord with your royal preëminence that you desire to know what was done in olden times by kings and emperors, and to know this [...] also for its [the state's] better molding by laws and statutes.[13]

As we arrive in the twelfth century, in addition to the modelling of exemplarity as a function of the *Kaiserchronik*'s quantifying episode framework, the dimension

---

10   Nancy Partner, *Serious Entertainments: The Writing of History in Twelfth-Century England* (Chicago, 1977), p. 3.

11   *The Etymologies of Isidore of Seville*, trans. by Stephen Barney and others (Cambridge, 2006), p. 67. Isidore of Seville, *Etymologiarum sive Originum Libri XX*, ed. by W. M. Lindsay, 2 vols (Oxford, 1911; repr. 1957): 'Historiae gentium non inpediunt legentibus in his quae utilia dixerunt. Multi enim sapientes praeterita hominum gesta ad institutionem praesentium historiis indiderunt, siquidem et per historiam summa retro temporum annorumque supputatio conprehenditur, et per consulum regumque successum multa necessaria perscrutantur' (I. 43).

12   Bede, *The Ecclesiastical History of the English Nation*, trans. by L. C. Jane (New York, 2007), p. 1. Bede, *Historia Ecclesiastica*: 'Sive enim historia de bonis bona referat, ad imitandum bonum auditor sollicitus instigatur; seu mala commemoret de prauis, nihilominus religiosus ac pius auditor siue lector deuitando quod noxium est ac peruersum, ipse sollertius ad exsequenda ea, quae bona ac Deo digna esse cognouerit, accenditur' (prologue, vol. 2, p. 2).

13   Otto of Freising, *The Two Cities: A Chronicle of Universal History to the Year 1146 A.D.*, trans. by Charles Christopher Mierow (New York, 2002), p. 87. Otto of Freising, *Chronica; sive, Historia de Duabus Civitatibus*, ed. by Adolf Hofmeister, MGH SS Rer. Germ., 45 (Hanover, 1912): 'Parui ergo libens et lubens vestro imperio tanto devotius, quanto regiae excellentiae concenientius esse considero ob rei publicae non solum armis tutandae, sed et legibus et iudiciis informandae incrementum antiqua regum seu imperatorum gesta vos velle cognoscere' (letter to Frederick I, p. 1; all quotations from Otto's *Chronica* are from this edition).

of the rhetorical presentation and communication of exemplarity arises: how does the *Kaiserchronik* use rhetorical devices to produce moral and didactic effects, and what are the sociocultural implications that shape the chronicle's transmission of exemplarity? Nancy Partner's 1977 book *Serious Entertainments* provided a useful approach to this complex of questions by showing conclusively how in the twelfth century — and in fact up until the late eighteenth century — the historiographer's task was not merely to record hard facts, but moreover to 'arrest the attention and divert the imagination' with a variety of different topics, among them 'accounts of exemplary lives and evidences of God's continuing interest in human affairs'.[14]

To achieve this, historiography had to aspire to the dignity of literature by employing the most beautiful style a writer could command.[15] Historiography and poetic writing both aspired to 'Wirklichkeitsbezug [...]: die wählende, strukturierende, verwandelnde und doch glaubwürdig wirkende Umsetzung der Ereignisse in die Modellhaftigkeit einer epischen Sprache'.[16] The historiographies of the twelfth century were read by their audiences as 'serious entertainment'[17] containing both the style and the material to educate and to delight. As Chinca and Young have argued, the *Kaiserchronik*, which is roughly contemporary with the chronicles Partner examines, seems to fit in with them.[18] And it is not the only text from the German lands from this time that can be read alongside Partner's texts: Reuter argued that the

> invention of a mythical past intended both as serious construction and as entertainment [can be found] in the anonymous author of the *Gesta Treverorum*, who supplied an elaborate pre-Roman history for his city, or in Godfrey of Viterbo, who in his works gathered together *exempla* from every possible source he could get his hands on.[19]

Chinca and Young propose positioning the *Kaiserchronik* alongside those texts,[20] which Reuter goes on to characterize as 'counterparts of Geoffrey of Monmouth or perhaps to the *Policraticus*'.[21] The main areas of interest and lines of argument Reuter sketches out for twelfth-century historiography from the German lands only corroborate Chinca and Young's claim: the 'question [...] where the community had come from and where it was going' is deeply ingrained in the *Kaiserchronik*'s

14   Partner, p. 2. She also lists: 'scenes of great triumphs and failures, inside information about princes both secular and ecclesiastical, matters of provincial but intense interest, scandalous gossip, tales of exotic places'.
15   See ibid., pp. 2–3.
16   Peter von Moos, 'Poeta und Historicus im Mittelalter: Zum Mimesis-Problem am Beispiel einiger Urteile über Lucan', *Beiträge zur Geschichte der deutschen Sprache und Literatur*, 98 (1973), 93–130 (p. 96).
17   Partner, p. 4.
18   Henry of Huntingdon, *Historia Anglorum* (second quarter twelfth century), William of Newburgh, *Historia Rerum Anglicarum* (mid- to late twelfth century), and Richard of Devizes, *Chronicon de Rebus Gestis Ricardi Primi* (late twelfth century); Chinca and Young, p. 16.
19   Timothy Reuter, 'Past, Present and No Future in the Twelfth-Century Regnum Teutonicum', in *The Perception of the Past in Twelfth-Century Europe*, ed. by Paul Magdalino (London, 1992), pp. 15–36 (p. 17).
20   See Chinca and Young, p. 16.
21   Reuter, pp. 17–18. For John of Salisbury's *Policraticus* as 'thesaurus exemplorum', see von Moos, *Geschichte als Topik*, pp. 134–38.

interest in aetiology. It is one of the texts that transmit — seemingly independently from one another — the story of Caesar's close affiliation with the Germans and their crucial importance for his rise to power. A couple of decades later, Godfrey of Viterbo, who also knew of Caesar's special relation with the Germans,[22] would expand this connection by tracing the genealogy of Henry VI back to Julius Caesar and the Trojans.[23] Finally, the *Kaiserchronik* displays a certain interest in traditions of local history that imbue particular regions or cities in the polycentric German Empire with historical authority,[24] like the Augustus episode for Cologne, Metz, and Trier (*KC*, 643–63); the Tiberius episode for Regensburg (*KC*, 685–89); the Lucretia episode, again for Trier (*KC*, 4305–16); the Adelger episode for Bavaria (*KC*, 6622–7135); or the Henry II episode for Bamberg (*KC*, 16,188–16,239). The *Kaiserchronik* was very much part of a 'wider northern European historiographico-literary scene'.[25]

The unperturbed oscillation of twelfth-century chronicles, Latin or vernacular, between rhetorical education and entertainment pertains to the broader question of their poeticity — a question highly relevant for the *Kaiserchronik*. The pairing of education and entertainment cannot, of course, simply be equated to the combination of fact and fiction, for it is the modern perspective that expects educational content to confine itself to factuality and wants to permit fictitious material only for the purposes of literature and entertainment. It has become clear that this analytical segregation was not a preoccupation shared by historical texts, and that both historiographical and more literary texts could fulfil Aristotle's poetic imperative as paraphrased by Peter von Moos in his influential study on Lucan's poeticity: '[...] daß [...] die symbolschaffende Organisation der rohstofflichen Fülle ereignishafter Erscheinungen zu einer allgemein intelligiblen Struktur, in

---

22   As the MGH edition by Georg Pertz from 1872 (see below) is far from complete, I refer here to the much older but also more comprehensive Godfrey of Viterbo, *Pantheon; sive, Vniuersitatis Libri*, ed. by Johannes Herold (Basle, 1559). It has been made accessible online by the Heinrich-Heine-Universität Düsseldorf (http://digital.ub.uni-duesseldorf.de/urn/urn:nbn:de:hbz:061:1–75610 [accessed 26 October 2017]). Caesar conquers the Germans: 'Rheno etiam flumine transmeato, Germanos ferocissimos, tam bello quam muneribus, omnes deuicit. Germanorum autem virtutem & fortitudinem, qui scire desiderat, Suetonium legat. Iosephus etiam & Egesippus, de ipsis tamquam de hominibus mori non timentibus incredibilem audaciam & fortitudinem atque uirtutem describerunt' (XII, col. 319). Caesar, the Romans, and the Germans share a common ancestry: 'Dum fortuna duces Germanos laeta decorat, Crescitque alta sonat super omnia climata Roma, Cuius ad imperium, praelia magna tonant. Hanc quasi reginam metuit satis hora marina, Terra Cisalpina timet, aduentate ruina, Sed loca Germana, quadia magna parant. Nam quos Troia suos olim generauit alumnos, Romans & Germanos uidet undique; summos, Et quasi consocios semper habebit eos' (X, col. 248).
23   Godfrey of Viterbo, *Speculum Regnum*, ed. by Georg Waitz, in MGH SS, 22 (Hanover, 1872), pp. 21–93: 'Ad dominum Henricum VItum regem romanorum et theutonicorum, filium dominum Frederici imperatoris de genealogia omnium regum et imperatorum Troianorum et Romanorum et Theutonicorum a tempore diluvii usque in hodiernum diem' (p. 21). For the use of rhetorical examples, particularly Alexander the Great, in Godfrey's *Pantheon*, see Anneke Mulder-Bakker, 'A Pantheon Full of Examples: The World Chronicle of Godfrey of Viterbo', in *Exemplum et Similitudo: Alexander the Great and Other Heroes as Points of Reference in Medieval Literature*, ed. by W. J. Aerts and M. Gosman, Mediaevalia Groningana, 8 (Gröningen, 1988), pp. 85–98 (pp. 88–92).
24   See Reuter, pp. 26–27.
25   Chinca and Young, p. 18.

der das Vergangene allein unter dem Gesichtspunkt der Verweisfunktion für eine zukünftige Entwicklung verallgemeinert wird.'[26]

Lucan is a useful example because critics since late antiquity have been arguing about whether he was a *poeta* or *historicus*. Von Moos uses this controversy to show that the most important link between historicity and poeticity is rhetoric. At the beginning of Christian Latin literature lies the classical practice of the rhetorical paraphrase of poetry, which in turn encompassed both poetic works, like Ovid, and works which were considered to be historiographical, like Virgil's *Aeneid*, but also books of the Bible. There is no discernible conceptual difference between, for example, metrical and non-metrical discourse, which would serve a modern audience as a touchstone: both were seen as interchangeable arts.[27] The medieval author follows the classical orator in his role as a rhetorical presenter, which translated into what Partner would call an amplification of his material.[28] Peter von Moos showed through the example of Lucan's *Pharsalia* and its reception in antiquity and the Middle Ages how poetry and historiography were regarded as just two different manifestations of the same rhetoric, which he defines as 'die Kunst des vergrößernden Realitätsbezugs'.[29]

How the *Kaiserchronik* modulates its own poetological position in the context of other twelfth-century texts is the concern of the next section, which takes the text's prologue, as the most poetologically and rhetorically charged part of the chronicle, as its focus.

2.2. The Prologue of the *Kaiserchronik*

2.2.1. The Historical Programme of Medieval Prologues

The prologue has — alongside epilogues and literary excursuses[30] — long been identified as the most important place in a medieval text for finding theoretical insights concerning the poetics of a genre.[31] In many cases, it remains the only appearance of this kind of discussion. The prologue is the place where the medieval author locates himself in the tradition of the texts that preceded his own.[32] Here, the conventions of traditional poetics and reflection on them meet and become visible.[33] When writing the prologue, the author has to rely on his own words and cannot simply take them over from a source, which, especially in a text like the *Kaiserchronik*, which is otherwise so heavily informed by its sources, makes taking a closer look at these passages all the more relevant.[34]

---

26   von Moos, 'Poeta und Historicus', p. 97.

27   See Curtius, *European Literature*, p. 148.

28   Partner, p. 206.

29   von Moos, 'Poeta und Historicus', p. 116.

30   Walter Haug, *Literaturtheorie im deutschen Mittelalter: Von den Anfängen bis zum Ende des 13. Jahrhunderts* (Darmstadt, 1992), p. 4.

31   See Ernst Friedrich Ohly, 'Wolframs Gebet an den Heiligen Geist im Eingang des Willehalm', *Zeitschrift für deutsches Altertum und deutsche Literatur*, 91 (1961–62), 1–37 (p. 19).

32   See Paul Zumthor, *Essai de poétique médiévale* (Paris, 1972), pp. 79–82.

33   See Haug, p. 3.

34   Eckart Conrad Lutz, *Rhetorica Divina: Mittelhochdeutsche Prologgebete und die rhetorische Kultur des*

In the case of the *Kaiserchronik*, no epilogue survives — if there ever was one: it is a characteristic trait of chronicle writing to be continued from generation to generation, as did in fact happen with the *Kaiserchronik*.[35] Thus, the lack of an epilogue as a reference point where the narrative can be poetically reflected on and closed is one of the typical implications of chronographical writing: while chronicles are written following a narrative sequence, they do not integrate it into their textual execution. Content is organized strictly chronologically and therefore lacks an internal reference framework that would make it possible to register the events depicted as part of a greater narrative whole.[36] This remains all the more true for a text like the *Kaiserchronik*, whose material organization is ultimately non-chronological but whose formal structure at least projects a strict chronological trajectory.

This section aims to provide a close reading of the poetologically and rhetorically relevant passages of the *Kaiserchronik*'s prologue. The guiding questions for this reading will be how the prologue is structured, and how it relates to other Early Middle High German texts and the broader rhetorical tradition in Latin as it would have been available to the author in the middle of the twelfth century.

The prologue of a medieval text does several things: it usually depicts 'the narrator in the persona of a poet addressing imagined readers as peers', it 'center[s] on language, literature, and knowledge', and finally, it is used by poets to 'situate [...] narrators or their narratives in relation to the past by means of conventional topoi that depict the past'.[37]

The first question to be answered will be whether or not the *Kaiserchronik* does in fact have a prologue that satisfies the standard rhetorical definitions of this *pars orationis*. Bernd Naumann claimed for Early Middle High German religious poems that they do not have 'Pro- und Epiloge als formal und inhaltlich eigenständige Gebilde, für die die mittelalterliche Rhetoriktradition bestimmte Forderungen aus der Antike übernommen oder neu ausgebildet hat'. Naumann goes on to note that the manuscripts usually do not mark the prologues of the texts he is looking at. It could be objected that this lack of marking proves simply that contemporary or later scribes saw no need to demarcate these components. And Naumann concedes that

Mittelalters (Berlin, 1984), p. 87.

35   The Bavarian continuation was probably written in the middle of the thirteenth century and survives in five manuscripts of recension C: Vienna, Österreichische Nationalbibliothek, Codex 2658 and Codex 12487; Landesbibliothek Karlsruhe, Cod. Aug. 52; Schloss Zeil, ZAMs 30; Munich, Bayerische Staatsbibliothek, Cgm 965. Schröder, p. 393, left Cgm 965 by Christoph Tegernseer from 1594 out of his edition of the Bavarian continuation 'wegen ihrer jugend und der absonderlichen manieren ihres urhebers'. The Bavarian continuation pushes the narrative up to the death of Frederick II in 1250. The second continuation, known as the Swabian continuation, only survives in ZAMs 30 and continues the imperial succession to Rudolf of Habsburg in the year 1274. Schröder, p. 409, feels confident in dating the Swabian continuation to 1281 — about a generation after the Bavarian continuation.

36   See Jörn Rüsen, 'Die vier Typen des historischen Erzählers', in *Formen der Geschichtsschreibung*, ed. by Reinhart Koselleck, Heinrich Lutz, and Jörn Rüsen, Beiträge zur Historik, 4 (Munich, 1982), pp. 514–605 (pp. 543–44).

37   Sunhee Kim Gertz, *Poetic Prologues: Medieval Conversations with the Literary Past*, Analecta Romanica, 56 (Frankfurt a. M., 1996), p. 19.

they may contain 'einführende und abschließende Verspartien, die inhaltlich und sprachlich (anderes Tempus, Zeitadverbien, Wechsel der verwendeten Pronomina bei der Publikumsadresse) vom Hauptteil abgehoben sind'. However, as he points out, it often remains unclear how long these passages are and where they cross over into the main part of the text.[38] As the early religious texts Naumann examines provide the largest rhetorical context in the German vernacular for the *Kaiserchronik*, a certain amount of caution seems appropriate.

The second question to be considered is how the first forty-two lines of the *Kaiserchronik* operate in relation to the text as a whole and to other vernacular and Latin texts of the time. Traditionally, the prologue would be the place for a medieval poet to 'display virtuosity' and at the same time use it as a 'metaliterary forum' to reflect on the medium and thus make the literary process visible for the audience that was about to embark on the reception of the text.[39] It also served as the rhetorical platform from which to prepare readers for the content of the text and to influence in advance their verdict on what they were about to receive.[40]

Rhetoric provides a broad array of literary devices to achieve this. As part of the *septem artes liberales*, rhetoric had been preserved from classical learning for the Middle Ages[41] and had by the twelfth century transferred its teachings and demands to historiography. Influential sources transmitting rhetorical tradition were, for example, Cicero's *De Inventione*, which was known as the *Rhetorica Vetus* and on which Thierry of Chartres, the teacher of John of Salisbury, wrote one of the earlier medieval commentaries in his *Heptateuchon*. Additionally of influence was the anonymous first-century BCE rhetorical handbook *Rhetorica ad Herennium*, which was until the sixteenth century also ascribed to Cicero as his *Rhetorica Nova*.[42] Quintilian's *Institutio Oratoria* and the relevant sections of the encyclopedic works of Martianus Capella or Isidore of Seville were influential, perhaps to a lesser degree.[43] Schulz identifies three basic rules of rhetorical *narratio* that entered medieval Latin historiography: the demands for truth, for brevity, and for lucidity,[44] which correlate of course with Cicero's famous instructions on how to deliver a good speech: 'Oportet igitur eam tres habere res: ut brevis, ut aperta, ut probabilis

---

38   Bernd Naumann, 'Ein- und Ausgänge: Frühmittelhochdeutsche Gedichte und die Predigt des 12. Jahrhunderts', in *Studien zur Frühmittelhochdeutschen Literatur: Cambridger Colloquium 1971*, ed. by Leslie Peter Johnson and others (Berlin, 1974), pp. 37–57 (pp. 38–39). The Middle High German *Hochzeit* would be a prime example of this problem.

39   Gertz, p. 20.

40   Henning Brinkmann, 'Der Prolog im Mittelalter als literarische Erscheinung', in *Studien zur Geschichte der deutschen Sprache und Literatur*, 2 vols (Düsseldorf, 1955–66), II (1966), 79–105 (p. 82).

41   Eckhard Kessler, 'Das rhetorische Modell der Historiographie', in *Formen der Geschichtsschreibung*, ed. by Koselleck, Lutz, and Rüsen, Beiträge zur Historik, 4 (Munich, 1982), pp. 37–85 (p. 59).

42   James Murphy, *Rhetoric in the Middle Ages; A History of Rhetorical Theory from Saint Augustine to the Renaissance* (Berkeley, 1974), pp. 106–10, 116–23.

43   Marie Schulz, *Die Lehre von der historischen Methode bei den Geschichtsschreibern des Mittelalters (VI.–XIII. Jahrhundert)*, Abhandlungen zur mittleren und neueren Geschichte, 12 (Berlin, 1909), pp. 133–34; Paul Klopsch, *Einführung in die Dichtungslehren des lateinischen Mittelalters* (Darmstadt, 1980), pp. 40–47.

44   Schulz, pp. 121–23.

sit.'[45] Writing a hundred years later, the Roman rhetorician Quintilian, whose *Institutio Oratoria* influenced medieval rhetoric until the mid-twelfth century before disappearing almost completely,[46] summarizes the purpose of the prologue in a straightforward mission statement:

> The sole purpose of the exordium is to prepare our audience in such a way that they will be disposed to lend a ready ear to the rest of our speech. The majority of authors agree that this is best effected in three ways, by making the audience well-disposed, attentive and ready to receive instruction. I need hardly say that these aims have to be kept in view throughout the whole speech, but they are especially necessary at the commencement, when we gain admission to the mind of the judge in order to penetrate still further.[47]

The ancient foundations of rhetoric had to undergo a many-layered process of appropriation to be applied in the Middle Ages.[48]

The main difference between the classical and the medieval perspectives of rhetoric for the purpose of historiography is the agency of divine *Providentia* in history, which turns historical occurrence into soteriological revelation and renders everything that happened before as necessary events that explicate the particularities of divine activity. Whatever happens in history is now semanticized by Providence and therefore confirmable in its factuality. History becomes 'objektiv wahrheitsfähig'. The task of rhetoric is no longer to constitute history, but merely to furnish the historiographical representation of this soteriological truth. To facilitate this, simply sticking to the facts may not prove sufficient. History not only has to be true; it also has to be probable.[49] Thus, Schulz is wrong when she claims that the occasionally surfacing *probabilitas* as a goal of rhetoric is simply being used synonymously with historiographical *veritas* due to a thoughtless mechanical adoption of rhetorical vocabulary.[50]

The textual explication of probable *verisimilitudo* is very much a complementary rather than an undesirable category of historical epistemology, as Quintilian writes when he echoes Cicero:

---

45   Cicero, *De Inventione*, in *On Invention, Best Kind of Orator, Topics*, trans. by H. M. Hubbell, Loeb Classical Library, 386 (Cambridge, MA, 1949), pp. 1–348 (I. 28, p. 56).

46   The reception of Quintilian's *Institutio Oratoria* in the Middle Ages really begun in the ninth century, but by the eleventh and twelfth century it had become readily available, even though its actual influence on the practice of medieval rhetoric remains unclear. See Franz Brunhölzl, 'Quintilianus', in *Lexikon des Mittelalters*, ed. by Bautier, Avella-Widhalm, and Auty, VII (Munich, 1995), cols 123–30.

47   See Quintilian, *Institutio Oratoria: Books I–III*, trans. by H. E. Butler, Loeb Classical Library, 124, 5 vols (Cambridge, MA, 1920; repr. 1963): 'Causa principii nulla alia est quam ut auditorem quo sit nobis in ceteris partibus accommodatior praeparemus. Id fieri tribus maxime rebus inter auctores plurimos constat, si beniuolum attentum docilem fecerimus, non quia ista non per totam actionem sint custodienda, sed quia initiis praecipue necessaria, per quae in animum iudicis ut procedere ultra possimus admittimur' (IV. 1. 5).

48   See Klopsch, *Einführung*.

49   See Kessler, pp. 59–62.

50   Schulz, p. 122.

> The statement of facts consists in the persuasive exposition of that which either has been done, or is supposed to have been done [...]. Most writers, more especially those of the Isocratean school, hold that it should be lucid, brief and plausible (for it is of no importance if we substitute clear for lucid, or credible or probable for plausible).[51]

Anticipating criticism for this, Quintilian justifies his focus on verisimilitude by pointing out that

> [t]here are many things which are true, but scarcely credible, just as there are many things which are plausible though false. It will therefore require just as much exertion on our part to make the judge believe what we say when it is true as it will when it is fictitious.[52]

By bringing the plausibility and power to convince of rhetorical speech into focus, Quintilian paves the way for one of the essential traits of the medieval historiographical application of rhetoric: truth is no longer constituted by the congruence of factual occurrences with their representation but through a *Kommunikationsgemeinschaft*[53] within which this representation can be accepted as truth. To achieve this, historiography must be geared toward the mental categories and cultural axioms that organize the reality of this *Kommunikationsgemeinschaft*[54] and can thus be utilized to reconstruct the past as 'true' history.[55] In the earlier twelfth century, Anselm of Laon, in his commentary on Lucan's *Pharsalia*, went so far as to single out verisimilitude and narrating plausibly as a binding obligation for every writer, historian and poet alike.[56]

However, despite the changed applications of rhetoric in the Middle Ages, its forensic, deliberative, and epideictic mandate remained largely unchanged: to provide a set of literary and linguistic tools apt for gaining the audience's attention, curiosity, and favour.[57]

2.2.2. The Rhetorical Structure of the Prologue

In light of these considerations, the question arises of whether the *Kaiserchronik*, and especially its prologue, reflects the narrative virtues and patterns of argument laid out above that would link it to the medieval interpretation and application

---

51   Quintilian, *Institutio Oratoria*: 'Nunc, quae sit narrandi ratio, subiungam. narratio est rei factae aut ut factae utilis ad persuadendum expositio [...]. Eam plerique scriptores maximeque qui sunt ab Isocrate uolunt esse lucidam breuem ueri similem. Neque enim refert, an pro lucida perspicuam, pro ueri simili probabilem credibilemque dicamus' (IV. 2. 31).

52   Ibid.: 'Sunt enim plurima uera quidem, sed parum credibilia, sicut falsa quoque frequenter ueri similia. Quare non minus laborandum est ut iudex quae uere dicimus quam quae fingimus credat' (IV. 2. 34).

53   Kessler, p. 50.

54   Karl-Otto Apel, *Transformation der Philosophie*, 2 vols (Berlin, 1994–99), II: *Das Apriori der Kommunikationsgemeinschaft* (1999), p. 429.

55   See Kessler, p. 50.

56   Mark Chinca, *Studies in the Poetics of Gottfried's Tristan*, Modern Humanities Research Association Texts and Dissertations, 35 (London, 1993), pp. 86–89.

57   Brinkmann, p. 83.

of classical rhetoric. With regard to content, the first forty-two lines of the *Kaiserchronik* break down into three distinct passages, which in the Vorau manuscript are marked by one-line initials.[58] Lines 1–14 address and admonish the audience, lines 15–26 summarize the content of the chronicle, and lines 27–42 take issue with 'scophelîchen worten' (*KC*, 31) and warn of the consequences of listening to them. Schröder indicates this in his edition by indenting the respective lines, as he does to mark the end of the prologue and the beginning of the historical narrative proper at line 43.

These are, of course, editorial measures, but a look at all the *Kaiserchronik* manuscripts of recension A reveals that they do in fact mark the break between lines 42 and 43, though usually not in a way different from markers used earlier to structure the prologue or later to shape the rest of the account. However, the text as edited by Schröder clearly presents an introductory passage, starting with the topical prayer-like invocation of 'des almähtigen gotes minnen' (*KC*, 1) and ending with the inchoative 'nû grîfe wir daz guote liet an' (*KC*, 42). This last line clearly indicates that the forty-one lines that preceded it are not to be considered as a diegetic part of the 'guote liet' but as some sort of proem, even though the according rhetorical terminology had in the twelfth century not yet been transferred into the German vernacular.[59]

A closer look at Naumann's criteria (tense, temporal adverbs, pronouns for addressing the audience) will help to consolidate the status of the first forty-two lines of the *Kaiserchronik* as an independent textual complex. Most of the prologue is written in the present tense. Prominent exceptions are 'mahten' (*KC*, 12) and 'wære' (*KC*, 14), where the mode shifts into the preterite subjunctive to ironically illustrate the futility of trying to teach the 'tumben' (*KC*, 6), and also the preterite indicative forms 'wâren' (*KC*, 21) and 'phlâgen' (*KC*, 22) where the historical content of the 'crônicâ' (*KC*, 17) is summarized. The rest is consistently written in the present tense, only to completely switch into the past tense after line 42.[60]

The use of temporal adverbs and personal pronouns confirms this division: in the passage that summarizes the content of the text, the phrase 'vor uns' (*KC*, 21) creates a sense of temporal distance between the audience and the events about to be presented. The linear progression of time unfolds 'unze an disen hiutegen tac' (*KC*, 23), at which point the distance is nullified as it converges with the event horizon of the 'crônicâ'. The audience is addressed by the narrator as 'iuh' (*KC*, 4) and 'iu' (*KC*, 25), and later the voice of the text includes itself in their number: 'uns' (*KC*, 16, 21, 36) and 'wir' (*KC*, 42). After this, the use of temporal adverbs marks not only a long jump back in time in relation to the audience's time — 'Hie bevor' — but also specifies the main categorical difference in temporal semantics: 'bi der haiden zîten' (*KC*, 43).

---

58   See Matthews, p. 6.
59   See Naumann, p. 38, n. 7.
60   e.g. 'anebette' (*KC*, 44), 'muosen' (*KC*, 47), 'wart' (*KC*, 50), 'tâten' (*KC*, 51), and 'sagent' (*KC*, 52).

The *Kaiserchronik* clearly has 'einführende Verspartien' in Naumann's sense, where the poet speaks about his audience and his intentions,[61] albeit in a very opaque way and — much to the chagrin of many a scholar — without making any statements about himself. But does this qualify as a prologue in the rhetorical sense of the term?

A prologue, or *prooemium*, has several possibilities for rhetorically preparing the reader or the audience.[62] Three attitudes of the audience have to be won, each to varying degrees depending on the quality of the theme of the coming speech or text: 'In ancipiti [causa] maxime benevolum iudicem, in obscuro docilem, in humili attentum parare debemus.'[63]

It would be futile to try to categorize the *Kaiserchronik* and its prologue according to one of the five forensic classes — Lausberg calls them 'Vertretbarkeitsrangstufen' — that classical rhetoric developed[64] and allow this result to shape the course of further enquiry, as a direct adherence to these principles is not to be expected. Instead, it seems more appropriate to look at the three parts of the prologue and try to identify the various rhetorical devices at work and then reconnect them to their deliberative background (or point out where and why this might not be possible).

The first two lines, for example, dedicating the *liet* (KC, 2) about to begin to 'des almähtigen gotes minnen' (KC, 1) echo the *invocatio* that was used to begin Latin charters of the time[65] but that was also quite common in other twelfth-century Middle High German texts like the *Wiener Genesis*, Heinrich von Veldeke's *Servatius*, or the *Rolandslied* and was often combined with claims about the truthfulness of the text.[66] According to Brinkmann, this kind of introduction has a double importance: it posits a generally shared and believed 'Lebenswahrheit' at the beginning of the text and thus helps to establish a common space for the author and his audience, which can subsequently be entered by the narrative proper.[67] After invoking the name of God and thus creating the universally shared space in line 1, which creates the space for his narrative to unfold in, line 2 introduces the narrator's first-person voice ('ich') and characterizes its object as a *liet*. The last line of the prologue picks this up in plural form when it announces: 'nû grîfe wir daz guote liet an' (KC, 42). Dickhut-Bielsky has cautioned against overestimating the self-identification of the *Kaiserchronik* as a *liet*, and rightly points out that the text displays a very fluid use of possible terminologies for sources and literature, as there was no fixed terminology for them in the twelfth century to begin with.[68]

---

61   Naumann, pp. 38, 42.
62   See Heinrich Lausberg, *Handbuch der literarischen Rhetorik: Eine Grundlegung der Literaturwissenschaft* (Munich, 1960), p. 150, §264.
63   Quintilian, *Institutio Oratoria*, IV. 1. 41.
64   *Honestum genus, anceps genus, admirabile genus, humile genus*, and *obscurum genus*; Lausberg, pp. 56–58, §64.
65   See W. Koch, 'Invocatio', in *Lexikon des Mittelalters*, ed. by Bautier, Avella-Widhalm, and Auty, v, cols 483–84. Phrases invoking Christ or God find their way into the beginning of legal documents in the sixth century.
66   See Matthews, p. 6.
67   See Brinkmann, p. 86.
68   Dickhut-Bielsky, p. 52.

Nevertheless, the mirrored self-identification as a *liet* seems too deliberate to dismiss it altogether. In the rest of the *Kaiserchronik*, the lexeme *liet* is overwhelmingly used analogously to *buoch* to confirm things to the audience: 'daz liet kundet uns daz' (*KC*, 622, also 1190; similarly 5176, 5671). In two other cases, it appeals to the audience to say a prayer for the benefit of someone deceased after the conclusion of a shorter narrative: 'swer daz liet vernomen habe | der sol einen pater noster singen'. In lines 10,619–20, this appeal is part of the curious reference to 'der des liedes alre êrist began' (*KC*, 10,626); in line 17,165, the appeal is for Emperor Lothair of Supplinburg.

It is also quite striking that several other roughly contemporary German vernacular texts, which share a quasi-historical conceptualization with the *Kaiserchronik*, speak of their accounts as *liet*. The *Eneasroman* (*ER*) uses *liet* almost exclusively to frame the source for its narrative, by repeatedly employing the phrase 'alsus saget uns daz liet' (48. 30, 110. 30, 214. 40, 276. 24, 349. 18).[69] Like the *Kaiserchronik*, Heinrich von Veldeke leaves it open whether the *liet* refers to his own narrative or the source from which he is drawing. In the *Alexanderlied* (*AXL*), Pfaffe Lamprecht uses *liet* twice to refer to his own work (1, 7279) and twice to refer to the work of his alleged source Alberic of Besançon (14, 19).[70] Only once (*AXL*, 1980) is it used following the pattern in which the *Kaiserchronik* and the *Eneasroman* use references to the *liet* as source and/or self-identification. Finally, *König Rother* uses the term in a similarly ambiguous self-referential manner (1503, 1826, 1906, 3490).[71]

Without wishing to labour the point, the semantics of *liet* can effortlessly take on several dimensions, none of them to the exclusion of the others. The word might suggest an oral performance of the *Kaiserchronik*, or at least try to implicate an oral dimension, if not in the presentation then at least in its conception as a collation of orally transmitted traditions. No one will disagree with Dickhut-Bielsky's conclusion that the *Kaiserchronik* is an entirely literarily conceptualized text.[72] The same can certainly be said of the other texts drawn upon above.

The written identity of the *Kaiserchronik* is first foregrounded in the second part of the prologue: 'Ein buoch ist ze diute getihtet, | daz uns Rômisces rîches wol berihtet' (*KC*, 15–16). Both 'buoch' and the two verbs connected to it, *tihten* and *berihten*, suggest a more poetically conceptualized approach to the compilation of the text.[73] This could, however, be more indicative of *liet* too being products of careful written compilation, only feigning their orality. As orality suggests an immediate report by someone who directly witnessed an event, this simulated connection of orality and witnessing can benefit from the high degree of authority

---

69   Heinrich von Veldeke, *Eneasroman: Mittelhochdeutsch/Neuhochdeutsch*, ed. by Ludwig Ettmüller, trans. by Dieter Kartschoke, RUB, 8303 (Stuttgart, 2004).

70   Pfaffe Lamprecht, *Alexanderroman: Mittelhochdeutsch/Neuhochdeutsch*, ed. by Elisabeth Lienert, RUB, 18,508 (Stuttgart, 2007).

71   *König Rother: Mittelhochdeutsch/Neuhochdeutsch*, ed. and trans. by Peter Stein, ed. by Ingrid Bennewitz, RUB, 18,047 (Stuttgart, 2000).

72   Dickhut-Bielsky, p. 52.

73   e.g. *Ortnit und die Wolfdietriche*, ed. by Arthur Amelung and Oscar Jänicke, Deutsches Heldenbuch, 3.1 (Berlin, 1971): 'Wolfdietrich in altem dichte hat siebenn hundert lied' (*Wolfdietrich A*, 334. 1).

granted to eyewitness accounts due to Isidore of Seville's connection of *historia* with optical perception through *videre* and *cognoscere*.[74]

The situation of any medieval text and its relations to its sources between orality and writing, and their competing authorities, remain a complex matter to be determined carefully considering each text's peculiarities.[75] On the one hand, everything fixed in writing benefits from the fact that the first content to be put down in writing in the vernacular was of a predominantly spiritual and religious nature, making its inherent authority a reference point for succeeding vernacular texts.[76] With its invocational sentence at the beginning, the *Kaiserchronik* clearly attempts to tap into this easily available authority pool. On the other hand, written records were often regarded with suspicion, especially when they dealt with the affairs of faraway lands, and orally transmitted eye-witness reports were granted a higher authority[77] notwithstanding their notorious unreliability.[78] Dickhut-Bielsky suggested shifting the focus from the dichotomy of orality and writing to that of German and Latin 'Schriftkultur', which converge in the *Kaiserchronik*.[79] While I think that this is in general a more productive way to look at the problem, I would not wish to diminish the possibility of the *Kaiserchronik*'s feigning its own orality in order to benefit from the authority ascribed to oral tradition. This should not, of course, exclude the possibility that there could actually have been oral traditions influencing the chronicle. A differentiation between feigned and actual orality does not seem possible at this point.

The oscillation in the *Kaiserchronik* between the four closely intertwined and interconnected concepts of orality and writing and of vernacularity and *latinitas* was mirrored by the results of a quantitative lexical examination executed with the search algorithm of the *Mittelhochdeutsche Begriffsdatenbank*.[80] The chronicle later

---

74   Isidore of Seville, *Etymologiae*: 'Dicta autem Graece historia ἀπὸ τοῦ ἱστορεῖν, id est a videre vel cognoscere' (I. 41). See also Mark Amsler, *Etymology and Grammatical Discourse in Late Antiquity and the Early Middle Ages*, Studies in the History of the Language Sciences, 44 (Philadelphia, 1989), pp. 165–66: 'He [Isidore] deploys the criterion of eyewitness truth to supplement his earlier explanation that *fabula* depicts what can never happen. [...] By distinguishing between eyewitness *historia* and secondary *annales*, Isidore associates *historia* with the Gospels as eyewitness accounts (John 19:35) and with the rhetorical device of *adtestio rei visae*'.

75   Stackmann, p. 65.

76   See Günter Butzer, 'Das Gedächtnis des epischen Textes: Mündliches und schriftliches Erzählen im höfischen Roman des Mittelalters', *Euphorion*, 89 (1995), 151–88 (p. 169).

77   See Jens Hirt, *Literarisch-politische Funktionalisierungen: Eine Untersuchung mittelhochdeutscher Kreuzzugsdarstellungen: 'Wilhelm von Wenden', 'Die Kreuzfahrt des Landgrafen von Thüringen', 'Wilhelm von Österreich' und 'Das Buch von Akkon'*, Göppinger Arbeiten zur Germanistik, 766 (Göppingen, 2012), p. 140.

78   See Johannes Fried, *Geschichte und Gehirn: Irritationen der Geschichtswissenschaft durch Gedächtniskritik*, Akademie der Wissenschaften und der Literatur: Abhandlungen der Geistes- und Sozialwissenschaftlichen Klasse, 7 (Mainz, 2003).

79   Dickhut-Bielsky, p. 55 (esp. n. 86). Similarly, see Ernst Hellgardt, 'Dietrich von Bern in der deutschen "Kaiserchronik": Zur Begegnung mündlicher und schriftlicher Traditionen', in *Deutsche Literatur und Sprache von 1050–1200*, ed. by Fiebig and Schiewer, pp. 93–110 (p. 95).

80   *Mittelhochdeutsche Begriffsdatenbank*, ed. by Universität Salzburg (1992–2017) <http://www.mhdbdb.sbg.ac.at/> [multiple accesses].

uses *liet* in eight instances to refer to the text or its presumed sources,[81] whereas in ninety-nine cases the term is *buoch*. However, in fifty of these cases the verb that marks the process of transfer from source to audience is *sagen*, which in thirteen cases is paired with *hôren*,[82] in thirty-three with *kunden*, and once with *jehen*.[83]

Now, these verbs imply the reading aloud of written books rather than some kind of oral tradition, and might at this point already have acquired an extended literal meaning like 'to inform'. The 'buoch tuot [...] kunt', which can also imply an oral element, in only two cases (*KC*, 277, 13,439); in one case, it 'zellet' (*KC*, 11,309) by providing a list of Cyrillus's virtues; and in one case, it actually 'urchundet' (*KC*, 16,271). With the *buoch* being the actor in these lines, the goal of the transfer process is almost exclusively marked by the first-person plural pronoun *wir* or its accusative and dative form *uns*.[84] The narrator is including himself in the text's audience and, vice versa, incorporating the audience in the hermeneutical act of source analysis. The book is being imagined as speaking to the audience and the author; the text becomes an actor who performs the hermeneutical act as much as the audience. This may relate to a performative way of presenting the content of the *Kaiserchronik*, with a reader reading the text aloud to an audience, but it also marks the combined effort to (re)construct history within the mental categories shared by author and audience, as is manifested in the text both in the process of poetical conceptualization and writing and in the receptive process of performance.[85]

With this background, the rhetorical devices employed as the prologue continues become clearer and help to determine whether the *Kaiserchronik*'s first forty-two lines can indeed be classified as a prologue in the rhetorical sense. Walter Haug certainly thought so, as he includes this passage among the Early Middle High German prologues that he analyses in search of insights into poetics.[86] He argues that the *Kaiserchronik* prologue includes several arguments drawn from the repertoire of 'Exordialtopik',[87] for example the demand to receive the text appropriately and the statement that it will be useful for the audience to listen to it because only the foolish would do without acquiring wisdom and reputation.[88]

Indeed, a closer analysis of the prologue unearths a sophisticated implementation of a multitude of rhetorical devices and strategies, for example when the narrator first addresses his audience: 'jâ mac iuh vil wole gezemen | ze hôren älliu frumichait' (*KC*, 4–5). The approach can be connected to the rhetorical strategy of *benevolum*

---

81   *KC*, 622, 1190, 5176, 5671, 10,619, 10,624, 15,072, 17,165.
82   'nû hôren wir diu buoch sagen', recurring throughout the text (e.g. *KC*, 13,417).
83   *KC*, 14,034, has *jehen* paired with *hôren*.
84   'daz buoch kundet uns', recurring throughout the text (e.g. *KC*, 15,335).
85   For more on the audience's participation in creating meaning in medieval texts, see Melville, pp. 98–104.
86   Haug, p. 66.
87   Ibid., p. 69. See Lutz, p. 88.
88   Haug, p. 69. Haug's interpretation is deeply coloured by Ohly's reading of the *Kaiserchronik*, and he interprets the core concepts of the prologue like *minne*, *wîstuom*, and *êre* as soteriologically charged and pointing at eschatological typologies.

parare,[89] first speaking to the audience *ab iudicium persona*, by appealing to their judgement and didactically pointing out the usefulness of the author's narrative to the audience.[90] He then constitutes them as a group in contrast to those who are not interested in hearing his *liet*:

> die tumben dunchet iz arebeit,
> sculn si iemer iht gelernen
> od ir wîstuom gemêren. (*KC*, 6–8)

History, or knowledge thereof, is developed *ex negativo* as a useful resource to have for one's own educational betterment. No audience will be overly inclined to count themselves among the 'tumben'. This corresponds to rhetorical speech *ab adversariorum nostrum persona*, which aims to denigrate the position of those opposed to the *causa* of the speaker, or in this case the narrator. The next lines continue in this rhetorical strain by disqualifying an unsympathetic audience as being 'unnuzze' (*KC*, 9) and scornful of 'guoter wizze' (*KC*, 10). Simultaneously, lines 7–14 advertise, in another well-established ploy of this rhetorical mode, *ex negativo* what a well-disposed audience can expect from the text:[91] an increase in wisdom and learnedness, but also 'êre' (*KC*, 13) and finally 'frum der sêle' (*KC*, 14). The emphasis on the moral value of receiving the text adequately is characteristic for this rhetorical figure, especially when employed in the literary sphere.[92] This does not strip the 'êre' of the soteriological connotations commonly attributed to it,[93] but it does put it into rhetorical perspective.

Consequently, the next rhetorical step, which dominates the second part of the prologue (*KC*, 15–26), is focused on arguments *ab nostra persona*,[94] in this case the text that is going to be presented to the audience. However, it remains ambiguous throughout the passage whether the *buoch* that is introduced in line 15 and referred to as a *crônicâ* in line 17 is indeed meant to be the *Kaiserchronik*. The text could indeed be referring to itself, like other twelfth-century authors such as Hartmann von Aue or Frau Ava who refer to themselves in the third person.[95] But the term could also refer to another book: the *Kaiserchronik*'s source, presumably in Latin, be it fabricated or real. German derivations of the ancient Greek χρονικός via Latin *chronica* would not have been unheard of in the middle of the twelfth century,[96] but they only became widespread in the thirteenth century.[97] The use of the Latinized form here does not necessarily mean that it refers to a Latin source instead of the

---

89   See Lausberg, p. 156, §273. I am using Lausberg in full awareness of the problems his systematic section-based approach to rhetoric causes. See Ulla Fix, *Rhetorik und Stilistik: Ein internationales Handbuch historischer und systematischer Forschung* (Berlin, 2008), pp. 152–53.

90   See Lausberg, p. 158, §277.

91   See ibid., p. 159, §278.

92   See Curtius, *European Literature*, p. 94.

93   e.g. Haug, p. 69.

94   See Lausberg, p. 157, §275.

95   See Matthews, p. 8.

96   See Lexer, s.v. *krônike*, *krônik* (I, col. 1749).

97   Ulrich von Etzenbach uses it extensively in *Alexander*, ed. by Wendelin Toischer, Bibliothek des Litterarischen Vereins in Stuttgart, 183 (Tübingen, 1888), 157, 1186, 1737, 15,933, 16,177, 16,700, 16,871, 17,321, 20,977, 24,692, 24,709, 25,559, 25,651, 25,776, 25,833.

Kaiserchronik. But it also does not imply a conscious decision to align the text with the broader tradition of Latin universal historiography.[98] If anything, it will have triggered associations with Isidore of Seville's definition of the chronicle in his seventh-century *Etymologiae*:

> 'Chronicle' (*chronica*) is the Greek term for what is called a 'succession of times' (*series temporum*) in Latin. Among the Greeks Eusebius, Bishop of Caesarea, compiled such a work, and the priest Jerome translated it into Latin. Χρόνος in Greek means 'time' in Latin.[99]

If accepted as a self-identification of the text, this suggests the kind of text that the *Kaiserchronik* was conceptualized and received as by author and audience, a fact often overlooked by all-too-eager proposals to change its name to an alternative more descriptive of the structure and perceived quality of its content.[100]

The way the text uses *buoch* throughout, as elaborated above, indicates strongly that these lines do indeed refer to the *Kaiserchronik*. The text refers to itself by verbalizing its own mode of oral recital by a reader to an audience.[101] Similarly, 'chundet uns' (*KC*, 18) anticipates the language later utilized throughout the text. But most likely, a medieval audience might not have been that concerned about analytically pinning down the *buoch* as a reference either to the *Kaiserchronik* or to its sources.

The ambiguity of the nature of the text is mirrored by the ambiguity of its purpose 'ze diute' (*KC*, 15), which means both that the text is intended for clear and helpful induction and explanation, and also that it is written in the German vernacular.[102] These two semantic dimensions are, of course, not mutually exclusive; in this case, they appear inseparably intertwined with each other: the text stands at the beginning of historiography in the German vernacular in order to convey history to its non-Latin-speaking audience. And to make history conceivable for this new audience, it is not sufficient to simply write in its language, but, as developed in the rhetorical tradition from Quintilian to John of Salisbury, to model the chronicle's subject matter in terms of its cultural axioms and historically preconceptualized expectations. The meaning of 'ze diute' encompasses both basic linguistic understandability and categorical cultural comprehensibility. The manuscripts of the A recension certainly do not help matters: Vorau, Stiftsarchiv, Ms 276 reads 'divte' (fol. 1ra); Wolfenbüttel, Herzog August Bibliothek, Cod. Guelf. 15.2 Aug. 2°

---

98 See Hellgardt, p. 95.

99 *Etymologies of Isidore of Seville*, p. 125. Isidore of Seville, *Etymologiae*: 'Chronica Graece dicitur quae Latine temporum series appellatur, qualem apud Graecos Eusebius Caesariensis episcopus edidit, et Hieronymus presbyter in Latinam linguam convertit. Χρόνος enim Graece, Latine tempus interpretatur' (v. 28).

100 See e.g. Christian Gellinek, 'The German Emperors' Chronicle: An Epic Fiction?', *Colloquia Germanica*, 5 (1971), 230–36. Gellinek suggests renaming it a 'deutsches Kaiserepos'.

101 See Dennis Howard Green, *Medieval Listening and Reading: The Primary Reception of German Literature 800–1300* (Cambridge, 1994), p. 101.

102 See Lexer, s.v. *diute, tiute* (I, col. 443). The etymological relatedness and semantic connectedness of modern German *deutlich* and *deutsch* — both *deuten* and *deutsch* are derivations of Old High German *diot* — still perpetuates this today. See *Kluge*, ed. by Seebold, s.vv. *deutlich, deuten, deutsch* (pp. 194–95).

reads 'tewtſch' (fol. 23rb); Heidelberg, Universitätsbibliothek, Cpg 361 reads 'dúte' (fol. 1ra); and Munich, Bayerische Staatsbibliothek, Cgm 37 reads 'devte' (fol. 1ra). Dickhut-Bielsky naturally argues for a translation with 'Deutung', 'Auslegung', or 'Erklärung'. I doubt that the *Kaiserchronik* is giving its audience another cue to engage in hermeneutical exegesis here, but Dickhut-Bielsky is certainly right to point out that the ambiguity and polyvalence of the wording might be intentionally implemented in the text.[103]

The chronicle goes on to explain its purpose with the verb *berihten* in the following line (*KC*, 16), the meaning of which goes beyond the modern German semantic value of *zu berichten* (as in to merely convey or relate information in a somehow formalized manner): in its Middle High German use, it strongly infuses order and structure into the object it refers to, in this case the Roman 'rîche[]' (*KC*, 16).[104] The passage goes on to identify the text as 'crônicâ' (*KC*, 17). So far in the second part of the prologue, the technical language of rhetoric has been scant, the focus clearly fixed on conveying hard information on the what, how, and when of the *Kaiserchronik*. But it closes with a clearly more rhetorical formula when the voice of the text announces: 'sô ich aller beste mac | sô wil ich iz iu vor zellen' (*KC*, 24–25). Here, the author clearly deploys a modesty topos, usually deployed in rhetoric when arguing *ab nostra persona*.[105] When he declares that he will tell 'iz' (his narrative) according to the best of his ability, he is not just alluding to his alleged limitations as a narrator but also drawing the audience's attention to his humility by acknowledging those limitations. Compared to classical authors,[106] but also to contemporary Latin and vernacular German texts, this happens in a reduced form, which suggests its implementation was perceived as more of a compulsory exercise, a testimony to the sustained commitment to rhetorical rules and norms.

2.2.3. Competing Texts

The third part of the prologue (*KC*, 27–42) develops a much-discussed didactic programme that is framed by polemical rhetoric, which rears its head again when the voice of the narrator bemoans a new malpractice that is introduced as only having become established 'in disen zîten' (*KC*, 27):

> manege erdenchent in lugene
> unt vuogent si zesamene
> mit scophelîchen worten. (*KC*, 29–31)

The infamous phrase 'mit scophelîchen worten' (*KC*, 31), which the *Kaiserchronik* puts at the core of the literature the passage criticizes, has usually been read together with the *Annolied* prologue and its polemic against heroic epic, which admonishes that, instead of being engrossed in the 'singen' (*AL*, 1. 1) of the heroic, military,

---

103 Dickhut-Bielsky, p. 54.
104 See Lexer, s.v. *be-rihten* (I, col. 191).
105 See Lausberg, p. 157, §275.
106 See Curtius, *European Literature*, pp. 83–86.

social, and political topoi and topics of epic poetry, people would do far better to consider their own mortality (*AL*, 1. 1–8).[107]

Coupled with Wissmann's linguistic analysis, which connects the *Kaiserchronik*'s *scophelîch* with the Old English *scop*, a singer of oral-heroic poetry who figures in many Old English epics,[108] a derogative interpretation of *scophelîch* has become the critical consensus. According to Kartschoke, it is used as a marker for the programmatic opposition between the more literarily conceptualized textual tradition of Christian authors and the minstrels, the carriers of oral poetry, held to only disseminate lies.[109] The most concise elaboration of this approach can be found in Hellgardt's examination of the Dietrich von Bern figure.[110] However, Matthews has more recently pointed out that the only other instance of the critical word — as 'schoflichen' — can be found in the twelfth-century *Trierer Silvester* (*TS*),[111] in a passage taken almost verbatim from the *Kaiserchronik*. By developing the etymological connection of *scophelîch* with its derivations and profiling its meaning as mainly 'creative', or 'shaping', he casts doubt on the idea that the passage necessarily targets oral-heroic poetry. Instead, he contends it should be read as an expression of hostility against narrative currents that distract audiences from listening to religious teachings.[112] But the classic reading of the passage as a polemic against heroic epics or oral tradition in general persists. For example, it remains instrumental for Goerlitz's argument. She aligns the polemical reading with the *Kaiserchronik*'s more general pejorization of Greekness[113] as a usurpation of imperial — by rights Roman — power. In her view, these two elements together prove that the chronicle's negative view of heroic epics not only extends to a narrative tradition but also to the entire historical timeframe to which this tradition of heroic epics is tied: the 'heroic age' of the great migrations between the fourth and the sixth century, which occurred at a time when there was no Latin but only a Greek Empire. Building on this, Goerlitz ascribes to the *Kaiserchronik* a general programme of denigrating and disqualifying this time as marked by its 'Romferne'.[114]

The continuing currency of the reading that the polemic is directed at heroic traditions is quite understandable. It fits in nicely with the established reading of the

---

107 See e.g. Christian Gellinek, *Die Kaiserchronik: Erzähltechnik und Kritik* (Frankfurt a. M., 1972), pp. 22–25.

108 Wilhelm Wissmann, *Skop*, Sitzungsberichte der deutschen Akademie der Wissenschaften zu Berlin, 2 (Berlin, 1955), p. 14.

109 Kartschoke, p. 34.

110 See Hellgardt, p. 95: 'Wenn aber von den hier attackierten Lügengeschichten gesagt wird, sie seien mit *scophelîchen worten* zusammengefügt, so verweist dieser Ausdruck eindeutig auf die Praxis mündlicher Dichtungstradition, und im hier gegebenen Kontext von Geschichte als Gegenstand der Darstellung wird man annehmen dürfen, daß dabei besonders an solche mündliche Dichtung gedacht ist, deren Inhalte für historisch wahr gehalten werden wollen und wurden, u.a. also z.B. an die Heldensage. Aus der polemischen Sicht des Kaiserchronikprologs aber wird der Wahrheitsanspruch mündlicher Dichtung bestritten und historisch gerade im Blick auf Gegenwart und Zukunft als verderblich gebrandmarkt.'

111 *Trierer Silvester*, ed. by Carl Kraus, in MGH Dt. Chron., 1.2 (Hanover, 1895), pp. 1–45.

112 See Matthews, p. 13.

113 For some examples of this tendency, see 1.1.4 in this book.

114 See Goerlitz, '(Un-)Wahrheit und (Nicht-)Erinnern', pp. 232–33, 238–39.

Kaiserchronik as a salvation-historical account and also connects to the earlier lines of the prologue where it promises 'frum der sêle' (*KC*, 14) to those who turn to the text attentively. Another factor supporting this reading is the *Kaiserchronik*'s criticism of the anachronistic conflation of the lifetimes of Dietrich and Etzel (*KC*, 14,176–87), as heroic epics were wont to do. However, if the passage were to be read as an attack on heroic literature, it would be a rather implicit one and, what is more, it would not reflect at all the treatment of historical protagonists in the rest of the *Kaiserchronik*, which constantly conflates, omits, or mixes up personalities. It has been pointed out that the passage follows Frutolf's similar observations on how, according to the *Getica* of Jordanes, Dietrich and Attila could not have been contemporaries.[115] A couple of decades later, Otto of Freising would echo Frutolf's remarks in language remarkably similar to the *Kaiserchronik*.[116] Both opt for impersonal formulations that leave open whom exactly they are criticizing. The topical offence that Frutolf, Otto, and the *Kaiserchronik* take had already been articulated in the middle of the eleventh century, when Canon Meinhard of Bamberg voiced his concerns about his superior, Bishop Gunther of Bamberg, and his choice of entertainment: in a letter written between 1057 and 1063, he complained to a colleague, who was temporarily absent from Bamberg in Carinthia, that Gunther did not care about the Church Fathers Augustine or Gregory, and was only interested in the exploits of Attila, the Amalungs, and others.[117] Gunther's cultural interests, however, not only provoked criticism but also made him the lauded patron of the very first lines of the *Ezzolied* (1–6).[118] What Meinhard might have thought of religious poetry like the *Ezzolied* now being written in the German vernacular remains undisclosed. Its

---

115 Ekkehard of Aura, *Chronica*, ed. by Georg Waitz, in MGH SS, 6 (Hanover, 1844), pp. 1–267: 'Haec Iordanis quidam grammaticus, ex eorumque stirpe Gothorum progenitus, de Getarum origine et Amalorum nobilitate, non omnia quae de eis scribuntur et referuntur, ut ipse dicit, complexus, exaravit, sed brevis pro rerum notitia huic opusculo inseruimus. His perlectis diligenterque perspectis, perpendat qui discernere noverit, quomodo illud ratum teneatur, quod non solum vulgari fabulatione et cantilenarum modulatione usitatur, verum etiam in quibusdam cronicis annotatur, scilicet quod Ermenricus tempore Marciani principis super omnes Gothos regnaverit, et Theodericum, Dietmeri filium, patruelem suum, ut dicunt, instimulante Odoacare, item, ut aiunt, patruele suo, de Veronapulsum, apud Attilam Hunorum regem exulare coegerit, hystoriographus narret, Ermenricum egem Gothorum multis regibus dominantem tempore Ventiniani et Valentis fratrum regnasse [...]' (p. 130).

116 Otto of Freising, *Chronica*: 'Quod autem rursum narrant eum Hermanarico Attilaeque contemporaneum fuisse, omnio stare non potest, dum Attilam longe post Hermanaricum constet exercuisse tyrannidem istumque post mortem Attilae octennem a patre obsidem Leoni augusto traditum' (v. 3, p. 232).

117 'Briefe Meinhards von Bamberg', in *Briefsammlungen der Zeit Heinrichs IV.*, ed. by Carl Erdmann and Norbert Fickermann, MGH Briefe der deutschen Kaiserzeit, 5 (Weimar, 1950), pp. 107–31, no. 73, p. 121: 'Quid vero agit domnus noster? quid suus ille exercitus galeatorum leporum? que bella, quas acies tractant? quos triumphos celebrant? Dii boni, quanta ibi colluvio non virorum sed muscarum! quam magnifici et vani strepitus! Nulla ibi gravitas, nulla disciplina! Et o miseram et miserandam episcopi vitam, o mores! Numquam ille Augustinum, numquam ille Gregorium recolit, semper ille Attalam, semper Amalungum et cetera id genus portare tractat. Versat ille non libros, sed lanceas, miratur ille non litterarum apices, sed mucronum acies.'

118 *Ezzolied*, in *Die kleinen Denkmäler der Vorauer Handschrift*, ed. by Erich Henschel and Ulrich Pretzel (Tübingen, 1963), pp. 2–27.

eponymous author would certainly have steered clear of accusations of occupying himself with secular and heroic matters, as the *Ezzolied* focuses on the miraculous qualities of Christ and the salvation-historical bringing together of the Old and the New Testament.

Looking at the Dietrich–Etzel passage of the *Kaiserchronik* with these observations in mind, and linking it to the texts attacked in the prologue, the conclusion that these must be heroic epics derived from Germanic oral traditions does not seem improbable. Hence, the *Kaiserchronik* has been identified as the first text to transfer 'Sagenkritik' into the German vernacular sphere.[119]

Yet this reading focuses only on one aspect of the polemic. Equally important is the preceding line with 'erdenchent in lugene' (*KC*, 29), which provides the mental frame for the *scophelîchiu wort*. From this, it becomes apparent that the chronicle takes issue with a certain 'Verbindung von Darstellungs- und Inhaltsebene'.[120] The context of the prologue suggests that the 'lugene' result in texts 'ân gottes minne', while the *Kaiserchronik* is of course, as the first line announces explicitly, dedicated to 'gottes minnen'. Millet interpreted the dichotomy evident in this contrast as a possible clash of secular and spiritual texts,[121] while Dickhut-Bielsky integrated it into his argument by reading it as an opposition between 'auslegungsbedürftiger und nichtauslegungsbedürftiger' literature.[122] The more recent trend in scholarship to move beyond the restriction to heroic epics is certainly welcome, but should be expanded by a closer look at the third trait characterizing the aim of the *Kaiserchronik*'s polemic, which can be found couched between the mental frame of 'lugene' and the mode of presentation in the 'scophelîchen worten'.

Both are quite literally conjoined by the phrase 'unt vuogent si zesamene' (*KC*, 30), which is presented as the process of modelling the 'lugene' (*KC*, 29) with 'scophelîchen worten' (*KC*, 31). The implications of this process, which appears to be the crucial link, have not to date received the attention they deserve. Considering them will add to the levels analysed by Dickhut-Bielsky by suggesting that in addition to presentation and content, there is also the level of the mode or technique of narration. Examining the literary discourse on a mode of narration that works with 'scophelîchen worten' will allow us to obtain a clearer view of how the texts the *Kaiserchronik* targets in its prologue are actually felt to construct their content and why this warrants reprimanding.

The *Kaiserchronik*'s phrase resonates with the very first reflection on writing in the vernacular all the way back at the very beginning of German writing: the ninth-century Benedictine monk Otfrid von Weißenburg is the first author to devise a vernacular perspective on rhetorical writing. In the prologue to his Old High German *Liber Evangeliorum*, a Gospel harmony written in the 860s and the

---

119 Elisabeth Lienert, *Die historische Dietrichepik: Untersuchungen zu 'Dietrichs Flucht', 'Rabenschlacht' und 'Alpharts Tod'* (Berlin, 2010), p. 36.

120 See Dickhut-Bielsky, p. 57.

121 Victor Millet, 'Das 12. Jahrhundert und die Heldensage', in *Aspekte des 12. Jahrhunderts: Freisinger Kolloquium 1998*, ed. by Wolfgang Haubrichs, Eckart Conrad Lutz, and Gisela Vollmann-Profe, Wolfram-Studien, 16 (Berlin, 2000), pp. 256–81 (pp. 256–58).

122 Dickhut-Bielsky, p. 58.

first substantial German text in rhyming couplets,[123] he contextualizes his work against the background of his classical predecessors:

> Tharana datun sie ouh daz duam: ougdun iro wisduam,
> ougdun iro cleini in thes tihtonnes reini.
> Iz ist al thuruh not so kleino giredinot:
> iz dunkal eigun funtan, zisamane gibuntan.
> Sie ouh in thiu gisagetin, thaz then thio buah nirsmahetin
> joh wol er sih firwesti, then lesan iz gilusti. (*Liber Evangeliorum*, 5–10)

As a semantic predecessor of the *Kaiserchronik*'s phrasing 'vuogent si zesamene' (*KC*, 39), the phrase 'zisamane gibuntan' (*Liber Evangeliorum*, 8) stands out. It indicates elaborate and artful framing of language, including but not limited to rhyming couplets and rhetorical refinement. This kind of language can usefully be applied to biblical accounts without any need for mediation: 'Ouh selbun buah frono irreinont sie so scono; | thar lisist scona gilust ana theheiniga akust' (*Liber Evangeliorum*, 29–30). While Otfrid is not at all opposed to artful language, but rather wants to unlock it for the German vernacular, he also aims to draw a clear line between his writing and uses of language that he does not deem dignified or beneficial, and whose prevalence in his time played a crucial part in motivating him to undertake his vernacular Gospel harmony.

Otfrid prefixes the *Liber Evangeliorum* with a Latin letter to Bishop Liutbert of Mainz asking him to examine and approve the work.[124] In this letter, Otfrid criticizes two different types of literary discourse between which he aims to situate his writing. Both of them pertain to the discourse established above on different levels. First, near to the end of his letter he remarks: 'He does not expect from us the flattery of smooth words, but the pious alignment of our thinking and many works made in pious eagerness, not empty lip service.'[125] Second, at the beginning of the letter he elaborates:

> As once the presentation of useless things insulted the ears of excellent men and the obscene singing of the lays disturbed them in their pious spirit, I have been asked by some brothers [...], to write them a vernacular harmony of the Gospels, so that the presentation of the holy text might push back a little entertainment with secular songs, and the people might learn, engrossed by the sweetness of the Gospels in their mother tongue, to turn away from useless things.[126]

---

123 See Otfrid von Weißenburg, *Evangelienbuch: Auswahl*, ed. by Gisela Vollmann-Profe, RUB, 8384 (Stuttgart, 1987), pp. 250–51; translations are my own.

124 Otfrid von Weißenburg, 'Ad Liutbertum', in *Frühe Deutsche Literatur und Lateinische Literatur in Deutschland 800–1150*, ed. by Walter Haug and Benedikt Konrad Vollmann, Bibliothek des Mittelalters, 1 (Frankfurt a. M., 1991), pp. 72–83: 'Hunc igitur librum vestrae sagaci prudentiae probandum curavi transmittere [...] Qui si sanctitatis vestrae placet optutibus, et non deiciendum iudicaverit, uti licenter fidelibus vestra auctoritas concedat: sin vero minus aptus parque meae neglegentiae paret, eadem veneranda sanctaque contempnet auctoritas' (p. 82); translations are my own.

125 Ibid.: '[...] verbum in eis suae laudis sonare, qui non verborum adulationem politorum, sed quaerit in nobis pium cogitationis affectum operumque pio labore congierem, non labrorum inanem servitiem.'

126 Ibid.: 'Dum rerum quondam sonus inutilium pulsaret aures quorundam probatissimorum

The object of criticism is different in the two passages. The second, earlier passage establishes a later well-trodden line of topical criticism of secular literature, which usually aims to highlight the spiritually beneficial quality of the writer's own text. Otfrid's deprecation foreshadows the polemic voiced in the prologue to the *Annolied* two hundred years later, but also the concerns of Meinhard, the song's contemporary, and later Frutolf, Otto, and the *Kaiserchronik*. But where they snipe at heroic epics, Otfrid, several centuries earlier, complains about the works of 'gentilium vates' like Virgil, Lucan, and Ovid flooding the entire world.[127] The *Kaiserchronik*'s polemic against 'lugene' (*KC*, 29) 'ân gotes minne' (*KC*, 34) could well be taking aim at these two kinds of texts (or texts which share both sets of traits).

The first passage from Otfrid's 'Ad Liutbertum' quoted above is much harder to pin down. Andreas Gardt suggested reading it as an implicit criticism of rhetoric that paves the ground for the argument that the vernacular as language is less ornate and artful, and thus better suited to expressing profound religious feelings and beliefs and not prone to be misused for 'labrorum inanem servitiem'. This, however, does not fit with what has been observed above about Otfrid's hopes of instrumentalizing rhetoric for vernacular writing, and appears to be an argument implemented with the hindsight of the discourses to come in later centuries.[128]

The opaque phrasing of *KC*, 30 also resonates with a very prominent Old French prologue, much more contemporary to the *Kaiserchronik* than Otfrid, namely what Chrétien de Troyes described as the process of the composition of his first great romance, *Erec et Enide* (*EE*), which was probably written around 1160:[129]

> Por ce dit Crestiiens de Troies,
> Que reisons est que totes voies
> Doit chascuns panser et antandre
> A bien dire et a bien aprandre,
> Et tret d'un conte d'aventure
> Une mout bele conjointure. (*EE*, 9–14)

Chrétien's famous *conjointure* signifies a 'juncture, a joining action [and] conscious craftmanship'.[130] It serves as the first indicator of the author's aiming for a 'well-ordered story' and a 'coherent narrative', and might even imply a 'latent architectonic

virorum, eorumque sanctitatem laicorum cantus inquietaret obscenus, a quibusdam [...] fratres rogatus [...] partem evangeliorum propria lingua occupati dulcedine, sonum inutilium rerum noverint declinare'.

127 Ibid.: 'petitioni quoque iungentes queremoniam, quod gentilium vates, ut Vergilius, Lucanus, Ovidius caeterique quam plurimi suorum facta decorarent lingua nativa, quorum iam voluminum dictis fluctuare cognoscimus mundum' (p. 72).

128 See Andreas Gardt, *Geschichte der Sprachwissenschaft in Deutschland: Vom Mittelalter bis ins 20. Jahrhundert* (Berlin, 1999), pp. 17–18. Gardt admits that this reading is very implicit and not very widespread in the Middle Ages and might very well have been triggered by Otfrid's making a virtue out of necessity.

129 See Chrétien de Troyes; *Erec und Enide*, trans. by Ingrid Kasten, Klassische Texte des Romanischen Mittelalters, 17 (Munich, 1971), pp. 12–15.

130 Commentary in Chrétien de Troyes, *Erec and Enide*, trans. by Dorothy Gilbert (Los Angeles, 1992), p. 253.

structure in the romance'.[131] Chrétien goes on to contrast his approach with 'Cil qui de conter vivre vuelent' (*EE*, 22), professional performers who played a key part in conveying the *matière de Bretagne* to the French,[132] but whom Chrétien criticizes for their incoherent and corruptive storytelling (*EE*, 19–21). But does the parallel go beyond the superficial lexical parallelism of *zesamene vuogen* and *conjoindre*? Both texts aim to distinguish themselves from only vaguely specified other texts and modes of narration that share an oral dimension and can, through their chaotic and incoherent arrangement, even be harmful to the audience: the narratives of Chrétien's antagonists are the product of 'depecier et corronpre' (*EE*, 21), and the texts the *Kaiserchronik* takes issue with cause 'daz diu sêle dar umbe brinne' (*KC*, 33). However, while Chrétien is claiming good composition as a sign of the quality of his narrative, in the *Kaiserchronik* it is precisely the other way round: composition marks the other texts. The language employed for this is not necessarily pejorative in itself. In the very first lines of Pfaffe Lamprecht's *Alexanderlied*, written at approximately the same time as Chrétien's first romance and a good decade after the *Kaiserchronik*, the terminology of an architectonically conjoining composition of narrative is clearly intended to signify the high quality of Lamprecht's work:[133]

> Diz lît, daz wir hî wurchen,
> das sult ir rehte merchen.
> Sîn gevuoge ist vil reht. (*AXL*, 1–3)

Another different, but emphatically positive reverberation of the artistic craft of story-composition can be found in the early lines of the Early Middle High German *Hochzeit*, written roughly contemporarily with the *Kaiserchronik*:[134]

> Swer diu zeichene wil began,
> der sol guoten list haben,
> also der smit vil guot
> die wiere in daz golt tuot. (*Hochzeit*, 7–10)

The imagination of textual production as artisanal craftsmanship was well established in Early Middle High German texts, and would usually be employed with positive connotations either to showcase the author's skill, as in the *Alexanderlied*, or to vie for the audience's favour, as in the *Hochzeit*.[135] But the *Kaiserchronik* uses language that refers to this kind of writing in a pejorative way.

---

131 Jean Frappier, *Chrétien de Troyes: The Man and his Work*, trans. by Raymond Cormier (Athens, OH, 1982), p. 45.

132 Jehan Bodel, *La Chanson des Saisnes*, ed. by Annette Brasseur, Textes littéraires français, 369, 2 vols (Geneva, 1989): 'Ne sont que .III. matieres a nul home atandant: | De France et de Bretaigne et de Rome la grant' (I, 3).

133 This did not spare him from ridicule when just under a century later, Rudolf von Ems wrote in his *Alexanderroman* that Lamprecht did not write of Alexander 'die rehten wârheit' (Rudolf von Ems, *Alexander, ein höfischer Versroman des 13. Jahrhunderts*, ed. by Victor Junk (Darmstadt, 1928; repr. 1970), 15,783–88).

134 *Die Hochzeit*, in *Frühe Deutsche Literatur*, ed. by Haug and Vollmann, pp. 784–847.

135 Sarah Bowden, 'Zur Poetik des mehrsinnigen Verstehens: Der allegorische Stil der Hochzeit', in *Literarischer Stil: Mittelalterliche Dichtung zwischen Konvention und Innovation*, ed. by Elizabeth Andersen and others (Berlin, 2015), pp. 305–21.

This leads to an alternative mode of imagining the process of composing text, one that contrasts with the *zesamene vuogen* of the antagonistic compositional mode and was available to vernacular German literature in the middle of the twelfth century. Many texts written in the decades before and after the *Kaiserchronik* invoke this mode in their very first lines. The *Wahrheit*, written at the same time, asks God to bestow upon the first-person voice of the text the 'sinne' to relate his message faithfully (1–9).[136] Similarly, the *Lob Salomons*, from the same time, invokes divine inspiration for its rendition:[137]

> Inclita lux mundi
> dû dir habis in dîner kundi
> erdin undi lufti
> unde alli himilcrefti,
> dû sendi mir zi mundi,
> daz ich eddilîchin deil muzzi kundi. (*Lob Salomons*, 1–6)

Where the *Wahrheit* asks more generally for 'sinne' (3), the author of the *Lob Salomons* specifically calls for the necessary words to be transferred to his mouth. Hence, the author is no longer a craftsman who artistically conjoins his text, but a mere rhapsode[138] who only proclaims (*kunden*) the divinely inspired words. The *Rolandslied*, whose author, Pfaffe Konrad, was long thought to be the author of the *Kaiserchronik*,[139] fully embodies this inspirational mode:[140]

> Schephære aller dinge,
> keiser aller künigine,
> wol du oberester êwart,
> lêre mich selbe dîniu wort.
> dû sende mir ze munde
> dîn heilige urkunde,
> daz ich die lüge vermîde,
> die wârheit scrîbe. (*Rolandslied*, 1–8)

While Lamprecht, whose 'lît [...] wir hî wurchen' (*AXL*, 1) and who embodies the compositional type, shifted the burden of the truthfulness of his account from his ability onto his source, but could not exclude erroneous storytelling (*AXL*, 16–18),

---

136 *Die Wahrheit*, in *Die kleinen Denkmäler der Vorauer Handschrift*, ed. by Henschel and Pretzel, pp. 50–61.

137 *Das Lob Salomons*, in *Frühe Deutsche Literatur*, ed. by Haug and Vollmann, pp. 702–17.

138 Rhapsodes were professional performers of oral epic poetry in ancient Greece. Many of the texts they performed prominently style themselves as being externally — divinely — inspired, as in the first line of Homer's *Odyssey*. Ironically, the word 'rhapsode' derives from ῥαψῳδεῖν/*rhapsodós*, which translates into 'to sew together' but refers more to the stringing together of several songs in oral performance than to a mode of textual composition. See Barbara Graziosi, *Inventing Homer: The Early Reception of Epic* (Cambridge, 2002), pp. 21–40.

139 A case most prominently made by Schröder himself, pp. 51–58, in the introduction to his edition. It was ultimately refuted by the thorough lexical comparison of the two texts in Karl Wesle, '"Kaiserchronik" und "Rolandslied"', *Beiträge zur Geschichte der deutschen Sprache und Literatur*, 48 (1924), 223–58.

140 Pfaffe Konrad, *Rolandslied: Mittelhochdeutsch/Neuhochdeutsch*, ed. and trans. by Dieter Kartschoke, RUB, 2745 (Stuttgart, 1993).

in the *Rolandslied* the possibility of inadvertently telling lies is foreclosed from the outset by the invocation of divine inspiration, turning its account into 'heilige urkunde', text of the highest conceivable authority.

The category of *sin* as *sensus*, denoting the receptive sensorium for God's message, necessary for this kind of inspiration, as laid out by Ohly,[141] features not only in the *Wahrheit* (3) but also in the *Himmlisches Jerusalem*: 'Nû sule wir beginnen | mit tiefen gesinnen' (1–2).[142] In the *Hochzeit*, the word turns from a receptive to a semanticizing function, but stays closely connected to God's communicative signage:

> umbe manich schône zeichen,
> dâ michil sin an stât.
> gesach in got, der ez begât. (*Hochzeit*, 4–6)

In the earlier *Ezzolied*, however, *sin* is still much more connected to the first-person voice of the text, which corresponds with the text identifying itself not as divinely inspired but rather as ordered to be made by Bishop Gunther of Bamberg:

> Ich wil iu lieben allon
> ein wâre rede vore tuon
> nâch dem mînem sinne. (*Ezzolied*, 13–15)

It is not possible to draw a precise line between an inspirational and a compositional mode of conception in prologues, or to pin down a definite linear development from one type to the other, but the tendencies are undeniable.

The language utilized by these Early Middle High German poets, most explicitly in the *Wahrheit* (3), the *Lob Salomons* (5), and the *Rolandslied* (4–8), invokes the words of Psalm 80. 11:

> Ego enim sum Dominus Deus tuus,
> qui eduxi te de terra Aegypti.
> Dilata os tuum, et implebo illud.[143]

Latin authors referred to this Psalm to create a conceptual dichotomy of literary invention that mirrors the two models employed in the prologues above. Quoting the Psalm, the anonymous author of the late seventh-century *Vita Sadalbergae Abbatissae Laudunensis* urges his readers: '[...] non quaerat in his Tullianam eloquentiam nec oratorum facundiam, non philosophorum flosculos et stoicorum diversas assertiones, sed veritatem et simplicitatem historiae.'[144] Not the flourish that the diverse compositional techniques impart to a text is to be expected, but rather the truth and simplicity of *historia*. The topical assertion of the *rusticitas* of the writer's style was a staple of medieval prologues, influenced by the rhetoric of

---

141 Ernst Friedrich Ohly, 'Gebet an den Heiligen Geist', in *Wolfram von Eschenbach*, ed. by Heinz Wupp, Wege der Forschung, 62 (Darmstadt, 1966), pp. 455–518.

142 *Das himmlische Jerusalem*, in *Kleinere deutsche Gedichte des 11. und 12. Jahrhunderts*, ed. by Werner Schröder (Tübingen, 1972), pp. 189–201.

143 Latin biblical quotations are from *Biblia Sacra Latina: Ex Biblia Sacra Vulgatae Editionis* (London, 1970).

144 *Vita Sadalbergae*, ed. by B. Krusch and W. Levison, in MGH SS Rer. Merov., 5 (Hanover, 1810), pp. 40–66 (p. 50; quotation modified to follow the reading 'historiae' of manuscript N).

late antiquity[145] and by Augustine's and Jerome's newly discovered appreciation of the Bible's stylistic simplicity.[146] But there is more to it. The following words from the *Vita Sadalbergae* emphasize the point that its simplicity is a conscious stylistic decision appropriate to the matter of the text: 'Neque enim aquila extensis alis semper ad aethera volitat, sed aliquoties assolet ut remissioribus pennis descendat ad terras; et inter regias saepe dapes, etiam vilia poma lactucaeque aggrestes optima quaeque censentur.'[147]

Both the Latin *Vita* and the German vernacular texts make recourse to the same biblical imagery to characterize their inception. These patterns are also pervasive in twelfth-century Latin texts contemporary with the *Kaiserchronik*, most prominently in the prologue to Otto of Freising's *Chronica*, where he calls his writing 'impertius' and himself 'indoctus' before elaborating: '[...] dum, sicut nonnunquam erroris fomes arguta sit subtilitas, sic semper veritatis amica sancta sit rusticitas.'[148] The topos is also used by Godfrey of Viterbo, whose *Pantheon* (1160s) has been identified as sharing many characteristics with the *Kaiserchronik*,[149] but arguably he eschews Otto's solemn analytical phrasing and embraces a more affected style when he declares:

> Hanc etiam simplicitatis et imperitie mee lectionem non summis magistris et philosophis didascalis audeo exibere, sed tibi layco moderate philosophanti et aliis quasi pueris tibi coetaneis ista simplicia dicta proposui et adaptavi. Mei etiam parvitas ingenii ad illa philosophantica culmina philosophantium non attingit.[150]

Specifying the *rusticitas* or *simplicitas* with which a text was authored in this way is, of course, in itself a rhetorical topos,[151] a case of 'affected modesty'[152] that does not preclude the use of rhetorical devices but aims to gain the audience's favour by avoiding undisguised arrogance and — in the case of the early German prologues — to heighten the text's authority by linking it to divine inspiration.

---

145 See Curtius, *European Literature*, pp. 411–13.

146 See Jerome, *Epistolae*, ed. by J.-P. Migne, Patrologiae Cursus Completus: Series Latina, 22 (Paris, 1845): 'Itaque miser ego lecturus Tullium ieiunabam; post noctium crebras vigilias, post lacrimas, quas mihi praeteritorum recordatio peccatorum ex imis visceribus eruebat, Plautus sumebatur in manibus. Si quando in memet reversus prophetam legere coepissem, sermo horrebat incultus, et quia lumen caecis oculis non videbam, non oculorum putabam culpam esse, sed solis' (no. 22: 'Ad Eustochium', 30). See also Erich Auerbach, 'Sermo Humilis', *Romanische Forschungen*, 64 (1952), 309–15. See Augustine, *Confessions*, ed. by James O'Donnell, 3 vols (Oxford, 1992): 'itaque institui animum intendere in scripturas sanctas et videre quales essent. et ecce video rem non compertam superbis neque nudatam pueris, sed incessu humilem, successu excelsam et velatam mysteriis. et non eram ego talis ut intrare in eam possem aut inclinare cervicem ad eius gressus. non enim sicut modo loquor, ita sensi, cum attendi ad illam scripturam, sed visa est mihi indigna quam tullianae dignitati compararem' (III. 5).

147 *Vita Sadalbergae*, p. 50.

148 Otto of Freising, *Chronica*, I. prologue, pp. 9–10.

149 See Ohly, *Sage und Legende*, p. 15; Nellmann, *Reichsidee*, p. 84; Chinca and Young, p. 16.

150 Godfrey of Viterbo, *Memoria Seculorum*, ed. by Georg Waitz, in MGH SS, 22 (Hanover, 1872), pp. 94–106 (p. 105).

151 See Lausberg, p. 157, §275β.

152 Curtius, *European Literature*, p. 83.

Where between all these positions does the *Kaiserchronik* stand? The statement of intent from the first two lines of the text reverberates in the climax of its damning polemic:

> In des almähtigen gotes minnen
> sô wil ich des liedes beginnen
> [...]
> nû vurht ich vil harte
> daz diu sêle dar umbe brinne:
> iz ist ân gotes minne. (*KC*, 1–34)

The *Kaiserchronik* is dedicated to 'gotes minnen'; the opposing texts are excluded from it and ultimately lead to damnation. And it is this commitment to the love of God that qualifies the *Kaiserchronik*'s account as preferable to the texts the prologue polemicizes against. Because of their lack of this 'minne', they only teach lies and pride:

> sô lêret man die luge diu chint:
> die nâh uns chunftich sint,
> die wellent sie alsô behaben
> unt wellent sie iemer fur wâr sagen.
> lugene unde ubermuot
> ist niemen guot. (*KC*, 35–40)

Of course, the invocation of 'gotes minne' is a readily available topos in Early Middle High German literature. The *Himmlisches Jerusalem*, which is transmitted with the *Kaiserchronik* in the Vorau manuscript, chooses almost identical words to start off its narrative: 'in sines namen minne | ditzes liedes sô beginne wir' (16–17). The love of God qualifies both accounts as truthful. It becomes clear that truth as a category is subject not to modern standards like verifiable evidence or empirical occurrence but to probability, acceptability, and imaginability within the historical logic of a creation conceived and represented in 'gotes minne'. In a way, the *Kaiserchronik*'s concept of 'gotes minne' becomes the textual agency realizing Quintilian's demand for verisimilitude.

The modern bewilderment occasioned by the discrepancy between the prologue's prominent claim to truthfulness and the chronicle's often fabulous content was evidently not shared by readers of the period in which the text flourished. Godfrey of Viterbo, writing only a couple of decades later,[153] could claim 'fabula non agitur, cronica vero cano'[154] without the apparent clash of claim and content being detrimental to his work's success: his *Pantheon* is transmitted in more manuscripts than Otto's *Chronica* and, just like the *Kaiserchronik*, continued to attract readers well into the later Middle Ages.[155]

---

153 Godfrey also proudly announces in the preface of his *Memoria Seculorum*, p. 105, that he spent forty years compiling material for his work, next to his obligations as envoy, lawyer, and notary at the imperial court of Frederick Barbarossa.

154 Godfrey of Viterbo, *Speculum Regnum*, p. 38.

155 See Thomas Foerster, *Godfrey of Viterbo and his Readers: Imperial Tradition and Universal Historiography in Late Medieval Europe* (Abingdon, 2016).

With *gotes minne*, an external and divine agency qualifies the content of the chronicle. Moreover, unlike the *Ezzolied*, Lamprecht's *Alexanderlied*, the *Hochzeit*, or Chrétien's *Erec et Enide*, the *Kaiserchronik* does not use any of the language associated with the artfully compositional style to describe its underlying poetological conceptions. The *Kaiserchronik* does not conceive of itself as an artefact. Foregrounding that quality is ascribed to literature that will ultimately lead its readers to damnation.

The findings of this chapter show how the *Kaiserchronik* conceptualizes itself in its prologue in contrast to other texts, which it attacks on three levels: first as being presented by peripatetic performers in a courtly setting, second as being untruthful within the logic of verisimilitude, and third as being overly artefactual in composition and too self-satisfied in rhetorical conception. Conversely, this means that the *Kaiserchronik* presents itself as an inspired text and its attacking of other texts aims less specifically at a certain genre of text — such as heroic epics — but instead at a more refined, compositional mode of storytelling. This criticism does not, of course, prevent the text itself from employing ample rhetorical devices to manufacture the impression of being beyond such artisanal preoccupations; in this respect, the *Kaiserchronik* quite possibly precedes Wolfram von Eschenbach's self-presentation in *Parzival* by some fifty years. Neither pole excludes the other; they simply represent a different emphasis on different rhetorical strategies for addressing the text's audience. This does not mean that the composer of the chronicle does not approve of rhetoric at all, but rather that he chooses to rhetorically foreground the inspirational aspect of literary composition.

This allows us to connect our poetological findings about the chronicle's self-stylization with our initial question of historiography. As shown above, the *Kaiserchronik* speaks of its account as if it were speaking of a second text. This text seems not to be exclusively the *Kaiserchronik* and presents the relationship between the chronicle and its sources in an ambiguous way. Almost as if it were referring simultaneously to itself and to its source, this self-stylization embodies the inspirational model the prologue espouses: it obfuscates the barriers between the *Kaiserchronik* as a text and the source texts as texts, and reduces the necessity of specifying the sources of individual stories or motifs. Once the text has become fused with its context or source tradition, the author's compositional intervention is reduced. This means that there is nothing in the *Kaiserchronik*'s account brought into it by the author, no *conjointure* that would construct history, but instead purely manifest truth: the truth to which the *Kaiserchronik* commits itself in its prologue and which is qualified by *gotes minne* as beneficial for its audience. Negating artefactuality and suppressing authorial intervention also catalyses the main task of the *Kaiserchronik*'s episodic paradigm, which is to create sameness in the account of historical events. This sameness is the prime condition for historical episodes to be available as historical examples with which to instruct the contemporary audience of the *Kaiserchronik*.

Moreover, the overall episodic framework functions to much the same effect. Since the constituent episodes of the content of the chronicle are neither framed by explanatory narrative nor by any attempt at explicit causal integration with one another or the overall historical trajectory of the Empire, but are rather presented by formulaic phrases and recurring patterns, the episode framework creates a distinct message: the form of the chronicle mirrors the form of history. There is no man-made artefactuality in the *Kaiserchronik*'s account of history, only the manifestation of truth sanctioned by *gottes minne*.

CHAPTER 3

❖

The First Dimension of Qualitative Change: The Religious Identity of the Empire

3.1. The Problem of Salvation History

The first category within which the *Kaiserchronik* has to negotiate qualitative change concerns the religious identity of the Empire. Over the timeframe that the *Kaiserchronik* covers, the Roman Empire changes its religious allegiance from a polytheistic pagan cult to the Catholic Christianity its medieval German audience would have lived and experienced every day. This change has to be mediated without disturbing the paradigmatic continuity of Romanness in the Empire. This chapter will first develop a critical take on the main methodological approach previously employed to illuminate the *Kaiserchronik*'s religious dimension, and then try to trace the narrative steps developed in the text to model the religious conversion of the Empire.

When looking at the *Kaiserchronik* in general, the idea that the form and the content of the text are somehow determined by the premises of salvation history has proven to be a popular, almost predictable approach, and the salvific negotiation of history in the chronicle has long been a focus of intense discussion. Salvation history was the guiding principle underlying Ohly's typological scheme of analysis, and from there it became one of the main pillars of *Kaiserchronik* scholarship. Indeed, as a historiographical concept it conveniently explains many of the text's idiosyncrasies and situates crucial elements of its content on a clear arc in a nicely ordered framework. However, it will become evident that this approach is not only overly neat but has also been overstretched in its application.

Even beyond main strands of research (as in Ohly and others), the assumption that the author's conscious or unconscious salvation-historical thinking shapes the content of the *Kaiserchronik* is so pervasive that it can serve as an implicit explanation for all kinds of theories about the work. For example, Stengel, in his reappraisal of the dating of the *Kaiserchronik*, places the text unhesitatingly in a long tradition of world chronicles reaching straight back to Jerome and Eusebius's first Christian chronicle.[1] Urbanek suggests that the anonymous author was imbued with a 'christlich heilsgeschichtlichen Sinn des Römischen Reiches' and therefore chose for his system of numerical symbolism numbers that have a salvation-historical meaning, such as 3 for the Trinity and 6 for the *aetates* of the world.[2]

Too many others to name individually have contributed from different points of view and with various queries at the heart of their examinations: Eberhard Nellmann developed the idea of the representation of an idealized *imperium christianum*.[3] Frank Shaw tried to localize the text in the same sphere as other historical narratives like the *Alexanderlied* or *Rolandslied*.[4] Others, such as Bertau, have completely denied the existence of a guiding historical principle in the text and see it as a mere collection of legendary tales, determined in its shape and content by the limited intellectual capacity of the environment in and for which it was compiled.[5]

The recurring idea of attributing salvation-historical and universal historical patterns to the text has come under increasing scrutiny from at least two angles. To begin with, the exact connection between the two terms has never been sufficiently established; 'salvation history' and 'universal history' are used unreflectively and interchangeably. Second, many of the scholarly arguments seem to be afflicted by the problem of confirmation bias: the unquestioned assumption that salvation-historical thinking governs the *Kaiserchronik* has led scholars to perceive, however vaguely, a teleological unfolding of history in the ordering system of the text; this perception in turn confirms the initial assumption, thus perpetuating the unquestioned initial assumption.

Indeed, the constant use of salvation-historical terminology appears to be more a case of what Hans Blumenberg calls 'terminological metastasis', in which the term is largely detached from its actual meaning and semantic context and is used to signify any kind of somehow religiously charged history.[6] This apparent gap between the *Kaiserchronik*'s content and the terminology used to describe it certainly warrants a closer examination of how this terminology has been used in the scholarly discussion to signify various, sometimes interconnected conceptions of history, and of what these terminological instruments entail. Only then will it be possible to decide whether the terms are suitable for use in connection with the *Kaiserchronik* and, where necessary, to develop a more specific set of terminologies to better specify the historical idea(s) and concept(s) that are productive in the text.

---

1   Edmund Stengel, 'Die Entstehung der "Kaiserchronik" und der Aufgang der staufischen Zeit', in *Abhandlungen und Untersuchungen zur mittelalterlichen Geschichte* (Cologne, 1960), pp. 395–417 (p. 395). Stengel claims that the *Kaiserchronik* could not have been written in the time of Conrad III, but argues for a later dating, either 1160–61 or 1164–65.

2   Urbanek, 'Herrscherzahl und Regierungszeiten', p. 236.

3   Nellmann, *Reichsidee*, pp. 95–115.

4   Frank Shaw, 'Das historische Epos als Literaturgattung in frühmittelhochdeutscher Zeit', in *Studien zur frühmittelhochdeutschen Literatur: Cambridger Colloquium 1971*, ed. by Leslie Peter Johnson and others (Berlin, 1974), pp. 275–91 (pp. 276–82).

5   Karl Bertau, *Deutsche Literatur im europäischen Mittelalter*, 2 vols (Munich, 1972–73), I (1972), 316–18, 337–44.

6   Hans Blumenberg, *The Legitimacy of the Modern Age*, trans. by Robert Wallace (Cambridge, MA, 1983), p. 63.

3.1.1. A Short Account of the Development of Salvation-Historical Historiography between the First and Fifth Century CE

The term 'salvation history' first appeared in the nineteenth century, as German *Heilsgeschichte*, to signify a unified *historia salutis*[7] that proceeds as a teleological linear process from the creation of man to the present and further on to the Last Judgement.[8] In its secularized form, this idea turned into world history, a most influential notion about the passing of time.[9] When, after the collapse of the Soviet Union, Francis Fukuyama proclaimed the 'end of history', he was echoing this historiographical tradition. History had reached its destination: in this case Western, liberal democracy, which would now be universalized into mankind's final form of government.[10] The soteriological concept of history at the foundation of salvation history does not work very differently from this, except that its *telos* is not Western democracy but the salvation of mankind from this temporal vale of tears. The way there does not lead through stages of different political systems, but is deliberately and premeditatedly implemented by God and bestowed upon mankind in different stages of religious revelation.[11]

Up to this point, the meaning of the term seems to be largely consistent with its usage in the scholarly discussion summarized above. The semantic dimension of salvation history contained in this discussion is, however, only the final stage in a historiographical process of representing and interpreting history through a complex lens. Essentially, it is an apologetic view of scriptural traditions and historical occurrences, and at this point the term's applicability to the *Kaiserchronik* becomes dubious. The prevalent reading of the chronicle often implies a linear reading of salvation-historical arguments. Salvation history, however, does not

---

7   See Hans Freiherr von Campenhausen, *Urchristliches und Altkirchliches* (Tübingen, 1979), p. 20. The term was first introduced in Johann Christian Konrad von Hofmann, *Weissagung und Erfüllung im Alten und Neuen Testamente: Ein theologischer Versuch*, 2 vols (Nördlingen, 1841–44). Von Hofmann was a student of Leopold von Ranke, which shaped his approach to the Bible as 'weissagende Geschichte' (I (1841), 52). See Martin Hengel, 'Heilsgeschichte', in *Heil und Geschichte: Die Geschichtsbezogenheit des Heils und das Problem der Heilsgeschichte in der biblischen Tradition und in der theologischen Deutung*, ed. by Jörg Frey, Stefan Krauter, and Hermann Lichtenberger, Wissenschaftliche Untersuchungen zum Neuen Testament, 248 (Tübingen, 2009), pp. 3–36 (p. 3).

8   See Bernd Janowski, 'Vergegenwärtigung und Wiederholung: Anmerkungen zu G. von Rads Konzept der Heilsgeschichte', in *Heil und Geschichte*, ed. by Frey, Krauter, and Lichtenberger, pp. 37–62 (p. 37).

9   von Campenhausen, pp. 20–25.

10   Francis Fukuyama, *The End of History and the Last Man* (London, 1992), p. 338: 'It is possible that if events continue to unfold as they have done over the past few decades, that the idea of a universal and directional history leading up to liberal democracy may become more plausible [...].'

11   For more on the discussion of modern historical theories as secularized Christian heuristics, see Blumenberg, p. 65: 'What mainly occurred in the process that is interpreted as secularization, at least (so far) in all but a few recognizable and specific instances, should be described not as the *transposition* of authentically theological contents into secularized alienation from their origin but rather as *reoccupation* of answer positions that had become vacant and whose corresponding questions could not be eliminated.' He is arguing against Carl Schmitt's notion of all resonant concepts of modernity as secularized theological concepts (*Political Theology: Four Chapters on the Concept of Sovereignty*, trans. by George Schwab (Cambridge, MA, 1985), p. 36).

begin at the beginning and does not progress in a linear pattern through historical occurrences. It starts with the core of salvation, Jesus, in the middle of history and works outward from that point, interrogating the past BCE for prophecies of his coming, and the past CE for signs of the continuing validity of his salvific mission. Working backward, it stops only at the creation of the world and the first humans; working forward, it passes through the present of the chronicler on a trajectory clearly aimed at the end times.

Campenhausen identifies the first salvation-historical narratives as early as the books of the New Testament. Both Matthew and Luke try to connect Jesus by means of long genealogical chains to Abraham (Matthew) and even all the way back to Adam (Luke). This widens the impact of Christ's salvation to include the entirety of the human race.[12] Looking back at the Old Testament, the salvation-historical perspective is indifferent to the original textual context, historical meaning, or even sequence of occurrence. Moreover, it tries to prise prophetic predictions from the Old Testament, at times forcibly breaking them out of their context and rearranging them into an alleged prophecy for the present without any regard for the Old Testament passages' historical context and composition.[13] The vehicles for this kind of prophetic reconnection are often typologies, which form the foundation on which Ohly builds his concept of extra-biblical typologies:[14] certain events, persons, or even single objects are extracted from earlier holy texts and, notwithstanding their historical meaning and context, deployed as prefigurative types for the various aspects of salvation now manifest with Christ's incarnation. The writings of the early Church and even the Gospels themselves are replete with such typological connections, for example when Matthew 12. 39–40 and Luke 11. 29–30 interpret the three days the prophet Jonah had to wait in the belly of the whale before being returned to land as a prefiguration of Christ's fate to remain in hell for the same time before returning to life.[15] Many parts of the New Testament only become clear when regarded through this lens. The notoriously odd passage in Matthew 21. 7, where Jesus apparently rides into Jerusalem on two donkeys, can be explained when read in conjunction with Zechariah 9. 9, where a righteous and victorious king rides toward Jerusalem 'on a donkey, on a colt, the foal of a donkey'; the historical-critical analysis of the text argues that Matthew here, in his eagerness to prove the fulfilment of the ancient prophecy in the events of Palm Sunday, missed the classical Hebrew stylistic device of a *parallelismus membrorum* and translated it with two donkeys instead of one.[16]

12   von Campenhausen, p. 25.
13   Ibid., p. 30.
14   Ohly, *Sage und Legende*, pp. 26–29.
15   von Campenhausen, p. 29.
16   See Barclay Newman and Philip Stine, *A Handbook on the Gospel of Matthew* (Stuttgart, 1988), pp. 637–41; John Nolland, *The Gospel of Matthew: A Commentary on the Greek Text* (Milton Keynes, 2005), pp. 833–37. The notion that Matthew would have made such a glaring mistake or deliberately sacrificed a better translation for a more explicit connection to Zechariah has been energetically refuted: Charlene McAfee Moss, *The Zechariah Tradition and the Gospel of Matthew*, Beihefte zur Zeitschrift für die neutestamentliche Wissenschaft und die Kunde der älteren Kirche, 156 (Berlin, 2009), pp. 80–83 (and esp. p. 88: 'Thus, this view, albeit advocated by some scholars, grants Matthew

The much-discussed *Visio Danielis* may serve as another more prominent example of this practice of decontextualizing biblical material in order to make it yield Christological prophecy. The Neoplatonic philosopher Porphyry,[17] who wrote around 300 CE, agrees with most modern scholars that the Book of Daniel was originally written in the middle of the second century BCE and is deeply rooted in contemporary controversies surrounding the infringements of the Judaic service at the Temple through the Seleucid ruler Antiochos IV Epiphanes; in this context, the book strives to justify Hasmonean claims for power against the Diadochean occupier.[18] Here, Antiochos is presented as the eleventh horn sprouting from the brow of the fourth beast, thus breaking the divinely ordained order of rule and veneration in Israel. The text expects him to die without foreign intervention (Daniel 11. 44–45), but as these prophecies fail to become literally true, they open themselves up to further interpretation by later generations of Christian exegesis.[19]

The Gospels are mainly interested in the concept of the 'son of man'[20] (Daniel 7. 13) and relate the prophetic content of the book tied to this term to the life of Christ, thereby turning it into one of the pillars of Christology.[21] Parallel to this, they no longer relate the fourth beast and its eleventh horn to Antiochos but to an 'Antichristos' who is yet to come and will bring a time of great blasphemy and corruption over mankind.[22] The most important propagator of this identification is St Jerome, who reassesses the passage in his commentary *In Danielem*[23] between 406 and 408 CE.[24] For him, Antiochos is the type of the salvation-historical truth revealed in the Antichrist.[25]

In addition to the typological legitimation of Christ, salvation-historical narrative was also fuelled by anti-Judaic sentiment, which grew strong in the early Church when it became apparent that most of the Jews would not accept Jesus as their Messiah: the idea took root of a truculent and unteachable people who killed the prophets sent to them by God to announce the coming of the Messiah, a prophecy which the Christians of course saw fulfilled in Jesus. The notion of the Jews as a

---

the desire to have prophecy fulfilled accurately but, by the same token, reduces his mental and theological capacity to simple causality. However, the author of the gospel of Matthew was anything but naïve and simple-minded, and his linguistic ability most likely exceeded such a low standard, he would not have made such a basic mistake').

17   Porphyry's copious anti-Christian works were later mostly destroyed and had to be reconstructed from the accounts of his Christian opponents. See *Porphyry's Against the Christians: The Literary Remains*, ed. and trans. by Joseph Hoffmann (Amherst, 1994).

18   See Klaus Koch, 'Das aramäisch-hebräische Danielbuch: Konfrontation zwischen Weltmacht und monotheistischer Religionsgemeinschaft in universalgeschichtlicher Perspektive', in *Geschichte der Daniel-Auslegung*, ed. by Bracht and du Toit, pp. 3–30 (pp. 6–7).

19   See ibid., pp. 23–24.

20   בן-אדם *ben-'adam*. See ibid., p. 22, with n. 29 on the problems of the term in its various translations from the Aramaic original.

21   See ibid., p. 8.

22   Ibid., p. 24.

23   See the introduction to this book.

24   See Courtray, p. 123.

25   Jerome, *In Danielem*: 'Hunc locum plerique nostrorum ad Antichristum referunt, et quod sub Antiocho in typo factum est, sub illo in ueritate dicunt esse complendum' (8, l. 14).

sinful people, incapable of accepting Jesus as the soteriological terminator of history, led to the expectation of some kind of impending judgement that would be passed upon them. At first, this expectation was projected forward into the impending end of days, but soon it was historicized by actual events[26] when the Romans sacked Jerusalem and destroyed the Temple in 70 CE.[27] Starting with Hegesippus as mediated by Eusebius, a long line of Christian apologists from Justin to Tertullian used this historical fact as a signifier for the truth of the Christian message and the supersession of the old Judaic covenant by the new Christian one. For them, the destruction of Jerusalem was nothing but the — albeit belated — final act and concluding chapter of Old Testament history. History so far had been understood as the history of the Jewish people being congruent with the history of God's presence and revelations in his creation.[28]

With the fall of Jerusalem and the ultimate expulsion of the Jews from the Holy Land after the Bar Kokhba revolt of *c.* 132–36 CE,[29] the soteriological reach of both the old prophets and of Jesus's imminent return, especially as represented by Luke, who managed to combine historiography with an eschatological vision,[30] seems to have been considered less and less productive.[31] No longer did reference to the prophets and the imminent expectation of the Parousia[32] of the early Church suffice to contain the queries Christians posed of their time,[33] which proved strangely reluctant to finally cross over into eschatology and appeared perfectly content to remain within the confines of historiography for just a while longer. But it fell to the Greek Irenaeus, who probably died around the year 200, to pick up the various strands and be the first to present a cohesive salvation-historical account. In his works, he develops the idea of a progressive education of humanity by God through a string of historical covenants that provide a framework with the capacity to integrate and unify the whole of biblical history.[34]

26   See von Campenhausen, pp. 32–35.
27   Flavius Josephus, *The Jewish War*, trans. by G. A. Williamson, ed. by Mary Smallwood (London, 1959; repr. 1981), describes the sack of Jerusalem in books V and VI, especially in book VI, which concludes: 'So fell Jerusalem in the second year of Vespasian's reign, on the 8th of Gorpiaios, captured five times before and now for the second time utterly laid to waste. Shishak king of Egypt, followed by Antiochus, the Pompey, and after that Sosius and Herod together, captured the City but spared it. Earlier the king of Babylon had stormed it and laid it to waste 1,468 years and 6 months from its foundation. [...] The Canaanite inhabitants were driven out by the Jewish king David, who settled his own people there; then 477 years and 6 months after his time it was utterly destroyed by the Babylonians. From king David, the first Jew to reign in it, to the destruction by Titus it was 1,179 years' (pp. 372–73). The system by which the figures in this section are derived remains obscure.
28   See von Campenhausen, pp. 36–37.
29   See Joan Taylor, *The Essenes, the Scrolls, and the Dead Sea* (Oxford, 2012), pp. 167–72.
30   See Garry Winston Trompf, *Early Christian Historiography: Narratives of Retributive Justice* (London, 2000), p. 109.
31   See von Campenhausen, p. 35.
32   See S. J. Duffy, 'Parousia, 2: In Theology', in *New Catholic Encyclopedia*, 15 vols (Washington, 1967), X, cols 1037–40.
33   See von Campenhausen, p. 59.
34   See ibid., pp. 51–52; Hengel, p. 13. Irenaeus, *Libros Quinque adversus Haereses*, ed. by William Wigan Harvey, 2 vols (Cambridge, 1857): 'Qualis igitur dispositio Filii Dei, talis et animalium forma: et qualis animalium forma, talis et [*sic*] character Evangelii. Quadriformia autem animaliam,

Due to the parallel development of early Christianity and Rabbinic Judaism,[35] ongoing persecution by the Roman pagan authorities, and Gnostic defections in the fourth century, this happened in a climate of sectarian conflict,[36] when with Eusebius's finishing of the *Ecclesiastical History*, Christianity started to become aware of its own historicity and the need to secure it.[37] In the freshly institutionalized Church, it found a new, appropriate carrier of historical meaning to which to attach this new historiography. However, the transformation of salvation history into ecclesiastical history did not imply a new quality of salvation at the disposal of the Church. It remained the same, identical with the salvation managed and bestowed by Jesus and the martyrs, thus constituting a space of perpetual presence of salvation between the first incarnation of Christ and his putative second coming.[38]

In this context, and building on the prior developments laid out above, a 'logic of retribution'[39] was able to take root in the newly forming Christian historiography. Eusebius, as the first Christian chronicler, for example, presents the fall of Jerusalem and the many miseries the Jews had to suffer after this as a direct punishment for the execution of Jesus;[40] Augustine sees the Judaic diaspora as an involuntary but therefore all the more credible testimony to the correctness of Jesus's role as Messiah.[41]

et quadriforme Evangelium, et quadriformis dispositio Domini. Et propter hoc quatuor data sunt testamenta humano generi; unum quidem ante cataclysmum sub Adam; secundum vero, post cataclysmum sub Noe, tertum vero, legislatio sub Moyse; quartum vero, quod renovat hominem, et recapitulat in se omnia, quod est per Evangelium, elevans et pennigerans homines et coeleste regnum' (III. 11. 11, vol. 2, p. 50).

35   See Philip Alexander, 'The Parting of the Ways from the Perspective of Rabbinic Judaism', in *Jews and Christians: The Parting of the Ways, A.D. 70 to 135: The Second Durham–Tübingen Research Symposium on Earliest Christianity and Judaism*, ed. by James Dunn (Tübingen, 1992), pp. 1–26 (p. 2). He shows how until the fourth century, Christian Jews and Rabbinism were competing within the broader scope of Judaism to determine its future shape, and how only after the triumph of Rabbinism Christianity and Judaism separated.

36   See von Campenhausen, p. 36.

37   See Trompf, p. 109.

38   See von Campenhausen, pp. 61–62.

39   Trompf, p. 3.

40   Eusebius of Caesarea, *Historiae Ecclesiasticae Libri X*, ed. by Friedrich Adolf Heinichen, 3 vols (Leipzig, 1827), III. 5, vol. 1, pp. 195–96. Eusebius of Caesarea, *The History of the Church*, trans. by G. A. Williamson, ed. by Andrew Louth (London, 1989): 'Passing over the details of the successive disasters that befell them from the sword and in other ways I think it necessary to mention only the miseries they suffered from starvation, so that readers of this book may have some knowledge at least of how their crime against the Christ of God a very little time later brought on them God's vengeance', and 'Such was the reward of the Jews' iniquitous and wicked treatment of God's Christ' (pp. 68, 73).

41   See von Campenhausen, p. 37; Bernhard Blumenkranz, *Die Judenpredigt Augustins: Ein Beitrag zur Geschichte der jüdisch-christlichen Beziehungen in den ersten Jahrhunderten*, Basler Beiträge zur Geschichtswissenschaft, 25 (Basle, 1946), pp. 176–77. For more on the discussion of Augustine's stance toward the Jews, see James Carroll, *Constantine's Sword: The Church and the Jews* (Boston, 2001), pp. 216–18, where he comes to an ambiguous evaluation of Augustine's teaching on the Jews. For a more positive assessment, cf. Paula Fredriksen, *Augustine and the Jews: A Christian Defense of Jews and Judaism* (New York, 2008), pp. 290–96. For Augustine's most important teachings on the Jews, see *De Civitate Dei*: '[E]t nunc quod per omnes fere terras gentesque dispersi sunt, illius

This system of retributive logic later found a more universal employment to explain the sustained presence of evil in a world that was, after the Constantinian shift in the early fourth century, largely Christianized.[42] Arguably most trenchant in this regard is the *Historiae adversum Paganos* by Orosius, student and friend of Augustine from Spain. Relying mainly on pagan sources and consciously eschewing biblical accounts, he narrates the history of the world before the incarnation of Christ as a *historia calamitatum* continually plagued by trials and tribulations. Only after Jesus's birth and death, with the spread of Christianity in the Roman Empire and the establishment of a Christian Church, did things take a turn for the better.[43] This idea remains alive in theological thought and argument until the twentieth century:

> This parousial hope gives meaning and consistency to history and manifests God's immanence to its linear development. If Redemption works in and through historical evolution, only when the redemptive decree of God has run its divinely plotted course will Christ come forth to His abiding presence in His church.[44]

In conclusion, three aspects of salvation-historical narrative can be identified. First, starting with Jesus in the centre, it encompasses the universality of history going back to the creation of the world and humanity, and going forward, passing through the present of the author and finally finding its conclusion in the end of days. Second, its main narrative matrix is apologetic. It starts with the soteriological apex of history and thenceforth interrogates historical occurrences along the time axis BCE for typological and prophetic prefigurations of Christ and along the time axis CE for affirmation of the ongoing validity and presence of Christ's salvation in history unfolding down to the present day. Third, following this basic assumption, it also seeks to assign salvation-historical meaning to persons, situations, and occurrences that work to the detriment of the soteriological premises it must maintain. They too must find their place in the axioms of the divine plan behind the factual unfolding of history.

unius ueri dei prouidentia est, ut, quod deorum falsorum usquequaque simulacra arae, luci templa euertuntur et sacrificia prohibentur, de codicibus eorum probetur, quemadmodum hoc fuerit tanto ante prophetatum' (IV. 34), and '[D]emonstrauit ergo deus ecclesiae in eius inimicis Iudaeis gratiam misericordiae suae, quoniam, sicut dicit apostolus, delictum illorum salus gentibus; et ideo non eos occidit, id est non in eis perdidit quod sunt Iudaei, quamuis a Romanis fuerint deuicti et obpressi, ne obliti legem dei ad hoc, de quo agimus, testimonium nihil ualerent. ideo parum fuit, ut diceret: ne occideris eos, ne quando obliuiscantur legem tuam, nisi adderet etiam: disperge eos; quoniam si cum isto testimonio scripturarum in sua tantummodo terra, non ubique essent, profecto ecclesia, quae ubique est, eos prophetiarum, quae de Christo praemissae sunt, testes in omnibus gentibus habere non posset' (XVIII. 46).

42   See von Campenhausen, pp. 58–61; Trompf, pp. 292–93.
43   Orosius, *Seven Books of History*, p. 8.
44   Duffy, col. 1039.

3.1.2. Comparing the Kaiserchronik to Orosius and Otto

Building on this outline, I intend now to elucidate these three points by comparing the *Kaiserchronik* to Orosius's *Historiae adversum Paganos* and Otto of Freising's *Chronica*. Orosius, on the one hand, is relevant as an early representative of a fully fledged salvation-historical narrative, his *casus scribendi* being an apologetical urge to explain the sack of Christian Rome by Alaric and his Visigoths in 410 CE and to defend Christianity against its pagan assailants, who in his time argued that the sack of Rome had occurred due to the Romans' neglect of the old, pagan gods.[45] Additionally, it has been established that Orosius's text was probably one of the direct sources the author of the *Kaiserchronik* was drawing from when he compiled his text.[46] Otto's *Chronica*, on the other hand, serves to demonstrate how a historiographical narrative that was written at roughly the same time and in the same cultural and political sphere as the *Kaiserchronik*, and that explicitly positions itself in terms of a salvation-historical rationale, could operate to achieve this goal.[47]

Of course, these texts — especially Otto's *Chronica* and the *Kaiserchronik*, despite their being so close to each other in time and place of origin — do not all operate on the same level of theological or historiographical sophistication, as Karl Bertau has demonstrated.[48] It is important not to set up comparisons between the *Kaiserchronik* and authors such as Orosius and Otto in such a way that that the *Kaiserchronik* will inevitably be found wanting.[49] In order to assess its cultural role and literary relevance in the twelfth century, it is more appropriate to establish whether and to what extent the *Kaiserchronik* adheres to the premises of salvation history.

For this purpose, three exemplary points of interest for a salvation-historical argumentation that feature in all three texts will be explored. First, the scope of the narrative: where does it begin, where does it end, what does it cover, and how does it comment on that, if it does so at all? Second, the treatment of the birth of Christ (to illustrate how the introduction into history of this soteriological determinant is handled): how does it affect the continuation of the historical narrative, and does it establish some sort of soteriological caesura? Third, the role played by Nero and his persecution of the Christian community as its first great historical antagonist in the narrative will be examined to determine how each text deals with the problem of the continuing presence of evil in factual history and how each one operates to integrate evil into a salvation-historical framework.

---

45   Orosius, *Seven Books of History*, pp. 7–12.

46   Ohly, *Sage und Legende*, p. 94.

47   For the most reliable resource on Otto's concept of history, see still Hans-Werner Goetz, *Das Geschichtsbild Ottos von Freising*, Beihefte zum Archiv für Kulturgeschichte, 19 (Cologne, 1984). But see also Walther Lammers, *Weltgeschichte und Zeitgeschichte bei Otto von Freising*, Sitzungsberichte der wissenschaftlichen Gesellschaft an der Johann Wolfgang Goethe-Universität Frankfurt am Main, 14.3 (Wiesbaden, 1977).

48   See Bertau, I, 337–38.

49   Bertau's approach being a prime example of this (I, 339–40).

3.1.2.1. Beginnings and Endings in Orosius's Historiae adversum Paganos,
Otto's Chronica, *and the* Kaiserchronik

Before offering a detailed description of the known world and its countries and regions, Orosius lays out the cornerstones of the historical programme of his chronicle at its beginning:

> But I have decided to trace the beginning of men's misery from man's original sin, merely gathering together a few short examples. 3,184 years passed from Adam, the first man, to Ninus, the so-called 'Great', when Abraham was born. These years are omitted by, or unknown to, all historians. There are then 2,015 years from Ninus, or from Abraham, to the time of Caesar Augustus: that is to the birth of Christ which took place in the 42nd year of Caesar's reign, when the peace was made with Parthia, the gates of Janus were closed, and wars ceased all over the world. During this time every form of action or inaction was either ground out by men of affairs or by those who wrote on them.[50]

Orosius is committed to narrating secular history, if only to show the unfolding of God's plan in history to the pagans, who would, he writes, not accept biblical records as historical evidence.[51] Because of this, he merely touches on occurrences solely transmitted in biblical texts, like the creation of the world and of Adam, the first man, though he of course maintains the importance of these events as the beginning of history.[52] As announced, the actual historiographical narrative commences '[a]nno ante urbem conditam MCCC' with 'Ninus rex Assyriorum'.[53] Over the course of the first book, Orosius briefly touches on the most important historical figures and events while virtually counting down to his main point of interest: the foundation of the city of Rome.[54] Rome succeeds and surpasses Babylon, which forms both a negative counter-image to and a positive template for Rome's role in history.[55]

After following the course of Roman history over one thousand years, Orosius catches up with his own present time, which he takes great pains to show in the best possible light:

---

50   Orosius, *Seven Books of History*, p. 34. Orosius, *Historiae*: '4 Ego initium miseriae hominum ab initio peccati hominis ducere institui, paucis dumtaxat isdemque breuiter delibatis. 5 Sunt autem ab Adam primo homine usque ad Ninum magnum ut dicunt regen, quando natus est Abraham, anni III.CLXXXIIII, qui ab omnibus historiographis uel omissi uel ignorati sunt. 6 A Nino autem uel Abraham usque ad Caesarem Augustum id est usque ad natiuitatem Christi. Quae fuit anno imperii Caesaris quadragesimo secundo, cum facta pace cum Parthis Iani portae clausae sunt et bella toto orbe cessarunt, colliguntur anni II.XV in quibus se inter actors scriptoresque omnium otia negotiaque triuerunt' (I. I. 4–6).
51   Orosius, *Seven Books of History*, pp. 7–8.
52   Orosius, *Historiae*, I. 3. 1–2.
53   Ibid., I. 4. 1.
54   He regularly begins his chapters in the first book with reckoning the years 'ante urbem conditam'.
55   Orosius, *Historiae*: 'Itaque haec ob hoc praecipue commemoranda credidi, ut tanto arcano ineffabilium iudiciorum Dei ex parte patefacto intellegant hi, qui insipienter utique de temporibus Christianis murmurant, unum Deum disposuisse tempora et in principo Babyloniis et in fine Romanis, illius clementiae esse, quod uiuimus, quod autem misere uiuimus, intemperantiae nostrae' (I. 3. 2–5).

We have shown, I believe, and demonstrated almost as much by pointing, as by my words, that innumerable wars have come to an end, a great number of usurpers have been put down, and the most savage tribes have been defeated, restrained, surrendered, and emptied of their strength with the minimum of bloodshed, no battles and hardly any killing.[56]

Otto of Freising is separated by a gulf of over seven hundred years from the Spaniard whom he quotes so frequently and whose description of the world he so warmly recommends to those who want to get to know its provinces, sites, and countries.[57] After the preface, in which he explicates his historiographical programme modelled on Augustine's schema of the two cities,[58] he begins his account of the history of the world with the creation of man, but does not share Orosius's almost scrupulous avoidance of biblical material.[59] Otto concludes his historical narrative in the seventh book, having arrived, like Orosius, in his own day and age with the rule of King Conrad III,[60] which he caps with a short history of monasticism.[61] In the context of the problem of salvation history, Otto's addition of a final eighth book after having already completed the historiographical part deserves special consideration. In it, he offers a short glimpse into the third and future mode *post presentem vitam* of mankind's spiritual fate within the two cities after the two antecedent periods *ante gratiam*[62] and *tempore gratiae*.[63] The Cistercian bishop thus logically concludes his rendition of salvation history by including a speculative account of the fate of the Catholic souls *post salvationem* in his *Chronica*.

Even at the most superficial glance, it becomes clear that the *Kaiserchronik* does not share this broad salvation-historical frame of reference. First, the text presents what appears to be a rather pedagogical programme in its prologue (*KC*, 1–42). Initially, it scoffs at the 'tumben' (*KC*, 6) for whom it is 'arebait' (*KC*, 6) to learn new things, and promises its reader an increase in 'wîstuom unt êre' (*KC*, 13). After

---

56   Orosius, *Seven Books of History*, p. 413. Orosius, *Historiae*: 'Manifestauimus, ut arbitror atque ostendimus non magis uerbo paene quam digito innumera bella sopita, plurimos extinctos tyrannos, conpressas coangustatas exinanitasque immanissimas gentes minimo sanguine, nullo certamine ac paene sine caede' (VII. 43. 17).

57   Otto of Freising, *Chronica*: 'Quarum provintias, situs, regiones qui velit cognoscere, legat Orosium' (I. 1, p. 38).

58   Ibid.: 'Cum enim duae sint civitates, una temporalis, alia eterna, una mundialis, alia caelestis, una diaboli, alia Christi, Babyloniam hanc, Hierusalem ille esse katholici prodidere scriptores' (I. prologue, p. 6).

59   Ibid.: 'Ad orientem igitur, quantum ex scriptis Geneseos conici potest, in terra Eden creata paradisus creditur. Ubi dum primus homo positus [...]' (I. 2, p. 38).

60   Ibid.: 'Sed quia mutabilium rerum ab Adam usque ad presentem annum, qui ab incarnatione Domini Mus Cus XLus VIus, ab Urbe condita Mus DCCCCus XVIIIus. Conradi nonagesimi tercii ab Augusto nonus, Eugenii tercii summi pontificis secundus est, seriem qualitercumque percensui multiplicesque mortalium miserias involvi [...]' (VII. 34, p. 369).

61   Ibid.: '[...] diversos religiosorum ordines, quorum, ut dixi, sanctitate a misericordissime iudice malignitas mundi subportatur, silentio preterire incongruum arbitramur, ut tantorum malorum turbulentiae clarorum virorum gesta insignia metam et articulum ponamus.'

62   Ibid., VIII. prologue, p. 391.

63   Ibid.: 'De tercio vero, quomodo videlicet haec ad summam beatitudinem profectura, illa ad ultimam miseriam defectura et casura sit, iudicante ac examinante in ultimo iudicio istissimo iudice utriusque urbis causam, in hoc octavo opere dicendum restat.'

this, it comments disdainfully on a new 'gewoneheit' (*KC*, 27) of concocting new narratives and arranging them 'mit scophelîchen worten' (*KC*, 31), and even goes on to imply that those who propagate such 'lugene' (*KC*, 29) will burn for it in hell (*KC*, 32–34). The prologue even goes so far as to express concern about these errors being taught to the following generation (*KC*, 35–38).

After this, the *Kaiserchronik* presents a short account of the foundation of Rome by Romulus and Remus (*KC*, 53–54) 'bi der haiden zîten' (*KC*, 43), without further relating it to prior events in history. Not even a genealogical connection back to Troy and the escaping Trojans is established. In the next two hundred lines, the narrative quickly introduces the Roman Senate (*KC*, 57–61) and at length presents the review of the pagans' week (*KC*, 67–208) as a system for venerating their seven gods. This shows clear signs of the established medieval calendar tradition going back to Isidore's account of the days of the pagan week.[64] After a short prefiguration of the Christianization of the Pantheon (*KC*, 186–208), the *Kaiserchronik* then elaborates on the *salvatio Romae*[65] (*KC*, 217–34) — in the text not identified as such — and then with line 247 dives into the first emperor-centric episode, dealing with Julius Caesar. Fifty-three emperor episodes and 17,037 lines later, the text stops in mid-sentence when Pope Eugene III (*KC*, 17,270),[66] Abbot Bernhard of Clairvaux (*KC*, 17,276),[67] King Conrad III of the Roman Empire (*KC*, 17,278),[68] and King Louis VII of France (*KC*, 17,274)[69] are readying for war to reconquer 'Rôas' (i.e. Edessa; *KC*, 17,250),[70] recently conquered by a figure called 'Sangwîn' (i.e. Imad ad-Din Zengi; *KC*, 17,249).[71]

64   Isidore of Seville, *Etymologiae*: 'Proinde autem ex his septem stellis nomina dierum gentiles dederunt, eo quod per eosdem aliquid sibi effici existimarent, dicentes habere a Sole spiritum, a Luna corpus, a Mercurio ingenium et linguam, a Venere voluptatem, a Marte sanguinem, a Iove temperantiam, a Saturno humorem. Talis quippe extitit gentilium stultitia, qui sibi finxerunt tam ridiculosa figmenta' (v. 30).
65   See Ohly, *Sage und Legende*, p. 40.
66   Pope Eugene III called for a Crusade to reclaim Edessa in 1145 and 1146, and also instructed Bernard of Clairvaux to campaign for such an endeavour in his sermons in France and Germany. See W. Maleczeck, 'Eugen III., Papst', in *Lexikon des Mittelalters*, ed. by Bautier, Avella-Widhalm, and Auty, IV (Munich, 1989), cols 78–80.
67   Bernard, Cistercian Abbot of Clairvaux and the most influential ecclesiastical authority of his day, was the leading instigator of the Second Crusade after the fall of Edessa. See R. Grégoire, 'Bernhard von Clairvaux, Leben und Wirken', in *Lexikon des Mittelalters*, ed. by Bautier, Avella-Widhalm, and Auty, I, cols 1992–94.
68   Conrad III led the German contingent in the Second Crusade in 1147–49. See O. Engels, 'Konrad III., dt. Kg.', in *Lexikon des Mittelalters*, ed. by Bautier, Avella-Widhalm, and Auty, V, cols 1339–40.
69   Louis VII led the French contingent in the Second Crusade in 1147–49. See Bernd Schneidmüller, 'Ludwig VII., Kg. v. Frankreich', in *Lexikon des Mittelalters*, ed. by Bautier, Avella-Widhalm, and Auty, V, cols 2183–84.
70   Schröder, p. 392, n. 4. Edessa was conquered by the atabeg of Mosul, Imad ad-Din Zengi, in 1144, which caused Pope Eugene III to call for the Second Crusade. See J. Ferluga, 'Edessa, Stadt in der heut. sö. Türkei, II: Die Grafschaft Edessa', in *Lexikon des Mittelalters*, ed. by Bautier, Avella-Widhalm, and Auty, VIII, cols 1568–69. The article, however, confuses Imad ad-Din with his son and successor Nur ad-Din.
71   Schröder, p. 392, n. 3. Like *Rôas* for Edessa, *Sanguinus* seems to have been a common Latinized name for Imad ad-Din. Otto of Freising, *Chronica*: 'Sanguinus enim Halapensis Syriae ac

This somewhat more detailed examination confirms the initial impression. The *Kaiserchronik* differs significantly in scope from the representatives of salvation-historical world chronicles. While they set out to encompass the entire history of creation, the *Kaiserchronik* is firmly focused on the Empire and its rulers. Moreover, even though they do all end up in the present time of the author — a characteristic trait of chronicles — their treatment of that present is tellingly different. Orosius uses it to once more reiterate the validity of his main point — that humanity suffered before the arrival of Christ, all present suffering has its place in God's greater scheme, and that things are actually much better now when compared to pagan times. Otto even surpasses the temporal end of history in the present by developing a vision of the soteriological future. The *Kaiserchronik*, however, simply breaks off without finding the opportunity to comment on present times or tie the ending back to the prologue. Thus, it cannot create a meaningful narrative structure to reflect upon its historiographical arc.[72] This opens the text up to criticism like Bertau's and makes it all the more puzzling why Ohly went to such lengths to associate the *Kaiserchronik* with the salvation-historical tradition.[73]

3.1.2.2. Christ and the Soteriological Apogee of History in Orosius's Historiae adversum Paganos, *Otto's* Chronica, *and the* Kaiserchronik

Having established the boundaries of history in all three cases, it now becomes necessary to consider the textual centre of gravity of the historiographical narrative in the three texts in question. It has been shown that Jesus Christ's appearance and acting on earth during the reign of Augustus mark the soteriological threshold at which God's creation passes into a new covenant and a new temporal continuum of salvation-historical reference. The following examples will further illuminate this phenomenon and shed light on how the *Kaiserchronik* — again — does not adhere to these premises.

Orosius explicitly states the importance of Christ's incarnation at this specific point in history:

> So in the same year when Caesar, whom God in His deep mysteries had marked out for this task, ordered that the first census be taken in each and every province and that every man be recorded, God deemed it right to be seen as, and become, a man.[74]

Augustus bringing peace to the Empire and closing the gates of the temple of Janus

---

Mesopotamie, excepta Antiochia et Damasco, princeps, Persarum vero et Medorum regis seu soltani vassallus, Edyssam, quae nunc Rohas dicitur, [...] cum infinita Saracenorum multitudine circumdedit ac in ipsa, ut dixi, nativitate Domini irrupit, cunctis ibidem cum epsicopo urbis Christianis in ore gladii occisis vel miserabili captivitate in servitutem redactis' (VII. 30, p. 356).

72   See White, p. 20.

73   Ohly, *Sage und Legende*, pp. 14–15.

74   Orosius, *Seven Books of History*, p. 316. Orosius, *Historiae*: 'Eodem quoque anno tunc primum idem Caesar, quem his tantis mysteriis paedestinauerat Deus, censum agi singularum ubique prouinciarum et censeri omnes homines iussit, quando et Deus homo uideri et esse dignatus est. Tunc igitur natus est Christus, Romano censui statim adscriptus ut natus est' (VI. 22. 6).

had set the historical stage for Christ's incarnation.[75] Only then did God determine to become man.[76]

> So 752 years after the foundation of the City, Christ was born and brought to the world the faith that gives salvation. Truly, He is the rock set at the heart of things, where there is ruination for whoever strikes against Him, but where whoever believes in Him is saved.[77]

The passage illustrates nicely the key position of Christ *medio rerum*. Temporally, his appearance marks the tipping point in history after which the fate of the world is gradually aligned with the will of God. Soteriologically, believing in him marks the watershed between those who are going to be saved and those who are going to be damned. Both angles shape Orosius's narrative on both sides of Christ's incarnation.

Similarly, in Otto's *Chronica*:

> 'But when the fulness of the time came, God sent forth his Son' into the world to lead back into the highway mortal men, who were wandering like the brutes through trackless and devious places. By taking upon himself the form of a man He proffered mortal men a highway; to recall those who were utterly astray from the error of falsehood to the light of reason, He revealed Himself in the truth; to make over anew the perishing he showed Himself as the true life [...].[78]

Otto echoes Orosius when introducing Christ as the decisive threshold that mankind has to cross on its teleological course toward salvation. He is not only the foretold saviour of his own creation; he is also the creator of the circumstances that allowed his incarnation in the first place. Otto elaborates expansively on why Jesus had to be born at this point in time and no earlier.[79] He finds a very succinct way to illustrate the seminal importance of Christ's birth for the course of history when he has different systems of reckoning of time culminate in the incarnation and then dismisses all of them and establishes that he will henceforth count the years starting anew from Christ's birth.[80]

75   Ibid.: 'Itaque anno ab Vrbe condita DCCLII Caesar Augustus ab oriente in occidentem, a septentrione in meridiem ac per totum Oceani circulum cunctis gentibus una pace conpositis, Iani portas tertio ipse tunc clausit' (VI. 22. I).
76   Ibid.: '[...] quia Dominus noster Iesus Christus hanc urbem nutu suo auctam defensamque in hunc rerum apicem prouexerit, cuius potissime uoluit esse cum uenit, dicendus utique ciuis Romanus census professione Romani' (VI. 22. 8).
77   Orosius, *Seven Books of History*, p. 323. Orosius, *Historiae*: 'Igitur anno ab Vrbe condita DCCLII natus est Christus salutarum mundo adferens fidem, uere petra medio rerum posita, ubi comminueretur qui offenderet, qui crederet saluaretur; uere ignis ardens,quem qui sequitur inluminatur, qui temptat exuritur' (VII. 3. I).
78   Otto of Freising, *Two Cities*, p. 217. Otto of Freising, *Chronica*: 'At ubi venit plenitude temporis, misit Deus filium suum, in terras, qui, ut homines per invia ac devia more pecudum oberrantes ad viam reducerent, viam se hominem assumendo hominibus prebuit, et ut a falsitatis errore exorbitantes ad rationis lumen revocaret, veritatem se ostendit, ut vero deficientes reficeret, vitam se vera exhibuit' (III. prologue, p. 130).
79   Otto of Freising, *Chronica*, III. prologue, p. 133, gives two reasons: (1) the spirit of mankind has to be unified to be prepared for higher insights, and (2) a unified faith should be planted into the heart of one mankind unified by the rule of one city, Rome.
80   Ibid.: 'Igitur novo homine, qui veterem evacuavit, nato, annalibus quoque a Nino ad Urbem conditam ac inde usque ad id tempus productis terminum demus, ab eiusque ortu annales nostros ordiamur' (III. 6, p. 143).

Again, the contrast to the *Kaiserchronik*'s approach is striking. The crucial importance of Augustus's rule — it creates peace and unifies the world to prepare it for the coming of Christ — so often and sophisticatedly stressed by Orosius and Otto, falls almost completely flat. In the entirety of the rather short Augustus episode (*KC*, 604–70), only one scant reference to Jesus can be found, when after Augustus has imposed a tribute to be paid by 'arm unde rîche | di dâ wâren in sînem rîche' (*KC*, 635–36), it is said:

> der cins stuont unz an den tac
> daz der wâre hailant
> von himele wart gesant,
> uns allen ze trôste,
> der uns von dem cinse relôste. (*KC*, 638–42)

What seems to be a salvation-historical prefiguration that the text can later build on to illustrate Christ's role as a saviour is, however, never revisited. The text seems to have little interest in synchronizing Augustus's rule with the birth of Christ. When Augustus dies — poisoned by the Romans (*KC*, 669–70), another idiosyncrasy of the *Kaiserchronik*'s historical account[81] — Jesus has not yet appeared. When he finally figures in the narrative, it is only in retrospect because he is already dead. Augustus's heir, Tiberius, has fallen ill: 'wurme also freissam | in sînem houbete wuohsen' (*KC*, 693–94), and no physician and no remedy are able to cure him (*KC*, 696–98). This is when the emperor learns of an 'aller wîsiste man' (*KC*, 701), said to be living in Jerusalem, who allegedly raised the dead and cured illnesses and therefore should also be able to save the emperor (*KC*, 703–09). He sends his emissary Volusianus (*KC*, 719) to find this marvellous 'arzât' for him (*KC*, 711), and only now does the *Kaiserchronik* finally identify the goal of his quest as the person the audience might already have suspected him to be:

> do er [Volusianus] in die burc ze Jerusalêm
> begunde rîten unte gên,
> dô frâct er die gesinden
> wa er Jhêsum mahte vinden,
> den vil guoten arzât,
> ob er wære in der stat,
> ob er dannoh lebete,
> oder wie er sih gehabete. (*KC*, 721–28)

Jesus's introduction happens so suddenly that it almost seems to have been conceived as some sort of surprise for the audience. Maybe the author is even playing a conscious game with their expectations: Jesus Christ, Son of God and saviour of all mankind, after being conspicuously absent from where he was expected to enter the narrative, is not introduced according to his historical and soteriological significance but as a mere physician of some renown who is sent for to heal the ailing emperor. The comic potential of this newly arranged configuration is even heightened by Veronica's eventual revelation that the man Volusianus is looking for is already dead (*KC*, 749–52). The question of whether the *Kaiserchronik* twists

---

81   See Ohly, *Sage und Legende*, p. 52.

the introduction of Christ into an elaborate narrative jest cannot be pursued here. What can be stated is that the *Kaiserchronik* finds a narrative role for Christ that is quite different from the Latin salvation-historical chronicles and mainly developed with regard to the *Kaiserchronik*'s own version of the legend of Veronica. Another reason for this particular treatment of Christ might be an attempt to historicize him by shifting him out of his soteriological position into a time and space where he might have entered the consciousness of the pagan majority for more mundane reasons, thus providing an alternative perspective on the factuality of Christ, unencumbered by Christian partisanship. Even Bertau — who is generally sceptical of the *Kaiserchronik*'s historiographical and literary qualities — is prepared to admit that the *Kaiserchronik* sometimes concerns itself — somewhat surprisingly and in a very peculiar way — with rationalistic enquiries into its narratives.[82] However, in twelfth-century Bavaria there seems to have been precious little need to provide additional historiographical validation of the evidence for Christ's existence.

Moreover, the following passages also fail to display any further interest in Christ's soteriological function in historiography. Veronica responds to the imperial emissary by asking whether he knew Jesus and then gives an account of his death and resurrection in a very matter-of-fact manner (*KC*, 735–55). In these and the following lines, the focus is clearly on the pagans not knowing Jesus and on opening a window for Veronica to introduce Christianity to the Roman Empire via the shroud in her possession (*KC*, 756–838).

3.1.2.3. Nero and the Problem of Evil in Orosius's Historiae adversum Paganos, *Otto's* Chronica, *and the* Kaiserchronik

Lastly, the presentation of Emperor Nero as the first persecutor of Christians will be compared. All three texts present him as the major antagonist of early Christianity; his predecessor, Claudius, merely expelled the Jews, and perhaps the Christians too, from Rome.[83] From a soteriological point of view, Nero's actions raise the question of why God permits the persecution of the people of his new covenant by the pagan Roman authorities and how salvation history, as an apologetic tool for rationalizing even adverse historical occurrences, reacts to them. From the very off, Orosius presents Nero in unambiguously negative terms: 'He was a follower of his uncle Gaius Caligula in all his crimes and vices and, indeed, surpassed him, for he practised wantonness, lust, extravagance, greed, and cruelty with every kind of crime.'[84] After this, Orosius lists some of Nero's most egregious alleged crimes, like

---

82   Bertau, I, 342: 'Mit Erstaunen bemerkt man: Der Erzähler scheint eine rationalistische Frage erwogen zu haben [...].'
83   Orosius, *Seven Books of History*, pp. 332–33. Orosius, *Historiae*: 'Anno eiusdem nono expulsos per Claudium Vrbe Iudaeos Iosephus refert. Sed me magis Suetonis mouet, qui ait hoc modo: Claudius Iudaeos inpulsore Christo adsidue tumultuantes Roma expulit; quod, utrum contra Christum simul uelut cognatae religionis homines uolerit expelii, nequaquam discernitur' (VII. 6. 15). As Fear points out (see Orosius, *Seven Books of History*, p. 333, n. 83), Orosius takes the account not from Josephus but from Suetonius, *De Vita Caesarum Libri VIII*, ed. by Robert A. Kaster (Oxford, 2016): 'Iudaeos impulsore Chresto assidue tumultuantis Roma expulit' (v. 25. 4).
84   Orosius, *Seven Books of History*, p. 333. Orosius, *Historiae*: 'Gai Caligulae auunculi sui erga omnia

the burning of Rome, and narrates the most flamboyant manifestations of his lust, greed, and cruelty, which he mainly takes from Eutropius and Suetonius. He then climaxes with Nero's persecution of the Christians:

> He added to this mound of iniquities his rash impieties towards God. For he was the first to execute and put to death Christians at Rome and command that they be hunted out and tortured in the same way throughout all the provinces. He tried to extirpate the very name of Christian, killing the blessed apostles of Christ, Peter and Paul, crucifying the former and putting the latter to death by the sword.[85]

In Orosius's logic of imminent divine vengeance, these crimes against the Christian community and its pillars cannot, of course, go unpunished:

> Soon great numbers of disaster piled up and beset the wretched city from all sides. For the following autumn, such a great plague broke out in the city that 30,000 funerals were entered into Libitina's books. On its heels disaster occurred in Britain, where two main towns were sacked amidst a stupendous slaughter of Roman citizens and their allies. Moreover, in the East the important provinces of Armenia were lost, Roman legions passed beyond the Parthian's yoke, and Syria was only retained with great difficulty. In Asia three cities, namely Laodicea, Hierapolis, and Colossae, were levelled by an earthquake.[86]

Fear's comments on his translation of Orosius show the narrative and chronographical tricks Orosius employs here to give his account of Nero's deeds the right salvation-historical spin. For example, he ignores the fact that Suetonius lists the persecution of Christians among Nero's good deeds,[87] anachronistically exaggerates

---

uitia ac scelera sectator immo transgressor, petulantiam libidinem luxuriam auaritiam crudelitatem nullo non scelere exercuit' (VII. 7. 1). Orosius directly quotes Suetonius, *De Vita Caesarum*: 'Petulantiam, libidinem, luxuriam, avaritiam, crudelitatem sensim quidem primo et occulte et velut iuvenili errore exercuit, sed ut tunc quoque dubium nemini foret naturae illa vitia, non aetatis esse' (VI. 26. 1).

85   Orosius, *Seven Books of History*, pp. 334–35. Orosius, *Historiae*: 'Auxit hanc molem facinorum eius temeritas impietatis in Deum. Nam primus Romae Christianos supliciis et mortibus affecit ac per omnes prouincias pari persecutione excruciari imperauit ipsumque nomen exstirpare conatus beatissimos Christi apostolos Petrum cruce, Paulum gladio occidit' (VII. 7. 10).

86   Orosius, *Seven Books of History*, p. 335. Orosius, *Historiae*: 'Mox aceruatim miseram civitatem obortae undique oppressere clades. Nam subsequente autumn tanta Vrbi pestilential incubuit, ut triginata milia funerum in rationem Libitinae uenirent. Britannica deinde clades e uestigio accidit, qua duo praecipua oppida magna ciuium sociorumque clade et caeda direpta sunt. 12 Praeterea in oriente magnis Armeniae prouinciis amissis Romanae sub iugum Parthicum missae, aegreque Syria retenta est. In Asia tres urbes, hoc est Laudicia Hierapolis Colossae, terrae motu conciderunt' (VII. 7. 11–12).

87   See Orosius, *Seven Books of History*, p. 335, n. 98. Suetonius devotes the sixth book of his *De Vita Caesarum* to Nero. After a short account of his childhood and how he became emperor, he first lists his good deeds, and then starting with the twentieth chapter moves on to list his vile deeds: 'Haec partim nulla reprehensione, partim etiam non mediocri laude digna in unum contuli, ut secernerem a probris ac sceleribus eius, de quibus dehinc dicam' (VI. 19. 3). The persecution of Christians is featured alongside Nero infringing on the debaucheries of the chariot drivers and banishing pantomimes from the city: '[A]fflicti supliciis Christiani, genus hominum superstitionis novae ac maleficae [...]' (VI. 16. 2).

the situation in Armenia,[88] and moves the date of the earthquake in comparison to his source (Jerome) so that it now happens after Nero's martyring of Peter and Paul and can thus be seen as a consequence of these transgressions against Christianity.[89] While Orosius does not offer an explanation for why Nero is allowed by the premises of salvation history to commit these crimes against Christianity, he deftly creates a counterweight of causally connected historical occurrences he can present as divinely administered retribution.

Otto's account takes the initial catalogue of Nero's sins almost directly from Orosius,[90] but interpolates one crucial passage in which he aims to explain the reason for the suffering of Christians under Nero's rule:

> To these disgraceful deeds he added impiety towards God: he was the first to institute a persecution of the Christians. This we believe was not done without the design of God, namely that His City might first have a foe of this sort, a foe whom even the city of earth would abhor on account of the crimes involved in his monstrously wicked deeds, a foe to whom nothing seemed dishonorable save honor.[91]

Within the soteriological system of the two cities, Otto reasons that the presentation of such a terrible adversary to the Christians was indeed God's will in order to bring the budding *civitas Dei* closer to the still sinful *civitas terrena* by means of an enemy whose atrocities and vile deeds surpass even what the *civitas terrena* is able to tolerate. He picks up this strand of salvation-historical argument when Nero dies. He narrates his suicide following Orosius's account,[92] but then adds another explanatory passage devised to connect it to a wider salvation-historical framework:

> Yet there were not lacking men [Augustine][93] to say that this which is contained

---

88   See Orosius, *Seven Books of History*, p. 335, n. 101.

89   See ibid., p. 335, n. 104.

90   Otto of Freising, *Chronica*, III. 15, pp. 153–54. Frutolf's account might have been the actual source for Otto. See Otto of Freising, *Chronica; sive, Historia de Duabus Civitatibus*, ed. by Adolf Schmidt and Walther Lammers, Freiherr vom Stein-Gedächtnisausgabe, 16 (Darmstadt, 1990), p. 243, nn. 99–99*.

91   Otto of Freising, *Two Cities*, p. 241. Otto of Freising, *Chronica*: 'His flagitiosissimis factis impietatem in Deum adiecit. Primus enim persecutionem in Christianos movit. Quod non sine consilio Dei factum credimus, ut videlicet civitas sua talem hostem primo haberet, quem ob flagitiorum suorum scelera civitas etiam mundi abhorreret, cui nichil preter honestatem inhonestum videbatur' (III. 15, pp. 153–54).

92   Otto of Freising, *Chronica*: 'Nero, qui audivit in Hyspania Galbam ab exercitu imperatorem factum, animo concidens, cum perturbare rem publicam molitur, a senatu hostis pronunciatur. Videns itaque maliciam suam ad effectum se perducere nin posse, fugiens ad IIIItum ab Urbe lapidem XIIII imperii sui anno se interfecit, in ipsoque familia Cesarum defecit' (III. 16, p. 155). Orosius, *Historiae*: 'at uero Nero postquam Galbam Hispania imperatorem creatum ab exercitu cognouit, totus animo ac spe concidit. Cumque incredibilia perturbandae, immo subruendae reipublicae mala moliretur, hostis a senatu pronuntiatus et ignominiosissime fugiens, ad quartum ab Vrbe lapidem sese ipse interfecit, atque in eo omnis Caesarum familia consumpta est' (VII. 7. 13).

93   Augustine, *De Civitate Dei*: 'Quidam putant hoc de imperio dictum fuisse Romano; et propterea Paulum apostolum non id aperte scribere voluisse, ne calumniam videlicet incurreret, quod Romano imperio male optaverit, cum speraretur aeternum: ut hoc quod dixit; Jam enim mysterium iniquitatis operatur, Neronem voluerit intelligi, cujus jam facta velut Antichristi videbantur. Unde nonnulli ipsum resurrecturum, et futurum Antichristum suspicantur' (xx. 19. 3).

in the writings of the apostle, 'And how ye know that which restraineth, to the end that he may be revealed in his own season,' [II Thessalonians 2. 6] and also, 'He that restraineth, let him restrain until he be taken out of the way,' was spoken of Nero, under whom Paul wrote; and they thought that Nero was not dead but had been withdrawn alive from human affairs until the last day, to appear in that generation which then was, and that he himself would be Antichrist.[94]

Nero is turned into a sort of proto-Antichrist in rapture, which explains why his actions are not only permitted but necessary in the greater plan of Divine Providence. Not only is he evil 'in eo ipso' and striving to destroy the *civitas Dei*;[95] he also has a salvation-historical role to play in the future as the potential adversary of Christ in the Apocalypse.[96] This displays the maximal breadth of salvation-historical argumentation: it ties the tribulations of the present to the biblically asserted future, and turns earthly plights into soteriological preparation for the things to come beyond the horizon of historiography once the eschatological *telos* of salvation has been reached.

The *Kaiserchronik*'s account of Nero echoes the introductions of Orosius and Otto when it characterizes him from the very beginning as 'der aller wirste man | der von muoter in dise werlt ie bekom' (*KC*, 4085–86). There can hardly be any retreating from this apodictic assessment of Nero's vile character. Subsequently, a string of Nero's atrocities is presented, structurally informed by Orosius and enriched with regard to content by legends from various sources.[97] The burning of Rome (*KC*, 4087–4100) is the most famous one, with historiographical validity going back all the way to Suetonius;[98] in the *Kaiserchronik*, it is expanded by Nero having tournaments conducted in the conflagration. The colourful array of vile deeds then continues with Nero's inquisitive killing of his mother (*KC*, 4105–13)

---

94   Otto of Freising, *Two Cities*, pp. 243–44. Otto of Freising, *Chronica*: 'Non defuerunt tamen, qui dicerent hoc quod in apostolo habetur: *Et nunc quid detineat, scitis, donec reveletur in suo tempore,* et illud: *Qui tenet, teneat, donec de medio fiat,* de Nerone, sub quo Paulus scripsit, dictum fuisse, arbitrabanturque Neronem non mortuum, sed humanis rebus vivum substractum usque ad ultimum tempus, in ea, qua tunc fuit, etate appariturum ipsumque Antichristum' (III. 16, p. 155).

95   Ibid.: 'Igitur dum Nero Christianos persequendo civitatem Dei destruere molitur [...].'

96   Revelation 12–14.

97   See Ohly, *Sage und Legende*, pp. 84–88: Ohly identifies Donizo's *c*. 1115 *Vita Mathildis* as the only text older than the *Kaiserchronik* to tell the tale of Nero killing his mother. Moreover, he manages to connect the toad episode to a grammatician's fable about the etymology of the Latin toponym *Lateranum* that can be traced back all the way to the early ninth century but finds its first narrative presentation in the *Kaiserchronik*.

98   Suetonius, *De Vita Caesarum*: 'Nam quasi offensus deformitate veterum aedificiorum et angustiis flexurisque vicorum, incendit urbem tam palam, ut plerique consulares cubicularios eius cum stuppa taedaque in praediis suis deprehensos non attigerint, et quaedam horrea circum domum Auream, quorum spatium maxime desiderabat, ut bellicis machinis labefacta atque inflammata sint, quod saxeo muro constructa erant. 2 Per sex dies septemque noctes ea clade saevitum est ad monumentorum bustorumque deversoria plebe compulsa. Tunc praeter immensum numerum insularum domus priscorum ducum arserunt hostilibus adhuc spoliis adornatae deorumque aedes ab regibus ac deinde Punicis et Gallicis bellis votae dedicataeque, et quidquid visendum atque memorabile ex antiquitate duraverat. Hoc incendium e turre Maecenatiana prospectans laetusque "flammae," ut aiebat, "pulchritudine" Halosin Ilii in illo suo scaenico habitu decantavit' (VI. 38. 1).

and his alchemically induced pregnancy and birth of a toad (*KC*, 4113–54). These bizarre anecdotes of evil are intertwined and tied together by short transitions (e.g. *KC*, 4101–04) and steered toward the apex of Nero's depravity and maledictions: the confrontation of the apostles Peter and Paul with their adversary Simon Magus, and their triumph and subsequent murder at Nero's command (*KC*, 4155–4253). His killing of the two, who are immediately received into heaven as saints (*KC*, 4254–64), seals his fate:

> sîn dinc ergienc im ubele
> nâh dirre marter hêre,
> begunder siechen sêre,
> ze aller êrist von pôdagrâ —
> sô stât gescriben dâ —
> dar nâh von der vergihte,
> dar nâh von miselsuhte;
> ze jungist begunder ze winnen. (*KC*, 4268–75)

Nero's ignoble fate is directly linked causally to his killing of Peter and Paul: God punishes him for the death of his apostles. The miserable death of a figure who is presented in an unfavourable light and eviscerated by repellent and foul-smelling diseases is a frequent motif not only in the *Kaiserchronik* but throughout medieval historiography. By tarnishing the circumstances of the death of the person in question, the chronicles imply a providential punishment for temporal sins that inaugurates damnation beyond the grave. One of the more prominent examples of medieval political thought on the topic that might be of relevance for the *Kaiserchronik* is, as Ohly pointed out,[99] John of Salisbury and his musings on the death of tyrants in his political work, *Policraticus*.[100] Here, he argues that tyrants might work in accordance with God's will — for example Cyrus and Darius, who conquered Babylon[101] — but also that the historical record shows how it is just and honourable to deceive and ultimately kill tyrants who threaten the state.[102] Their deaths are decreed by God according to their rule as either just rulers or malevolent tyrants.[103] Combined with the medieval fear of the *mors peccatorum pessima*, that is to die without final blessing, the last rites, and the forgiving of sins,[104] a powerful narrative tool emerges in the hands of contemporary chroniclers: to illustrate the quality of a historical personality's life, they can render his or her death accordingly.

99 Ohly, *Sage und Legende*, pp. 18–20.

100 John of Salisbury, *Policraticus*, VIII. 18.

101 Ibid.: 'Vnde propheta; Ingedientur portas Babilonis duces, uidelice Cirus et Darius; ego enim mandaui sanctificatis meis et uocaui fortes meos in ire mea et exultantes in gloria mea [Isa. 13,2–3]. Ecce quia sanctificatos uocat Medos et Persas, non quod sancti essent, sed Domini aduersus Babilonem implebant uoluntatem' (VIII. 18, p. 359).

102 Ibid.: 'Ex quibus facile liquebit quia semper tiranno licuit adulari, licuit eum decipere et honestum fuit occidere, si tamen aliter cherceri non poterat' (VIII. 18, p. 364), and 'Sicut ergo dampnatum hostem licet occidere, sic tirannum' (VIII. 19, p. 371).

103 Ibid.: '[...] sed quomodo omnium domuerit tirannidem aut represserit clementia Dei, qui pro decreto iustitiae, quando uult, flagellum inducit in delinquentium penam et, quando uult, quos fecit penitentes admittit ad ueniam' (VIII. 19, p. 371).

104 Olaf Rader, *Friedrich II.: Der Sizilianer auf dem Kaiserthron: Eine Biographie* (Munich, 2010), p. 485.

A grim and miserable death signifies a life marked by debaucheries and sinfulness, and indicates the damnation of the soul.[105]

The *Kaiserchronik* most prominently deploys this narrative schema in the case of the heretic Arius (*KC*, 13,437), who dies on a privy before he can defend his heresy at the Synod of Ephesus because 'daz gewaide was von im gevallen' (*KC*, 13,476–77). Nero's death falls into the same category. Unambiguous signifiers of his damnation caused by his vicious life accompany each step of his passing. The fate of his body after his death illustrates particularly well just how high a price he has to pay for his sins:

> die liute wolten in ûz tragen,
> bi den fuozen zôh man in in den burcgraben.
> Die tievel kômen dar
> mit ainer micheln scar
> in swarzer vogele pilede.
> In ainem michelem genibele
> nâmen si die sêle:
> die helle bûwet si iemer mêre.
> Der lîchname was unraine.
> Die wolfe frâzen sîn gebaine. (*KC*, 4291–4300)

Nero is physically and metaphysically completely eradicated. His soul now dwells eternally in hell, and wolves devour even his mere bones. The gravity of his sins corresponds proportionally to the graphicness of his demise. However compelling the textual representation of Nero's deeds and his ultimate fate in the *Kaiserchronik* are, it must nonetheless be stated that the text does not move beyond the implementation of a simple narrative of just punishment for blatantly sinful behaviour. Salvation-historical problems concerning why Nero is allowed to act in the way he does and what part his actions play in the greater scheme of things are apparently of no concern and of no interest to the *Kaiserchronik*. His punishment appears to happen almost automatically, due to very basic theological premises that are engrained deeply enough in the cultural and theological sphere in which the text was written and received to work, without being actually discussed in the text itself.

It has been demonstrated that the *Kaiserchronik* does not adhere to the parameters of the salvation-historical presentation of history provided by texts such as Orosius's *Historiae adversum Paganos* and Otto's *Chronica*, which display its classic application. The *Kaiserchronik* either shows no interest in the narrative potential and historiographical problems created by salvation-historical expectations with regard to the unfolding of history, or it finds alternative and even idiosyncratic ways to integrate objects of soteriological reference for its own narrative purposes. While this does not exclude the presence of salvation-historical thought in individual episodes, as will be shown below, it can be concluded that salvation history should be disregarded once and for all as an overarching hermeneutical lens for reading the

---

105 The many different renditions of the death of Emperor Frederick II about one hundred years after the *Kaiserchronik* was written exemplify this prominently. See Rader, pp. 486–89.

Kaiserchronik. In general, greater caution should be exercised when using salvation history as a perspective on historical writing. The above analysis has shown that far more is required in order to demonstrate that a text has a salvation-historical structure than merely identifying a vaguely theologically and teleologically charged historiography.

3.1.3. *Contingent and Contained Salvation History: The Sack of Jerusalem*

This is not to say that salvation history does not play any role at all in the *Kaiserchronik*. There are passages that display clear soteriological content. But while they do exist, it is doubtful that they were as formative and productive for the chronicle as the scholarly tradition usually assumes. Nevertheless, this claim remains incomplete until such passages have been duly considered and positioned with regard to the results of the above analysis.

The second part of the already discussed Tiberius episode provides perhaps the most systematically salvation-historical passage of the text: the indicators identified and commented on above as not being present in the text are fully fleshed out here. Biblical prophecy introduces Titus and Vespasian's march on Rome, which is introduced as a metadiegetic allusion to Luke 19. 41–44. Drawing on Christ's lamentation of the things to come for Jerusalem, the *Kaiserchronik* expands the prophetical content of this passage. It aims to prepare the ground for an interpretation of the Roman sack of Jerusalem as fulfilment of New Testament prophecy:

> dâ nâhet in daz zît
> daz in dâ vor gesaget was.
> daz êvangeljum kundet uns daz:
> dô unser hêrre vuor in die burc ze Jerusalêm,
> unt zuo der marter solte gên. (*KC*, 862–66)

Almost every line provides crucial information and creates a sense of historical specificity and textual focus that is otherwise largely absent from the chronicle. Line 862 sets the stage for prophetic fulfilment; the following lines specify the source of the prophecy to be fulfilled. The personal pronoun 'in' (third-person dative plural) is used twice to clearly target the prophecy at the Jews, and contrasts with the first-person dative plural 'uns', which indicates the audience of the prophecy: the object and the witnesses of salvation-historical fulfilment become linguistically separated from each other. Lines 865–66 situate the utterance of the prophecy clearly in time and space: Jerusalem, shortly before Jesus arrives there on Palm Sunday to set in motion the events leading to the crucifixion five days later. These lines help both to localize the events referred to in the biblical memory of the audience and to create a salvation-historical vantage point that imparts meaning to the following passages.

> die stat er an sah,
> daz wort er wainende sprach:[106]
> 'Owî kint von Jerusalêm,
> waz iu ze laide muoz geschehen!

---

106 Almost verbatim from the Bible: 'Et ut adpropinquavit videns civitatem flevit super illam dicens' (Luke 19. 41).

> wainet niht mînen tôt:
> mîn vater hât iz von himel alsô geordenôt.
> ir meget wol wainen diu dinc
> die her nâh kunftic sint. (*KC*, 873–80)

Prophecy is now complemented by divine predestination. The future to which the text refers is not the crucifixion, as is suggested by the language of line 877, but the events about to unfold in the primary narrative of the Tiberius episode. When Jesus refers to God as 'mîn vater' (*KC*, 878), he actualizes the main point of friction between Judaism and Christianity and then clarifies that the suffering of the Jews is preordained. Jesus's prophecy permeates several layers of time. Metadiegetically situated in the biblical past, he nevertheless verbalizes the assumed biblical knowledge of a twelfth-century audience, thus providing a transition from two firmly established spheres of knowledge into the primary diegesis of the events leading to the sack of Jerusalem in 70 BCE. This temporal intersection is exemplified by the three layers of weeping in the text. Jesus himself is 'wainende' (*KC*, 874) when he denounces the lamenting of his passing by the Jews that is yet to come (*KC*, 877). He extends his lamentation forward to the sack of Jerusalem in 70 CE, where his prophecy and the audience's reception of the text are about to converge and where the crying of the Jews will be more appropriate (*KC*, 880).

The last lines of the *Kaiserchronik*'s paraphrase of Christ's prophecy could almost have been taken directly from Luke's biblical record, in which the impending doom of Israel is causally linked to the Jews' refusal or failure to recognize Jesus as their foretold Messiah:

> ir werdet zevuoret,
> allez iwer geslehte zestôret,
> iwer salbe sâme in Israhêle
> engesamenôt sih niemer mêre;
> want ir des zîtes niht erkantet
> dô iu got fride zu hûs sante.[107] (*KC*, 886–73)

The excursus from Tiberius's age back into Jesus's lifetime comes to an end with a final assertion of the fulfilment of biblical prophecy in historical events about to occur: 'Diu gotes wort wurden wâr' (*KC*, 897).

The following accounts of Josephus's miraculous escape and the Romans' conquering and razing of the city are repeatedly infused with commenting excursuses that erect a cohesive explanatory background — something otherwise exceedingly rare in the *Kaiserchronik* — that clearly points to the salvation-historical meaning of the depicted events. The mass suicide is depicted as another factor legitimating the divine retribution about to be meted out by the Romans (*KC*, 1002–08). In this instance, the *Kaiserchronik* fully subscribes to the salvation-historical concept that the

---

107 Compare the Bible: 'Quia si cognovisses et tu et quidem in hac die tua quae ad pacem tibi nunc autem abscondita sunt ab oculis tuis quia venient dies in te et circumdabunt te inimici tui vallo et circumdabunt te et coangustabunt te undique ad terram prosternent te et filios qui in te sunt et non relinquent in te lapidem super lapidem eo quod non cognoveris tempus visitationis tuae' (Luke 19. 42–44).

fall of Jerusalem marks a pivotal moment that divides history into a before — 'da vôr' (*KC*, 1004) — in which the Jews are the beloved people of God and an after in which they have lost this position. According to this logic, the destruction of Jerusalem becomes nothing but the belated final act and concluding chapter of Old Testament history. Up to this point, salvation history has been understood as the history of the Jewish people being congruent with the history of God's presence and revelations in his creation.[108] Now, with this position out of the way, the Christians can succeed.

After the Romans storm the city, the text underlines the replacement of the Jews by the Christians as God's chosen carriers of salvation-historical responsibility. Through repeated use of the adverb 'ê', it illustrates the total reduction of the Hebrews from their former position in God's favour and *in extenso* as carriers of historical semantics and soteriological teleology:

> die ê wâren chuone
> die wurden alle blôde,
> die ê wâren siges helede
> die wurden alle fremede;
> der schalke werc si worhten
> die man ê vorhte.
> [...]
> duo wurden die gesceiden
> di der ê wâren heime. (*KC*, 1055–66)

After this, the *Kaiserchronik* invokes the 'althêrren' (*KC*, 1068), the paragons of the soteriologically still relevant *alte ê* like Saul, Jonathan, David, and Salomon, but transposes the heritage of their authority to the Christians: 'von ir wîsheit | frouwet sih noh diu cristenheit' (*KC*, 1073–74). The text concludes this salvation-historical commentary with a final explication of the Hebrews' fall from God's grace:

> jâ stuont diu stat ze Jerusalêm
> mit michelen êren
> unz si merterten unsern hêrren:
> do nemaht ir hêrscefte niemer sîn. (*KC*, 1080–83)

The transgression against the Son of God facilitates the epochal shift. In the end, the surviving Hebrews are carried away in chains to be sold as slaves and to take up the societal place the medieval audience knows them to hold in their own time: an uprooted, marginalized diaspora.

> wie maht in iemer wirs gescehen?
> in ze laster unt ze scanden.
> si sint in fremeden landen
> unz an den jungisten tac,
> daz in niemen gehelfen mac. (*KC*, 1100–04)

In the last lines of the episode, the text picks up the topical helplessness of the Hebrews, introduced during Jesus's prophecy at its beginning ('iu kumt der tac |

---

108 See von Campenhausen, p. 37.

daz niemen dem anderem gehelfen mac'; *KC*, 881–82). With this, it closes a frame that emphasizes the preordained nature of the divine retribution that is visited upon the Hebrews. Simultaneously, it projects the temporal duration of their suffering as far as the soteriological end of history itself, the 'jungisten tac'.

To summarize, when it comes to the soteriological fate of the Hebrews, the *Kaiserchronik* proves itself quite capable of marshalling the narrative tools of salvation history — biblical prophecy, divinely preordained retribution, exacted fulfilment, eschatological perspective, and the concomitant historical commentary. Taken together, they display a historiographical awareness unique to the second part of the Tiberius episode. But the retributive logic of the passage on the sack of Jerusalem does not have any effect beyond the Tiberius episode. It does not inform other episodes or help to construct an overarching soteriological argument running through the rest of the *Kaiserchronik*.

Comparing the text's version with its sources sheds light not only on the indebtedness of salvation-historical elements to the source traditions but also on what the *Kaiserchronik* lacks in order to be a cohesive salvation-historical narrative. The notion that Jesus's prophecy according to Luke was fulfilled in the events of 70 CE had entered Christian historical conceptions at an early stage. Starting with Hegesippus as mediated by Eusebius, a long line of Christian apologists from Justin Martyr to Tertullian used this historical fact as a signifier for the truth of the Christian message and the supersession of the old Judaic covenant by the new Christian one.[109] From historiography the idea found its way into the late sixth-century homilies of Gregory the Great and the Venerable Bede. Ohly believes that the concept as it is presented in the *Kaiserchronik* is firmly rooted in contemporary sermons like, for example, those by Honorius Augustodunensis. Moreover, both the memory of the fall of Jerusalem and the potential for its polemical exploitation find their space in the Christian year in the sermons for the tenth Sunday after Trinity.[110]

The second part of the Tiberius episode, which tells of Vespasian and Titus's sacking of Jerusalem, owes much to Flavius Josephus's account of the Jewish War. Josephus is held in high regard by the author of the *Kaiserchronik*, as he praises his didactic quality as a source (*KC*, 1041–44). This explicit appreciation of an author whose text directly or indirectly influenced the *Kaiserchronik*'s historical account is unique.[111] It is later echoed by Pope Silvester in the Constantine episode, when he utilizes Josephus's established authority to refute a polemic argument during his disputation with the wise Jewish men (*KC*, 8693–95).

Two episodes — the collective Jewish mass suicide (*KC*, 965–1001) and the desperate mother who kills and cooks her own child (*KC*, 909–60) — originate in

109 See von Campenhausen, pp. 36–37. For more on the early role of the fall of Jerusalem in Christian writing, see Heinz-Martin Döpp, *Die Deutung der Zerstörung Jerusalems und des Zweiten Tempels im Jahre 70 in den ersten drei Jahrhunderten n. Chr.*, Texte und Arbeiten zum neutestamentlichen Zeitalter, 24 (Tübingen, 2002).
110 See Ohly, *Sage und Legende*, p. 58.
111 Ohly, ibid., pp. 60–61, suspects several layers of intermediate transmission, in particular an array of homilies since the ninth century: Haymo of Halberstadt, Radulphus Ardens, Honorius Augustodunensis, Werner of St Blase, and Sicard of Cremona.

Josephus, and the rest of the sack of Jerusalem is largely constructed on the basis of Josephus's account of events.[112]

From the other longer narrative sources Ohly had identified for the Veronica legend and the Tiberius episode as a whole,[113] only the *Vindicta Salvatoris* seems to have informed the second part, albeit to a limited extent.[114] This seventh- or eighth-century text originated in Aquitaine and is one of the Latin revenge legends that took shape as demotic interpretations of history to create a satisfying sense of retribution for the murder of Christ by the Jews among their audiences.[115] Indeed, in the *Vindicta Salvatoris* the logic of retribution is so persuasive that even the Jews themselves subscribe to it. They accept their death as a punishment, which leads some of them to kill themselves and others to subject themselves to the judgement of Vespasian and Titus, demanding: 'Judge for us how we ought to die, because we delivered Christ to death.'[116] The text is very explicit in developing motifs surrounding the death of Jesus Christ into prophetic and typological connections to the events surrounding the sack of Jerusalem.

> And they went down into Judea and came into Jerusalem and seized your kings and sent them to judgement, so saying: 'Just as they did with Christ, so also let us do to them. They hung our Lord on a green tree and let us hang them on a dry tree; they killed Him without fault and let us kill them with the foulest death; they took his tunic and divided it into four parts and let us rent them into four parts and give their bodies to the beasts of the earth and birds of the air; they sold Christ for thirty silver pieces and we give thirty of them for one piece of silver and let their names be obliterated from the earth.[117]

Here, in Volusianus's account to Tiberius, Vespasian and Titus deliberately devise the atrocities that they are going to inflict upon the Jews in Jerusalem as inverted mirror images of the circumstances of Christ's death.

Another motif that runs through the *Vindicta Salvatoris* is the Christians' repeated proclamation that their redeemer lives. This is most prominently performed by Veronica: 'And I shall worship Him and serve Him as long as I live because He, my Redeemer, lives and I shall see God, my Saviour on the last day.'[118] She

---

112 *Judean War*, III. 359, VI. 207. Ohly, *Sage und Legende*, p. 62, lists more texts transmitting this tradition.

113 The *Curia Sanitatis Tiberii*, the *Vindicta Salvatoris*, and the Latin prose Pilate. See Ohly, *Sage und Legende*, pp. 54–56.

114 See ibid., p. 60.

115 See Heinz Schreckenberg, *Die christlichen Adversus-Judaeos-Texte und ihr literarisches und historisches Umfeld*, Europäische Hochschulschriften: Reihe XXIII, 172 (Frankfurt a. M., 1990), pp. 463–64.

116 *Vindicta Salvatoris*, 15–17, pp. 266–70, esp. 'Iudicate nobis quomodo mori debemus quia Christum ad morte tradidimus' (18); translations are from the edition.

117 Ibid.: 'Descenderuntque in Iudeam et uenerunt in Hierosolimam, adprehenderunt reges tuos es miserunt eos in iudicio, ita dicentes: "Quomodo fecereunt de Christo, ita es nnos faciamus illos. Suspenderunt dominum nostrum in lignum uiride, et nos suspendemus eos in arido; occiderunt ille sine culpe, et nos occidamus illos morte turpissima; acceperunt tonciam eius et fecerunt de ea partes .IIII., et nos scindamus eos in quattuor partes et damus carnes illorum bestiis terre et uolatilibus caeli; uendiderunt Christum .XXX. argentos, et nos damus pro uno argenteo .XXX. ex illis et deleantur nomina illorum de terra"' (30–31, p. 290).

118 Ibid.: 'Et ego adorabo eum et seruiam ei usque dum uiua sum quia ipse, redemptor meus, uiuit

echoes Volusianus's previous exclamation upon first setting eyes on the shroud of Veronica,[119] and Joseph of Arimathea's confession of his belief in the bodily resurrection on Judgement Day.[120] The threefold repetition of the same phrase by exemplary Christians shows a clear concern to pursue a salvation-historical shaping of the text's account. In these expressions, Christian certainty of resurrection and eternal life, both for Christ and for oneself, is intertwined and projected toward the eschatological future. Both the death of Christ and the sack of Jerusalem are interpreted as historical events with an eschatological unfolding, thus marking the text's salvation-historical trajectory. Similar notions are expressed in the *Kaiserchronik*, but they do not feature in the same structural form and remain contained within the source-bound premises of discrete episodes like the Tiberius episode.

In a sense, Heinrich von Veldeke's *Eneasroman*, written twenty to thirty years after the *Kaiserchronik*, is more of a salvation-historical narrative. After Heinrich's narrative has found its diegetic conclusion with the great celebration of the wedding and coronation of Eneas and Lavinia (*ER*, 344. 5–347. 9), the narrator cannot bring himself to stop. The historical role of his material as a prequel to the foundation of Rome demands that the story should be carried on. From Eneas the text speeds through the rule of his sons, Ascanius and Silvius Eneas, in Alba Longa (*ER*, 350. 2–33) to Silvius's descendants Romulus and Remus (*ER*, 350. 34–351. 9), quickly referencing the foundation of Rome, fast-forwarding to Caesar, his conquests, and his assassination (*ER*, 351. 11–26), and finally concluding with Augustus and his just and peaceful reign:

> do vil wol waren behuot
> wittewen vnd waisen
> von vnrechten fraisen,
> von arme vnd reiche. (*ER*, 351. 27–30)

The role of these auspicious circumstances is of course — as in Otto or Orosius — to introduce the incarnation of Christ:

> bî des zîten wart der gotes sun
> geboren ze Bethelehêm,
> der sint gemartert wart ze Jersalêm
> uns allen ze trôste,
> wander uns erlôste
> ûz der freislîchen nôt,
> wandern êwigen tôt
> mit sînem tôde ersterbete,
> den Âdâm an uns erbete.
> alsô hât her uns erlôst.
> daz is uns ein michel trôst,
> ob wirz selbe behalden. (*ER*, 352. 2–13)

et in nouissimo die uidebo Deum saluatorem meum' (26, p. 284).

119 Ibid.: 'Viuit dominus et uiuit anima mea' (24, p. 280).

120 Ibid.: 'Et ego credo quod ipse redemptor meus uiuit, et in nouissimo die de terra surrecturus sim, et in carne mea uidebo ipsum Deum saluatorem meum' (21, p. 276).

On his tour d'horizon through history from Eneas to Augustus, Heinrich von Veldeke follows the same lines as the *Kaiserchronik* lays out in its pre-episodic part and early episodes, but — unlike in the *Kaiserchronik* — the apogee toward which Heinrich's narrative is targeted is the incarnation. The birth of Christ might be completely irrelevant for the diegetic world of Eneas, Lavinia, and Turnus, but to firmly anchor his text in the Christian present's cultural axioms he has to extend it on the salvation-historical axis through Roman history up to the fulfilment of God's salvific promise.[121]

3.2. From Pagan to Christian Rome

3.2.1. Christian Conversion

3.2.1.1. Early Contacts with Christianity: Tiberius, Faustinian, and Philip

The process of qualitative change affecting the religious identity of the Roman Empire is a process of conversion, and for long stretches the *Kaiserchronik* can be read as a history of conversion from pagan polytheism to Christianity and the formation of the Christian identity of the Empire. The *Kaiserchronik* develops certain episodes into important signposts along the way: from the city of pagan temples and statues in the review of the pagan week or the Gaius episode; to the first imperial brushes with Christianity in the Tiberius, Faustinian, and Philip episodes; to the persecutions by Nero, Decius, and Diocletian; on to the full onslaught of official imperial conversion under Constantine and Silvester; and through the retarding interlude from Julian to Theodosius, whose reign marks the end of the linear and teleological conversion to Christianity in the *Kaiserchronik*. The section on continuity in chapter 1 has already done much to set up the starting point from which the gradual process of Christianization is launched in the *Kaiserchronik*:[122] the pagan gods were demons all along, and the pagans' worship of their idols is ultimately nothing but a fraud set up by devils to corrupt the pagans. To arrive in the Christian present of the twelfth century, the *Kaiserchronik* now has to introduce a momentum of conversion that transforms the thoroughly pagan Rome into a Christian place.

The curious disinterest in the incarnation of Christ and his life and deeds has already been pointed out.[123] It is not Christ's birth, life, death, or resurrection that puts Christianity on the narrative map of the *Kaiserchronik* but — as befits the emphasis on the historical continuity of the Roman Empire — Christianity's first contact with imperial authority in the Tiberius episode. Tiberius's healing elicits great rejoicing from the Romans (*KC*, 836–38), and he speaks of Christ as the *hêrre* (*KC*, 851) of whom the Jews have unlawfully robbed them. So, even though

---

121 For more on salvation-historical patterns in Heinrich von Veldeke's *Eneasroman*, see Karen Opitz, *Geschichte im höfischen Roman: Historiographisches Erzählen im Eneas Heinrichs von Veldeke*, Beihefte zur Germanisch-Romanischen Monatsschrift, 14 (Heidelberg, 1996). pp. 199–216. Also, slightly dated: Marie-Luise Dittrich, *Die Eneide Heinrichs von Veldeke: Quellenkritischer Vergleich mit dem Roman d'Eneas und Vergils Aeneis*, 2 vols (Wiesbaden, 1966), I, 560–64.

122 See 1.2.1 in this book.

123 See 3.1.2.2 in this book.

Tiberius's conversion to Christianity is not made explicit, as it is in the source material from the *Vindicta Salvatoris*,[124] the language he uses, which includes him in the collective deprived of their Lord, strongly implies it.

The first time Christianity appears as a collective in the diegetic historical paradigm of the *Kaiserchronik* is two episodes later, in the Faustinian episode, when it is pointed out that Zachary had been sent to Greece by St Peter 'der christenheit ze trôste' (*KC*, 1476).[125] It is not entirely clear whether this indicates an already existing Christian community there that — presumably assailed by persecution by the Roman authorities — is supported by Zachary's new monastery, or whether this is not rather to be understood as a more general statement about the monastery's beatific presence and function for the sake of Christianity. Both the nascent Christianity of the first century and the contemporary Christianity of the twelfth century as part of a universal and transhistorical Christian world could be covered by this statement. But the explicit establishment of Christianity as a converting and proselytizing movement is — like Zachary's mission to Greece — firmly tied to St Peter, the '[g]runtveste der christenheit' (*KC*, 2465). During his first disputation with Simon Magus, Peter relates the core of the apostolic mission he embodies:

> unser hêrre der heilant
> hât sîne jungere in die werlt gesant
> ze toufen unt ze lêren,
> die heiden ze bechêren. (*KC*, 2247–51)

The narrator later confirms that Peter is doing just that and also curing the infirm from leprosy and palsy and raising the dead (*KC*, 4043–54). The Christian mission and miracle-working permeate Peter's actions throughout the Faustinian episode, which develops him into the main protagonist in contrast to the most important sources, the Latin Pseudo-Clementine *Recognitiones* and the *Vita Clementi*, which both, as their titles suggest, focus on Clement.[126] Peter's mission is presented most prominently in certain individual acts of baptism, for example when he heals the old woman who took Faustinian's unrecognized wife Mechthild into care after her shipwreck (*KC*, 2857–74).

One of the first clashes between newly baptized Christians and pagan Roman polytheists is staged when a group of 'koufliute von Rôme' (*KC*, 1770) travel to Jerusalem, where they become Christians, and return to Rome in the company of Barnabas, who has been commissioned by Peter to bring the gospel to Rome

---

124 *Vindicta Salvatoris*: 'Credidit ille et baptizatus est et omnis domus eius tota' (35, p. 292).

125 See Ohly, *Sage und Legende*, p. 82. There are earlier instances of the lexemes *christen* (in *KC*, 199) and *christenheit* (in *KC*, 1074), but in both cases they point toward the universally accepted Christianity of the twelfth-century present and say little about the state of Christianity in the early episodes of the *Kaiserchronik*.

126 See Ohly, *Sage und Legende*, pp. 78–82. Ohly had doubts about whether the author of the Faustinian episode had any other sources than the *Vita*, but Hans Fromm showed that the author must in fact have had recourse to the *Recognitiones*, as only they and not the *Vita* provide the Simon Magus material in the way the *Kaiserchronik* processes it ('Die Disputationen in der Faustinianlegende der "Kaiserchronik": Zum literarischen Dialog im 12. Jahrhundert', in *Deutsche Literatur und Sprache von 1050–1200*, ed. by Fiebig and Schiewer, pp. 51–69 (p. 53)).

(*KC*, 1798). Their interaction, upon their arrival back home, with the Romans they encounter in a 'dinchûs' (*KC*, 1830) and who press them for news from Jerusalem (*KC*, 1828–37) is depicted in the text as a call-and-response exchange. Each proclamation of the 'koufman' (*KC*, 1838, 1844, 1858) is answered by the 'Rômære' (*KC*, 1842, 1856, 1868). The merchants, who had been introduced as 'von Rôme', and were still called 'Rômære' as long as they were not actually back in Rome (*KC*, 1826), suddenly find themselves in opposition to their compatriots as they re-enter the city. The qualitative marker that now divides them is religion. The merchants have undergone a qualitative change and become Christians. Their Christianity does not suspend their Romanness, but their confrontation with other Romans does. The Romans answer the Christianized merchants' praise of Christ's wondrous qualities and deeds in a tripartite progression of acknowledgment: first with disbelief (*KC*, 1843), then conceding that Jesus must have been a 'guot arzât' (*KC*, 1857), and finally announcing that Jesus 'einem ir gote gelîch wære' (*KC*, 1869). They do not, however, arrive at the desired conclusion, which is recognizing Christ's new monotheistic position, so Barnabas has to intervene (*KC*, 1872–1902), trying to convince them of Christ's singular and divine nature, which results in angry responses from the Romans and finally in Barnabas and the merchants being kicked out of the 'dinchûs' (*KC*, 1904). The polytheists are only capable of gradually conceding Christ's special properties, but stay firmly within the premises of their pagan worldview to rationalize them as the traits of a skilled physician or of just another god. The merchants, by contrast, moved past these epistemological limitations when they allowed themselves to be Christianized by the evidence that Lazarus gave them when they came to Bethany (*KC*, 1791–97).

In the end, even Emperor Faustinian is baptized by Peter, when the latter reunites him with his sons and with his wife and presents it as a true miracle from God (*KC*, 3931–34). However, Faustinian's conversion does not occasion much of an effect on the religious constitution of the Empire, as he and his wife almost immediately afterward gift all their estates in Rome to Peter and then take holy vows to withdraw into a monastery (*KC*, 4035–37). Faustinian's brother and successor, Claudius, whose transgressions against Faustinian's wife initiated the entire narrative, quickly falls under the sway of Peter's antagonist Simon Magus, who advises the emperor to bar Peter from ever entering Rome again (*KC*, 4067–72). Faustinian's conversion thus remains contained on a personal level, and the Christian mission remains limited to the activities of Peter and his companions. The Empire and the Romans remain pagan. They do not resent and ultimately poison Claudius because he suppresses Christianity but because he falls in with a wizard and because he fornicates with their women (*KC*, 4073–82).

As well as the introduction of conversion, the *Kaiserchronik* also lays down some basic tenets of Christian dogma as a way of introducing the new and still-struggling religion. This happens mostly but not exclusively in the two disputations taken from source material and included in the *Kaiserchronik*. The first disputation, between St Peter and Simon Magus in a *dinchûs* in Caesarea, concerns the nature of God and Christ and negotiates — perhaps unwittingly — the clash of orthodox and Gnostic

Christian concepts in the earliest days of the Church.[127] The second disputation
— the *wîlsælde* disputation — happens between the unrecognized Faustinian, who
confronts Peter, and the latter's young companions, who are Faustinian's long-lost
and likewise unrecognized sons. They debate whether fate is determined by stars
and planets or rather by man's choice to lead either a virtuous or a wicked life. Some
of the more salient dogmatic points: Christ wishes Christians to drive out evil and
reap souls for him (*KC*, 1898–1902); separation of family is good if done following
the will of God (*KC*, 2282–2308); God rules alone and is all-powerful, angels are
subordinate to him (*KC*, 2385–2424); idle hands are sinful (*KC*, 2637–46); Christ is
the beginning and the end, his mercy fills the earth (*KC*, 2939–48); Christ as creator
and redeemer (*KC*, 2976–84); Christ is a gatherer of souls (*KC*, 3024–27); whoever
teaches God's truth will be rewarded with eternal life in God's kingdom (*KC*,
3133–51); God is onefold, without beginning or end, and indivisible, indestructible,
and therefore eternal (*KC*, 3241–69); God as omnipotent creator and protector of
the world, virtues, and all goodness (*KC*, 3292–3301); man has to decide whether to
surrender his soul to God or face damnation (*KC*, 3359–74); nothing exists without
God, but men are free to do either good or evil (*KC*, 3413–54).

One passage during the *wîlsælde* disputation in particular sheds an intriguing light
on Christianity as a conceptually and qualitatively new religion in the historical
logic of the *Kaiserchronik*. The old man (Faustinian unrecognized) claims that all
events in a man's life are ordained by *wîlsælde* — fate — as determined by the hour
of his birth and by the movements of the 'septem planêtê' (*KC*, 3544) and that
there is no escaping this (*KC*, 3514–54). He cites Pythagoras as the authority for
the astronomical underpinnings of his argument, and scolds his opponent Aquila
(unbeknown to Faustinian, one of his sons) for not having applied himself enough
to have a sufficient grasp of astronomy to understand his point (*KC*, 3532–33).
As with his earlier statement that his opponents should choose their arguments
according to their ability from the 'siben listen frîen' (*KC*, 3201), Faustinian anchors
his argument firmly in the context of ancient erudition and philosophical learning.
Aquila responds to this with a historical reference:

> Unser althêrren
> flizzen sih hie vor verre,
> daz si ettelîh wunder vur brêhten,
> dâ man ir iemer bî gedêhte;
> philosophi gwisse vunden
> wîle unde stunde,
> duo der hêrre Pytagoras
> in di hôhe der himele maz,
> daz wâren grôze sinne,
> sô menniske niht bezzers mahten vinden.
> si wâren alle wîse genuoch. (*KC*, 3563–73)

With 'hie vor' and the reference back to their shared 'althêrren', Aquila's speech
creates historical distance between the time they are inhabiting right now and the
time of the creation of the arts and sciences by the 'althêrren', among them the

authority Pythagoras, whom Faustinian had brought up earlier. Their discoveries are 'wunder' that surpass all human invention. The verbs *vinden* and *vurbringen* are used to characterize the human activity that creates new knowledge. While *vinden* implies the finding of something that is already there, *vurbringen* marks the completion of a finite process. Both verbs indicate that the humans of the past have in their erudition fully mapped out the space that human ingenuity can hope to subject to discovery. It allows no more space or time for further progress, as expressed in line 3572, which points to the impossibility of expanding these discoveries in the future. Thus, the only way to turn is to the creator behind the phenomena that human ingenuity subjected to the arts and sciences.

> der aver den wîstuom truoch,
> daz himel und erde gescaffen wart,
> und alle di werlt in sînem tenre beslozzen hât,
> dem die engel lobent in dem himele,
> und elliu sîn gescaft hie nidere
> vurhtet unt êret;
> unde die er selbe denne hât gelêret,
> unt in eroffenet hât sîne tougen,
> dem sculn wir mêr glouben
> ir lêre sculn wir vesten unde tragen. (*KC*, 3574–82)

Aquila reveals that God is not only the creator of all the elements ('himel und erde') that human ingenuity has strived to describe and to measure, but also that he is the mediator of the knowledge ('er selbe [...] hât gelêret') needed for this. The intellectual achievement of the 'philosophi' (*KC*, 3567) in the first part of Aquila's speech is contrasted to God's creative work. But this contrast does not imply mutual exclusion, but rather the envelopment and strengthening of one by the other. Belief in God can in turn confirm and maintain 'ir lêre', with 'ir' referring back to both the 'philosophi' and to God's 'gescaft' (*KC*, 3578), which of course fall together. In short: after human ingenuity has expanded as far as conceivably possible in the physical world, it can now only turn to God to gain any further insights into the metaphysical world that lies beyond the temporal creation. This turns the introduction of Christianity not only into a qualitative change in religious identity but also into the breaking of an epistemological barrier hitherto impenetrable by human intellectual enquiry.

After the arguments of Niceta and Aquila have left the old man unmoved, Faustinian's youngest son, Clement, who is also unrecognized by his father and in turn does not recognize him, challenges the old man's pagan religious practice, pointing out that it is inconsistent to believe that all events in life are preordained by the movements of the stars while at the same time making sacrifices to the gods in the hope of bettering one's lot on earth (*KC*, 3681–3700, 3744–60). Faustinian's initial response provides valuable insights into the medieval imagining of ancient pagan practice: Faustinian concedes that sometimes the gods treated him well and sometimes ill (*KC*, 3701–04). Bringing sacrifices to the gods is described as a demand of 'unser ê' (*KC*, 3705). While 'unser' sets the pagans apart as a collective constituted by law and custom from the Christians, who are represented by

Faustinian's opponents, 'ê' characterizes religious observance as a lawful duty. In the Christian context, *ê* is of course mainly used as a term for the two Testaments of the Bible, but it can also describe the norm and the form of religious belief.[128] Of the gods that Faustinian mentions, most are already familiar from earlier episodes (Mars, Mercury, Jupiter, Venus, Saturn; *KC*, 3709–42); others are introduced for the first time (e.g. Luna; *KC*, 3706–08). Believing in them is a question of *erkennen* (*KC*, 3681–84), just as it is for the Christian God (*KC*, 74, 739, 3019, 8184). The language that marks the practice of both monotheistic Christianity and pagan polytheism overlaps significantly. Since these indicators do not point toward a qualitative difference between the two belief systems, that must be sought instead in the content of religious practice as sketched during the disputation. And indeed, as is to be expected, pagan polytheism does not compare well to Christianity. Faustinian's list mainly adheres to one simple pattern: naming the god, specifying what is sacrificed to the god, and why. There is a simple transactional relation implied: the god is offered sacrifice in exchange for support, protection, or blessing. The virtuousness of the gods is centred on them and has no moral implications for their followers (*KC*, 3739–42). There is no consideration of ethical or social concerns, and also no uneasiness about the lack thereof.[129] The relationship is purely individual and limited to the contractual exchange mechanisms enacted in sacrifice and reward. This reduced representation resonates with earlier Christian polemics and critical representations of pagan polytheist veneration. For example, when Eusebius describes Constantine's considerations over which god to turn to in order to acquire their help:

> He sought a god to be his helper and depended on the soldiers and size of his army only in second place. For he thought that that was of no use anyway without the help of a god. He considered the divine aid to be invincible and unconquerable. So now he thought seriously about which god he should enlist as a helper, and it crossed his mind that most previous rulers had put their hopes in several gods when they came to power and had worshipped them with offerings of wine, sacrifices and votive offerings.[130]

This leads us to Emperor Philip. While on the one hand Tiberius's conversion is only implied, and Faustinian's conversion is immediately contained, Philip on the other hand is explicitly introduced as the first Christian ruler (*KC*, 6099–6101).[131] Considering the circumstances of the conversions of Tiberius and Faustinian, this statement can be considered as accurate within the *Kaiserchronik*'s imperial paradigm and not just in regard to the classical source tradition, which conventionally

128 See Lexer, s.v. *êwe* (I, cols 715–16).
129 See Ramsay MacMullen, *Christianizing the Roman Empire: A.D. 100–400* (New Haven, 1984), p. 13.
130 Translation from Sam Lieu, 'Constantine's "Pagan Vision": The Anonymous Panegyric on Constantine (310): Pan. Lat. VII(6): Introduction', in *From Constantine to Julian: Pagan and Byzantine Views*, ed. by Samuel Lieu and Dominic Montserrat (London, 1996), pp. 63–76 (p. 73). Eusebius of Caesarea, *De Vita Constantini: Über das Leben Konstantins*, ed. by Bruno Bleckmann, trans. by Horst Schneider, Fontes Christiani, 83 (Turnhout, 2007), I. 27–28.
131 See 1.1.4 in this book.

introduces Philip as the first Christian emperor.[132] He also has Pope Sixtus baptize his son, and together they do their best to 'bekêren | getoufen unde gelêren' (KC, 6107–08) as many pagans as possible. It is their Christianity that raises the ire of Decius, a 'fraislîch man' (KC, 6115). He cannot stand the prospect of 'dehainer slahte cristen' (KC, 6119) ruling the Empire, and so proceeds to kill father and son and their entourage in their palace. As Ohly has pointed out, this marks a new element in the tradition motivating Decius's later persecution of Christians, which had until then mainly been traced back to political antagonism.[133] The confrontation is framed in a remarkable passage of rhyming couplets that — in alternating parallelisms carrying contrasting pairs — contrast Philip's virtuousness with Decius's wickedness:

> Dêcius mit menige,
> der cunic mit venie;
> Dêcius mit gewæfen,
> der cunic mit almuosen;
> Dêcius mit gewalte,
> der cunic mit ainvalte;
> Dêcius mit grimme,
> der cunic mit guoter minne;
> Dêcius mit sêre,
> der cunic wegete sîner sêle. (KC, 6133–42)

The passage is one of the few strongly formally crafted passages in the text, which appear only on a handful of occasions, for example in the anaphoric doxology on the virtues of Charlemagne (KC, 15,075–83). Ohly connected this specific form of anaphoric antitheses to the sermons of Honorius Augustodunensis.[134] Philip's virtues here — 'mit almuosen', 'mit ainvalte', 'mit guoter minne' — are of course decidedly Christian in nature. The sermon form complements the content. Together with the christening of his son and his work to convert as many pagans as possible, these virtues are Philip's only defining qualities, yet the text singles him out, because of his role as the first Christian king, to receive this treatment. Unlike his antagonist Decius, Philip is not referred to by his given name but by his title, 'cunic', as if to emphasize the circumstance that he is indeed the first Christian king. The new motivational structure behind Decius's persecutions becomes more amplified when he decrees that 'nehain cristen' (KC, 6159) should remain in Rome under his reign. And it is the continued Christian work of Pope Sixtus, who 'die haiden lêrte, | toufte und bekêrte' (KC, 6167–68) — the same three activities that previously marked Philip's reign and Peter's travels through the Empire — that triggers the string of martyrdoms that the Kaiserchronik presents in the rest of the Decius episode.

132 See Ohly, Sage und Legende, p. 128. The historiographical tradition of identifying Philip the Arab as the first Christian emperor goes back to Eusebius's Historia Ecclesiastica and later Jerome's Chronicon, and was also promulgated by Orosius in his Adversum Paganos. Launching from these widely read and available texts, the idea became a staple of medieval Christian historiography between the fifth and eighth century CE.
133 Ohly, Sage und Legende, p. 129.
134 Ibid., p. 130.

3.2.1.2. Imperial Conversion: Constantine and Silvester

After emperors like Tiberius, Faustinian, or Philip have established preliminary points of contact between the Empire and Christianity, the actual conversion of the Romans to Christianity comes upon the Empire under Constantine. Without any causal integration or diegetic trigger, Constantine's personal conversion begins with a misunderstanding. Suffering from a great 'siehtuom' (*KC*, 7814), and having rejected cures he has deemed immoral (*KC*, 7818–41), in his sleep Constantine receives a divine vision of St Peter and St Paul. As a pagan (*KC*, 7810), he does not recognize them, but they appeal to him to turn to Pope Silvester as his 'gaistlîch vater' (*KC*, 7857) in order to be cured of his ailment. When Constantine sends his messengers to Silvester, both pope and emperor are initially confused about the implications of the meeting Constantine asks for. The pope rejoices, believing his time for martyrdom has come (*KC*, 7876–79), while the emperor believes that Silvester must be some sort of 'arzât' (*KC*, 7885). Why else would the two wise men from his vision have pointed Silvester out to him as a way of becoming 'gesunt' (*KC*, 7863) again? Only when they meet does Silvester realize 'daz iz allez von gote chom' (*KC*, 7905). He proceeds to verify the identity of the two men from Constantine's vision as indeed St Peter and St Paul — 'ain was grâ | [...] | der ander was chal' (*KC*, 7916–18) — and then explains the purpose of Constantine's vision to him:

> daz sint die hailigen hêrren,
> die dich an dem lîbe machent gesunden
> unt die sêle lôsent von den sunden.
> sô bin ich der arzât,
> der dir daz gotes wort vor saget;
> got hât dirz getân ze minnen:
> er wil dich im selben ze ainem dienestman gewinnen.
>
> (*KC*, 7925–31)

As the cure from his bodily ailment equates to the absolution of his soul from sin, Silvester does indeed become an 'arzât' to Constantine. He communicates God's explicit wish that the emperor should become his 'dienestman', which implies an almost feudal understanding of the relationship between God and emperor. Constantine does not hesitate, negotiate, or display any sign of doubt or disbelief. At once, he agrees to turn to God completely (*KC*, 7933), and is subsequently baptized by Silvester.

The initial misunderstanding is a categorical one. Constantine thinks of his suffering as a physical one, hence Silvester must be a physician. The category he applies is secular and physical. Silvester thinks of Constantine as a pagan emperor, who — like other pagan emperors before him — must have an interest in killing Christians. He thinks in religious and soteriological categories. Interestingly, the *Trierer Silvester* (*TS*), which was written about half a century later but draws heavily on the *Kaiserchronik*'s Silvester material, adds another dimension to make this categorical clash even more prominent. Constantine describes the two men from his vision to Silvester as 'zwein goten gelich getan' (*TS*, 202), whereupon

Silvester clarifies that 'iz waren niet wen zwene gote, | iz waren zwene gotis knechte' (*TS*, 208–09). Here, from Constantine's pagan perspective, Peter and Paul appear not as saints but as gods. This polytheistic perspective is not contained in the *Kaiserchronik*'s account, where Constantine describes the two men from his vision as 'êrlich unt wolgetân' (*KC*, 7899). This might suggest that the *Trierer Silvester* focuses on the figure of the pope and emphasizes his role in converting the pagan Constantine, while the *Kaiserchronik* can only admit that Constantine was indeed pagan but nevertheless 'vil bescaiden' (*KC*, 7811). The categorical difference in their perception of the situation serves as a stark contrast to the extensively displayed unity in which Constantine and Silvester act throughout the rest of the episode.

After Constantine's conversion, pope and emperor jointly issue a string of decrees in a seven-day process, often holding one another's hands to emphasize their union. This process in many ways mirrors the review of the pagan week from the pre-episodic part of the *Kaiserchronik*. Where the calendar firmly semanticized Rome as pagan, both as a space and as a collective in time and space, the seven-day legislative ritual of Constantine and Silvester now reprograms the Empire's condition. This process serves as the most prominent marker of Rome's qualitative transition from a pagan place, ruled by pagan temples, rituals, and idolatry, into a Christian place, ruled by the seven days as ordained in the process of God's creation and by the religiously inspired laws of pope and emperor. The process also integrates several concepts and notions about pagan polytheism as the *Kaiserchronik* so far has conceived of it, and dissolves them through Christian legislation and repurposes them for monotheistic practice.

Interestingly, the beginning of this seven-day process is not explicitly marked. Only as the text arrives at the second day does the pattern become apparent (*KC*, 7970). But before this, the unmarked first day sees the christening of Constantine, which immediately leads to his being cured of his 'siehtuom' (*KC*, 7943–57). Through baptism, Constantine is reborn as a Christian as he literally sheds his former pagan self:

> die hût im elliu ab viel,
> jâ wart im der lîp sîn
> als ain niwe gebornez chindelîn. (*KC*, 7945–47)

The chronicle inverts the biblical metaphor of the wolf in sheep's clothing (Matthew 7. 15) to illustrate the personal change in Constantine that inaugurates the broader change in the religious identity of the Empire. Next, the *Kaiserchronik* explicitly harkens back to the gods in the city as presented in the review of the pagan week. This reference prepares the implementation of the seven-day scheme. Finally, and as Silvester had recognized earlier, the conversion of the Empire is attributed to the will of 'der waltinde got' (*KC*, 7957). This is echoed by the framing of the event on the next day, the 'anderen tage' (*KC*, 7970): Constantine attends Mass in St Peter's and prays: 'owol dû waltinder got, | dû mich von der haidenscefte hâst erledigot' (*KC*, 7980–81). Constantine's personal conversion is explicitly attributed to God and the repeated qualification of God as 'waltinder' stresses God's active presence and shaping hand in history as the Empire is turning toward Christianity. Subsequently,

Constantine participates in the Eucharist, whereupon Pope Silvester takes his hand (*KC*, 7985–87). Together, they issue an edict that prohibits pagan worship of the idols and decrees the veneration of one God and creator *ex nihilo* (*KC*, 7989–97). This mandated monotheism will be further fleshed out through the symbolic and legislative actions on the following days: on the third day, emperor and pope together praise the Holy Ghost, and the pope again takes Constantine's hand, whereupon the emperor sits 'an daz gerihte' and from this position decrees the baptism of those who believe 'an den wâren got' (*KC*, 8008–16). Seemingly triggered by nothing more than Constantine's decree, many Romans recognize pagan worship as what the *Kaiserchronik* conceives it to be: a fraud ('wol rechanten si dar inne, | daz si lange wâren betrogen'; *KC*, 8019–20). On the fourth day, the legislative unity of emperor and pope is again emphasized, this time when Constantine takes Silvester's hand (*KC*, 8029) and proceeds to command the destruction of the pagan temples in Rome (*KC*, 8032–35). The idea that devils act under the guise of pagan polytheism to deceive and corrupt humans — most explicitly articulated in the Pantheon, Astrolabe, and Julian passages[135] — is mirrored by the fact that the devils have to accept their powerlessness and, as a consequence, Christianity spreads in Rome (*KC*, 8036–39). The fifth day begins with a service to the twelve apostles and coincides with great pagan festivities (*KC*, 8042–47). Again, Constantine gets into legislative mode when he sits in 'gerihte' (*KC*, 8048), and declares 'swer der heidenscefte mêr phlæge' (*KC*, 8052) to be enemies of the emperor 'unt aller Romære' (*KC*, 8054). This line is significant because it explicitly positions the Romans as a collective in opposition to the pagans. Constantine's declaration makes clear that at this point, the qualitative recoding of the Roman citizenry as a Christian collective is complete. Adhering to pagan beliefs now positions an individual outside the premises of Romanness.

The sixth and seventh days mainly see the installation and furnishing of Silvester's ecclesiastical papal court (*KC*, 8065–83) and of Constantine's temporal aristocratic court (*KC*, 8084–8115). The latter includes the explicit marking of the Roman aristocracy — all those who gird themselves with swords (*KC*, 8102–06) — with crosses, and their commitment to fight against the devil and to protect Christianity (*KC*, 8107–10).

Finally, the proceedings are brought to a climax by the coronation and consecration of Constantine on a Sunday (*KC*, 8116–34). His consecration is a singular process in the Roman part of the *Kaiserchronik*, since he is the only emperor to be exalted in this way before Charlemagne and the other German emperors. Subsequently, he delivers a speech that encapsulates many of the more general concepts of pagan polytheism in the *Kaiserchronik* and appeals to the Roman public to turn to Christianity.

> owol ir Românî,
> nu verstêt iuh wol dâ bî:
> got ruochete sich erbarmen
> uber unsich mennisce arme:

---

135 See 1.2.1 in this book.

> er sant uns sîn selbes sun,
> zerlôsen uns von den sundun.
> ê betten wir algemaine
> an holz und staine;
> daz war des tievels getroch.
> nû tuot irz durch den wâren got. (*KC*, 8138–47)

The reduction of the pagan idols to their materiality as 'holz und staine', and the characterization of pagan worship as 'tievels getroch', prefigures the events of the Astrolabius passage, whose main narrative points refer to these concerns. The temporal arrangement of the passage is also telling. The pairing of 'ê' and 'nû' sets a pagan past against a Christian present. The two periods are qualitatively separated by religious practice: idols of wood and stone versus the liturgy in the name of the true God. The contrast of two temporal layers is synchronized with the use of grammatical number in Constantine's speech. Having initially addressed the Romans as a collective and appealed to their understanding in the second person plural (*KC*, 8139) in the present tense, Constantine goes on to include himself in this group by consistently speaking in the first person plural (*KC*, 8141–45) when he relates the previous pagan practices of Rome in the past tense. At the end, he reverts to the second person and the present tense (*KC*, 8147). Constantine includes himself in the pagan past of Rome, but when he comes to the Christian present, he does not include himself in his exhortative speech. This should not be construed as some sort of exemption but much more as a stylistic device to better target and appeal to the Romans, who have just made the transition to Christianity or are about to make it. Constantine himself, while sharing their pagan past, has no need of persuasion, as his response to Silvester's initial approach illustrated. His appeal becomes even more explicit later on, when he urges the Romans: 'rechennet ainen wâren got, | den Silvester hât gebredigot' (*KC*, 8184–85). Constantine's address is immediately followed by 'mêr denne siben tûsunt' (*KC*, 8197) Romans converting to Christianity.

This great conversion event triggers an intervention from Constantine's mother, Helena, who remains pagan and wishes for Constantine to become pagan again. This development leads to a series of disputations that are supposed to resolve the religious crisis of the Empire and in which Pope Silvester takes on the role of defender of the Christian faith. To make Helena's pagan case at the disputation, twelve 'wîse redenære' (*KC*, 8571) are selected, 'di under juden und under haiden wâren' (*KC*, 8576). Jews and pagans are both presented together as 'des tieveles geverte' (*KC*, 8109). However, during the disputation it becomes clear that all the speakers who are presenting the pagan case are in fact Jewish, as they are either explicitly marked as such or their questions reflect Jewish criticisms of Christianity.[136] Like the earlier Faustinian disputations, these disputations present

---

136 See Christiane Witthöft, 'Zwischen Wahrheitssuche und Wunderglauben: Die christlich-jüdischen Disputationen der Silvesterlegende in der "Kaiserchronik"', in *Disputation 1200–1800: Form, Funktion und Wirkung eines Leitmediums universitärer Wissenskultur*, ed. by Marion Gindhart and Ursula Kundert, Trends in Medieval Philology, 20 (Berlin, 2010), pp. 291–310; Vera Milde, 'si entrunnen alle scentlîchen dannen: Christlich-jüdischer Disput in der Silvesterlegende der "Kaiserchronik"', in

some basic tenets of Christianity by confronting a defender of the faith with various adversarial figures of what has been referred to by scholarship as the 'hermeneutical Jew' who interrogates a number of established dogmatic problems with Christianity.[137] In the *Kaiserchronik*, most of these arguments try to cast doubt on the monotheistic nature of Christianity and the doctrine of the Trinity,[138] on the virginity of Mary,[139] the mechanics of redemption,[140] or the nature of Christ.[141] All of these arguments are well established within the Christian *adversus Judaeos* literature. These fictitious disputations did not aim to actually represent Jewish counter-arguments or to convert Jews. Nor were they dialogues in the modern sense of two parties exchanging arguments with the aim of persuading the other or establishing common ground. Their result was literally not open to debate; the fact that the Christian side would prevail was part of the conceptualization of the genre from the outset. Moreover, the texts engaged with points of uncertainty within the changing Christian belief system and developed an arsenal of arguments for defending them. In order to accomplish this, they established a system of allegorical and typological readings of both Testaments of the Bible. They aimed to consolidate their arguments within the Christian community and to create a sense of religious superiority among Christians. Thus, Christians, not Jews, were the actual targets of these texts.[142]

At the conclusion of the disputation, the *Kaiserchronik* does introduce a differentiation between Jews and pagans. Over the course of the Jews' enquiries, it has become clear that they are deliberately telling untruths and know that their accusations against Christianity are wrong. Initially, the disputation seems to take place on some sort of common ground between Silvester and his disputants: the books of the Old and New Testament are the universally recognized authority, and the ability to read them is the shared hermeneutical means for gleaning theological insights. However, as soon as the Jews' arguments are refuted by Silvester's Christian or Christological readings of the Bible, the Jews, without further explanation or resistance, accept his interpretation of Scripture and make a hasty retreat (e.g. *KC*, 9085–86, 9193, 9246–51). The most explicit instance of this occurs when Silvester refutes Jubal:

Juden in der deutschen Literatur des Mittelalters: Religiöse Konzepte — Feindbilder — Rechtfertigungen, ed. by Ursula Schulze (Tübingen, 2002), pp. 13–34.

137 Marcel Müllenburg, Britta Müller-Schauenburg, and Henrik Wels, 'Und warum glaubst du dann nicht? Zur ambivalenten Funktion der Vernunft in Religionsdialogen des 12. Jahrhunderts', in *Integration und Desintegration der Kulturen im europäischen Mittelalter*, ed. by Michael Borgolte and others, Europa im Mittelalter, 18 (Berlin, 2011), pp. 261–324.

138 e.g. Archisynagogus Abiathar (*KC*, 8602–8777) and Bishop Jonas (*KC*, 8778–8905).

139 e.g. Godolias (*KC*, 8906–9035) and Aunan (*KC*, 9088–9193).

140 e.g. Kusi (*KC*, 9194–9310), Didascali (*KC*, 9311–9437), Aroel (*KC*, 9438–9525), and Tara (*KC*, 9580–9641).

141 e.g. Doech (*KC*, 9036–87), Benjamin (*KC*, 9526–79), Jubal (*KC*, 9642–9807), and Zeleon (*KC*, 9808–9957).

142 See Schreckenberg, p. 539. See also Daniel Lasker, *Jewish Philosophical Polemics against Christianity in the Middle Ages* (New York, 1977).

er hiez im Daviden bringen,
do zaict er im dar inne
'tollite portas principes vestras' [Psalm 23. 7].
der jude reblaichet und gesaz. (*KC*, 9744–47)

This and all of Silvester's other refutations employ Scripture from the Old Testament, both because it would have had more impact on a twelfth-century audience and because the likely Latin source tradition of the disputation lays this out as a ground rule. While this ground rule is never made explicit, the *Kaiserchronik* does clearly adhere to it. Tellingly, in refutation of Jubal, Silvester quotes Scripture in Latin, which remains the language of authority in the disputation, and also orders the physical production of the Book of Psalms. It is almost as if not only his citation but also the physical appearance of the book drives his point home immediately. This also fits in with the *Kaiserchronik*'s tendency to conclude its disputations not on a discursive level but with a performative act or an external intervention, like Arius's untimely death by divine decree (*KC*, 13,475–83) or Silvester's miraculous resurrection of the bull (*KC*, 10,303–26).[143]

The Jews' reactions to Silvester's refutations imply that they knew all along that his Christian reading was in fact the one true reading of the Bible; the common ground suggested by the shared reference to the Bible has in fact been a comprehensively Christian ground all along. It further suggests that the Jews know they are in the wrong. Zeleon's final argument is undermined and makes the deceit of the Jews public when Silvester tricks him into perjuring himself. With their arguments, the Jews have knowingly tried to deceive not only the Christians but also the pagans, whom they were supposed to represent as a whole in the disputation. As Silvester destroys Zeleon's argument and makes his perjury visible, even the convinced pagan Helena, whose opposition to Constantine's Christianization triggered the whole disputation, recognizes the truth: 'an dem worte verstuont sich aller êrist diu chunigîn, | daz si mit dem geziuge betrogen was' (*KC*, 9943–44). Once more, the development culminates in mass-conversion events in which Silvester not only baptizes his twelve disputants and the two judges who adjudicated the disputations, but also 83,500 more pagans who were present, and finally Helena herself (*KC*, 10,359–81).

The events of the Constantine and Silvester episodes anchor Christianity firmly in the heart of Roman identity. Constantine's baptisms, his acts of legislation in conjunction with Silvester, his long speech to the Roman public, and Silvester's disputations and further baptisms mark the threshold that leads the *Rômære* of the *Kaiserchronik* from a pagan into a Christian chronotope.

143 See Almut Suerbaum, 'Erzählte Geschichte: Dialog und Dialogizität in der "Kaiserchronik"', in *Aspekte des 12. Jahrhunderts: Freisinger Kolloquium 1998*, ed. by Wolfgang Haubrichs and others, Wolfram-Studien, 16 (Berlin, 2000), pp. 235–55 (pp. 242–45).

3.2.2. Roman Christian Fragility

Long after Constantine and later Theodosius push the Romans firmly into the Christian chronotope, it comes as something of a surprise when Charlemagne is presented as the victor who brought Christianity to the Romans with his sword:

> von dem tage iemer mêre
> sô wuohsen Karle sîn êre,
> want er mit sînem swerte uberwant,
> daz er Rômære betwanch,
> daz si gote wurden undertân.
> vil manige sêle er dem tievel benam. (KC, 14,821–26)

Charlemagne's second arrival in Rome is described as a salvific act: by conquering the city, apparently by military force, even though this is not explicated in the text, he has now secured Rome for Christianity and saved many souls from damnation. This assessment appears entirely detached from the long and arduous process that the *Kaiserchronik* has otherwise painstakingly laid out, whereby the Empire is transformed from a pagan and polytheistic entity into a Christian one. Once again, the contingency of the text's episodic structure overrules any syntagmatic connection of events. Even so, there are instances to be found in the text before and after Charlemagne's Christian conquest of Rome that underpin the notion of Rome and *in extenso* Italy as a place in which Christianity is imperilled and whose inhabitants constantly threaten to relapse into pagan rites.

Doubt emerges among the Romans for the first time when Pope Silvester, who earlier in the text facilitated the greatest and most decisive of all conversion events, has to defend them against a dragon:

> sumelîche cristen,
> di mit gote nihte wâren veste,
> die sprâchen, wâ ir grôzer got wære?
> wie im daz gezæme?
> und wi er ouch daz verdolte,
> daz sie sô getânes tôdes retweln solten? (KC, 10,521–26)

The religious backsliding of the Romans makes sense primarily as providing another obstacle for Silvester to overcome. Not only did his resurrection of the bull at the end of the disputation with the Jewish wise men trigger a massive conversion experience for many pagans, but his whole rule has generally been characterized by his proselytizing and catechetical work (KC, 10,511–14). It therefore makes perfect narrative sense for his achievements to be challenged toward the end of his episode as the dragon threatens Rome. But this threat also creates a precedent for Roman Christian fragility on which later episodes can capitalize. Later during the *Kaiserchronik*, when cisalpine Rome has largely outlived its historical usefulness, this weakening of the Romans' hard-won Christian identity makes them more easily available as narrative antipoles to the Germans who are now in charge of the Roman Empire. A good example for this can be found in the Otto I episode, when an insurgency of Milan against the pope in Rome is characterized as a pagan endeavour and the papal legates report to the emperor

> daz die von Mailân
> die Cristen viengen,
> die haidenscaft mit in begiengen. (*KC*, 15,864–66)

This puzzling characterization of the Milanese as pagans has been described as a sign of the chronicle's carelessness by Schröder,[144] while Neudeck set it in the context of the author's desire to present Otto as a successful fighter against the pagans, which necessitated the characterization of the Milanese in these terms.[145] Most recently, Matthews has pointed out that the designation of the Milanese as pagans is confined to the reported speech of the papal legates who convey the news of their actions to Otto. Matthews sees this as deft exploitation of the potential of reported speech to present different perspectives on events. He contrasts the perspective of the papal legates, who slander the Milanese as pagans, with the perspective of the narrator and Otto, who take a more secular approach.[146]

In my opinion, this fragility of Christianity south of the Alps is a consequence of the twofold qualitative change in the identity of the Empire. In the Charlemagne episode, the Empire has not only changed into a fully Christian entity: the perspective on its political identity is also changing, from a Roman-cisalpine to a German-transalpine one. The configuration of the conflict with Milan puts the pope and the emperor on the same side but reintroduces the notion of *haidenscaft* in the heart of the Christian Empire: Italy. This resonates with the shiftiness of the Romans in times of conflict, for example when Emperor Otto II has to fight the Greeks in southern Italy (*KC*, 15,998–16,063). As rulership of the Empire migrates north of the Alps, Rome is painted in a rather ambivalent light. On the one hand, it is turned into a place constantly at risk of sliding back into heathendom or of undermining the emperor's authority. On the other hand, it is the Rome of the papacy and of the tombs of the apostles, which attract Charlemagne more than fraternal duty when he first visits the city (*KC*, 14,334–36). There seems little need for the chronicle to reconcile these two qualities of the city. Depending on the angle, both perspectives are applicable and create a Rome that becomes increasingly malleable now that it has lost its function as the seat of Roman central rule.

Looking at the qualitative development of religious identity in the *Kaiserchronik* has revealed two important insights: rejecting salvation history as a scaffold for the trajectory of its historical account, the chronicle deliberately models crucial passages within its episode paradigm to frame the process of transition from pagan to Christian empire. While points of imperial contact with Christianity mark the spread of the religion within the Empire, the disputations provide space to expand on dogmatic points of Christology, theology, and liturgy. In these instances, the chronicle displays an actual interest in presenting the new religion as something qualitatively new and different in its Roman pagan environment.

In this context, Bakhtin's concept of the chronotope again proves useful. Under Constantine and Silvester, the clearly marked transformation process lets the

144 Schröder, p. 368.
145 Neudeck, p. 81.
146 Matthews, pp. 109–13.

Kaiserchronik's Rome emerge first as a pagan and then as a Christian chronotope. Here, it is not a protagonist that moves in time through three-dimensional space,[147] but rather Rome as the space itself that is moved through time, analogously to a protagonist. As this movement is necessarily mutual, a change in the religious composition of time is accompanied by a concomitant change in the space in which the religious change unfolds, resulting in what Bakhtin described as time and space 'thickening' and becoming artistically visible.[148]

Several strands of motifs concerning Roman polytheism are bundled together here so as to be transferred into a Christian system of meaning. By deliberately mirroring the seven-day pattern of the review of the pagan week from its beginning, the *Kaiserchronik* now switches the default identity of the Romans from pagan to Christian. However, neither Constantine and Silvester, nor Theodosius, in whose episode both internal and external threats to the newly established Christian identity are repelled, mark the end of a teleological arc toward complete and final Christianization of the Roman Empire. The motif of Roman Christian fragility emerges just as the focus on the Roman Empire's political identity shifts to a transalpine German perspective. The circumstances that create this change also lead to the final point this book aims to address: the question of how this shift of perspective on the political identity of the Roman Empire in the *Kaiserchronik* is presented and negotiated.

---

147 As shown in the case of Serapion; see 1.1.4 in this book.
148 See Bakhtin, p. 84.

CHAPTER 4

❖

The Second Dimension of Qualitative Change: The Political Axis

4.1. Romans and Germans

The focus of the final chapter of this book will be on the qualitative change that occurs on the level of the political identity of the Roman Empire in the *Kaiserchronik*: from an ancient polity centred on the city of Rome and Italian or Mediterranean localities, to a polity firmly associated with the German *gentes* and the lands north of the Alps.

Scholarship has already dedicated much attention to the Germans and their role and profile throughout the *Kaiserchronik*. This is because, as a German vernacular chronicle, it has mainly interested Germanists, who have looked at it in the hope of gaining insights into the process of emergence of the German nation, its language, and its culture. Wolfgang Haubrichs has analysed the contribution of the *Kaiserchronik* to the emergence of vernacular terms for Germanness,[1] Heinz Thomas has added observations on the role of Caesar from the perspective of a historian,[2] and most recently Uta Goerlitz has written on the literary construction of (pre-) national German identity from the eleventh to the sixteenth century. On the construction of German identity in the *Kaiserchronik*, she summarizes:

> In den bisher betrachteten Partien der 'Kaiserchronik' hat sich das volkssprachige Konzept, das von den alten 'Deutschen' entworfen wird, eben nicht als jenes eindeutige, programmatisch durchgehaltene nationale Bild eines alten 'deutschen Volkes' und eines 'Landes' erwiesen, als das es häufig aufgefaßt wird. Vielmehr hat sich herausgestellt, daß dieses literarische Bild ein in sich differenziertes ist, für welches das Spannungsverhältnis konstitutiv ist, in das die Komponenten 'deutsch' sowie — um bei den vier tragenden Landen der Caesar-Episode zu bleiben — 'bayerisch', 'fränkisch', 'sächsisch', und 'schwäbisch' zueinander in

1   Wolfgang Haubrichs, 'Theodiscus, Deutsch und Germanisch — drei Ethnonyme, drei Forschungsbegriffe: Zur Frage der Instrumentalisierung und Wertbesetzung deutscher Sprach- und Volksbezeichnungen', in *Zur Geschichte der Gleichung 'germanisch-deutsch': Sprache und Namen, Geschichte und Institutionen*, ed. by Heinrich Beck and others, Ergänzungsbände zum Reallexikon der Germanischen Altertumskunde, 34 (Berlin, 2004), pp. 199–228.
2   Heinz Thomas, 'Julius Caesar und die Deutschen: Zu Ursprung und Gehalt eines deutschen Geschichtsbewußtseins in der Zeit Gregors VII. und Heinrichs IV.', in *Die Salier und das Reich: Gesellschaftlicher und ideengeschichtlicher Wandel im Reich der Salier*, ed. by Stefan Weinfurter, 3 vols (Sigmaringen, 1991), III, 245–78.

> Beziehung gesetzt sind. Hinzu kommt die Dialektik zwischen diesen Komp-
> onenten und dem Faktor 'römisch'. Kollektive Identitätskonstruktion erfolgt in
> der 'Kaiserchronik' daher auf unterschiedlichen Ebenen, deren Verhältnis zu
> beachten ist.[3]

With Goerlitz's focus on Germanness as multifaceted and non-unitary, the question
remains as to whether the *Kaiserchronik* actually models qualitative change in the
relationship between the Roman Empire and its two most prominent *gentes*: the
Romans and the Germans. This touches on the long, ongoing discussion about
why and how the final part of the chronicle — the part after Charlemagne — is
qualitatively different. I have referred to this question at several instances over the
course of this book and will show here how it ties in with the broader issue of the
political identity of the Empire.

To achieve this, the final chapter will proceed in two steps. In the first section,
the relationship of the city of Rome and its people to the emperor and the Empire
will be examined. The second section will focus on the two pivotal episodes of the
emperors Caesar and Charlemagne, so as to glean some insight into the question of
whether and how they actually negotiate a qualitative change in the political fabric
of the Roman Empire.

4.1.1. Kings, Emperors, and Rulers in the Kaiserchronik

The twelfth century witnessed not only an increased interest in the textual explor-
ation of Rome and its ancient sites but also in their rediscovery for political purposes.
When Henry IV was dealing with Roman interest-groups in the late eleventh
century, he made the mistake of subsuming them all into one homogeneous group
without being willing or able to acknowledge the internal divisions in Rome or
the divergent interests of groups like the aristocratic oligarchs or the clergy. His
son Henry V, on the other hand, showed a keen awareness of these problems when
he opted for more nuanced salutations when dealing with the Romans in the early
twelfth century. By echoing the nomenclature Roman officials used for themselves,
which derived from ancient titles but of course had little in common with the
offices of the Roman Republic or even the Empire, Henry V could make it clear
when he wished, for example, only to address the representatives of the civic and
not the ecclesiastical Rome.[4] It was also Henry V who revived imperial interest in
Roman sites as stages for public actions. He mainly utilized St Peter's Church in
the Vatican, but more remarkably also the Capitoline Hill of the city of antiquity.
In early 1117, Henry V entered Rome to mediate in the conflicts between the
Roman citizens and their pontiff. After trying unsuccessfully to confront the pope
in St Peter's, Henry and his entourage ascended the Capitoline Hill the following
day and gave great gifts to those who supported him. The Capitoline Hill was the
political and religious centre of ancient Rome, as Isidore of Seville had defined it

---

3   Uta Goerlitz, *Literarische Konstruktion (vor-)nationaler Identität seit dem Annolied: Analysen und
Interpretationen zur deutschen Literatur des Mittelalters (11.–16. Jahrhundert)*, Quellen und Forschungen zur
Literatur- und Kulturgeschichte, 45 (Berlin, 2007), p. 160.
4   See Jürgen Petersohn, *Kaisertum und Rom in spätsalischer und staufischer Zeit: Romidee und
Rompolitik von Heinrich V. bis Friedrich II.*, MGH Schriften, 62 (Hanover, 2010), pp. 14–16.

in his *Etymologies*, and it had been an integral part of ritual triumphal processions.[5] The Capitoline Hill had, however, since fallen into disrepair and during the early Middle Ages was at least in parts famously populated by goats.[6] In a sense, the Capitoline Hill had by this time returned to the bucolic state described in the Roman prehistory of the *Aeneid*, in which cows and cattle roam where the magnificent urban sites of the imperial Rome of Virgil's time were later to be erected.[7]

While the Capitoline Hill had since the late eleventh century been used as a site for markets and legal courts, it is doubtful if this provides a sufficient semantic charging of the site to explain Henry's interest in it as a political stage. Some idea of the ancient importance of the place must have been present and available to Henry and his partners in Rome, even though they only become textually manifest in the decades after his early death. This rediscovered importance can be grasped in texts like the *Mirabilia Urbis Romae*, the closely connected *Graphia Aurae Urbis Romae*, and also the *Kaiserchronik*. The *Mirabilia Romae* were written before September 1143 by an author familiar with ancient literature and rhetoric and the topography of Rome.[8] For a long time, the *Mirabilia* were attributed to Benedict of St Peter, but more recent scholarship has cast doubt on this, and the author has since mostly been treated as anonymous.[9] The *Mirabilia* were quickly translated into German, and are very likely to have been one of the sources for the *Kaiserchronik*.[10] Two of the six short narratives that form the middle part of the *Mirabilia* show some similarities with episodes from the *Kaiserchronik*: the rededication of the Pantheon by Boniface, and the murder of Emperor Philip by Decius and the subsequent ploy of his son to prevent Philip's treasure from falling into the usurper's hands by handing it over to Pope Sixtus instead. The text also shares the *Kaiserchronik*'s great interest in ancient pagan monuments like temples[11] and its expressed intent to preserve knowledge about the past for posteriority.[12]

---

5   Isidore of Seville, *Etymologiae*, xv. 2; Petersohn, p. 28.

6   See Richard Krautheimer, *Rome: Profile of a City, 312–1308* (Princeton, 1980), p. 285.

7   Virgil, *Aeneis*, ed. by George Long, 3 vols (London, 1883), vii. 359–61.

8   See Nine Miedema, *Die Mirabilia Romae: Untersuchungen zu ihrer Überlieferung mit Edition der deutschen und niederländischen Texte*, Münchener Texte und Untersuchungen zur deutschen Literatur des Mittelalters, 108 (Tübingen, 1996), pp. 6–11.

9   Benedict of St Peter was first identified as the most likely author by Louis Duchesne, 'L'Auteur des Mirabilia', *Mélanges d'archéologie et d'histoire*, 24 (1904), 479–89 (p. 486). See also Bernhard Schimmelpfennig, *Die Zeremonienbücher der römischen Kurie im Mittelalter* (Tübingen, 1973), pp. 8–12; Dale Kinney, 'Fact and Fiction in the "Mirabilia Urbis Romae"', in *Roma Felix — Formation and Reflections of Medieval Rome*, ed. by Carol Neuman de Vegvar and Éamonn Ó Carragáin (Abingdon, 2008), pp. 235–52 (p. 236).

10   See Miedema, p. 263, p. 364, n. 26; Ohly, *Sage und Legende*, p. 41.

11   John Kenneth Hyde, 'Medieval Descriptions of Cities', *Bulletin of the John Rylands Library*, 48 (1966), 308–40 (p. 322).

12   *Codice topografico della città di Roma: Saec. XII–XIV*, ed. by Roberto Valentini and Giuseppe Zucchetti, 4 vols (Rome, 1940–53), iii, Fonte per la storia d'Italia, 90 (1946), p. 65: 'Quantae etiam essent pulchritudinis auri et argenti, aeris et eboris pretiosorumque lapidum, scriptis ad posterum memoriam, quanto melius potuimus, reducere curavimus.'

The *Mirabilia* also became a core part of the *Graphia Aurae Urbis Romae*, which must have been compiled shortly thereafter, but probably not before 1154.[13] The *Graphia* combine a free reworking of material from the *Mirabilia* with three other texts: a history of Rome from Noah to Romulus; the *Graphia-Libellus*, a puzzling treatise that produces a largely fictional account of the ancient imperial court; and an older passage known as the 'Three Formulas' that contains oaths for swearing-in ceremonies.[14] The provenance of the *Graphia* was long contested, before Bloch managed to identify the Benedictine monk Peter the Deacon of Monte Cassino as the author.

These texts, which show great interest in the antiquities of Rome and its imperial past, colour the context in which the *Kaiserchronik* was first compiled.

4.1.2. The Introduction of Rome

Considering the increase of political and cultural interest in Rome at the time of the *Kaiserchronik*'s composition and the importance of the city as a place for the chronicle's narrative, it is surprising how little time the text devotes to actually presenting the city. Roughly contemporary texts like the *Eneasroman* (24. 24–29) or *Herzog Ernst* (2212–47)[15] contain rich descriptions of cities like Carthage or Grippia respectively. In both texts, a grand panoramic scene is presented to the audience, with shared points of interest being walls, towers, and fortifications, as well as the relevant city's topographical situation in the surrounding landscape, especially in relation to bodies of water such as the sea, rivers, or moats. Both descriptions are also accompanied by references to the authoritative source material that vouches for the veracity of the account presented. Of course, at least in the case of Grippia, a caveat applies. As a fantastic place, inhabited by crane-headed *monstra* far removed from the realm of empirical experience and accessibility for the text's audience, it requires a more detailed introduction. This introduction is strongly influenced by fairy tales and by the newly made Western acquaintance with the East as a projection of the fantastic Orient. Moreover, the description has its own narrative function beyond mere description, as it is in itself part of the text's creation of an atmosphere of subliminal dread and impending doom that is about to befall Ernst and his companions as they explore the city.[16] While this makes the comparison less effective on a contextual level, the aim of the comparison here is more on a structural level, designed to show what narrative strategies to describe cities would have been available to the author of the *Kaiserchronik*.

13   See Herbert Bloch, 'Der Autor der "Graphia Aureae Urbis Romae"', *Deutsches Archiv für Erforschung des Mittelalters*, 40 (1984), 55–160 (esp. p. 59).
14   See Petersohn, pp. 49–50; Bloch, p. 56. See also Ernst Percy Schramm, *Kaiser, Rom und Renovatio: Studien zur Geschichte des römischen Erneuerungsgedankens vom Ende des karolingischen Reiches bis zum Investiturstreit* (Darmstadt, 1957), pp. 193–97.
15   *Herzog Ernst: Mittelhochdeutsch/Neuhochdeutsch*, ed. and trans. by Mathias Herweg, RUB, 19,606 (Stuttgart, 2019).
16   David Blamires, *Herzog Ernst and the Otherworld Voyage: A Comparative Study* (Manchester, 1979), pp. 29–32.

The lack of textual mapping of Rome in the *Kaiserchronik* was noticed by Matthews, who concludes that the 'description and perception of city space [...] were not exploited to the extent possible' and more attention is given to 'shaping space [...] in terms of defining places within it or of movement through it, and relating it to the exemplary roles of pope and emperor'.[17] This leads to the core of the problem. Both *Herzog Ernst* and the *Eneasroman* have a clearly defined, eponymous main protagonist. Both protagonists are itinerant for significant stretches of their narratives, and the narrative focalization moves with them to discover the foreign cities. Once discovered, they require introduction and description.

The situation in the *Kaiserchronik* is rather different. Starting with the prologue, Rome is set to be the stage of the text's events (*KC*, 16). The foundation and the basic political situation of Rome are sketched in just a few lines. Both quantifiable historical distance — 'Hie bevor' (*KC*, 43) — and qualitative historical difference — 'bi der haiden zîten' (*KC*, 43) — are marshalled to contrast the situation of the narrator and his audience with the historical situation at the beginning of the narrative. The main marker of this twofold historical alterity is the presence of 'abgot diu unrainen' (*KC*, 45) and of the pagans who worship them according to the law of their kings (*KC*, 46–48). Interestingly, the foundation of Rome by Romulus and Remus (*KC*, 49–54) is set apart temporally from the antediluvian age of 'promiscuous idolatry'[18] in which the only source of order was the rule of a king whose authority was vaguely tied to pagan worship. The city's foundation by Romulus and Remus happens 'nâch der werlte' (*KC*, 50), with *werlt* in its temporal usage meaning 'age' or 'century'.[19] The stratification of time again marks both a qualitative and a quantitative leap forward to prepare the stage for the foundation of Rome. After this, another temporal leap is indicated by 'sît' in line 55, which positions the fearful service of 'elliu die rîche' to Rome and its Senate of 'driu hundert althêrren' (*KC*, 56–57) as a later occurrence than the city's foundation. No historical process of conquest that might causally link the two is referenced. Only the temporal adverb 'sît' indicates a succession of events, but without explicating their qualitative relation. Rome's introduction into the narrative automatically brings with it the city's supremacy over other countries. Or, as Heinrich von Veldeke puts it:[20]

> ez enmohte niht so ergan,
> sint hete Rom den giwalt,
> daz man ir den chinz galt
> unde man in ir sande

17   Matthews, p. 57.
18   Chinca and Young, p. 11.
19   See Lexer, s.v. *werlt* (III, cols 782–84). In his mid-twelfth-century *Rede vom Glauben*, 7, Der Arme Hartmann translated the Latin phrase *in saecula saeculorum* with 'von werlde zo werelde' (in *Die religiösen Dichtungen des 11. und 12. Jahrhunderts*, ed. by Friedrich Maurer, 3 vols (Tübingen, 1964–70), II (1965), 568–628).
20   Carthage was not to reign supreme 'vber alliv div riche' (*ER*, 28. 1) as Juno had decreed when she supported Dido in founding Carthage. This role would fall to Rome, the city later founded by Eneas's descendants.

> von uil manigeme lande.
> daz was sit uber manich iar,
> daz wizzent gnvoge livte fur war. (*ER*, 28. 4–10)

Rome's supremacy was common knowledge and did not require elaboration. The many lands ('von uil manigeme lande') that pay tribute to Rome in the *Eneasroman* correspond to the *Kaiserchronik*'s 'elliu die rîche' (*KC*, 56), which fearfully serve Rome after it has been founded by Romulus and Remus, and also to 'elliu diu lant' (*KC*, 61), to which the 'althêrren' of the Roman Senate promulgate their decisions. Line 58 elaborates the relationship between the Senate and the lands subjected to Rome. The 'althêrren' are caretakers of their *zuhte* (discipline) and *êre* (reputation). The lines connecting the prologue to the review of the pagan week map out — in a brief space — a three-stage model of qualitative historical development in which an initially chaotic pagan world is put into order first by the foundation of Rome and then by the rule of the Senate.

Unlike Rome, Carthage and Grippia receive extensive descriptions of their cityscapes because they are both new and exotic places for the texts' protagonists to explore. Both Herzog Ernst and Eneas travel through changing scenery while being the focal point of the narrative. In the *Kaiserchronik*, however, Rome serves as an environment for the text's episodic narrative and the episodes' ever-changing characters. The backdrop of the city is, in a sense, the only constant for most of the text. As the deeds of the emperors and popes and of the many different protagonists of the *Kaiserchronik* are inextricably linked to the city, it could be argued that Rome in its relation to and as carrier of Roman authority is the central protagonist of the *Kaiserchronik*, at least until the notion of the Empire is detached from the city and crosses the alps to the North.

4.1.3. Of Kings and Emperors

If Rome serves as an anchor-point for the Roman Empire's central authority, it has to be considered how this authority figures in the *Kaiserchronik* and how it relates to the ideas of Germanness and Romanness. Kingship as such is a ubiquitous notion in the *Kaiserchronik*, and hence it is hardly surprising that it has attracted a great deal of scholarly attention. Indeed, it was scholars rather than the text itself that identified the *Kaiserchronik* as a chronicle of emperors.

The ruler of the Roman Empire is mostly represented by the word *kunic*. However, the differentiation from the word *kaiser*, which means 'emperor' and is also regularly employed, is very imprecise, if it exists at all. The *Mittelhochdeutsche Begriffsdatenbank* yields 136 hits for *kaiser*, with only one instance of *kaiserinne* (referring to the wife of Henry III).[21] Furthermore, the database yields 568 hits for *kunic*, 63 for *küniginne*, and 16 for *küniclich*, but only 2 for *künicrîche*. With 319 hits, *rîche* and its derivatives are the favoured spatial term for the Empire whose story the *Kaiserchronik* sets out to narrate.[22]

---

21   At the time of their imperial coronation in 1046, this would have been Agnes of Aquitaine, Henry's second wife, whom the *Kaiserchronik* does not name, however.

22   *Mittelhochdeutsche Begriffsdatenbank*, ed. by Universität Salzburg <http://www.mhdbdb.sbg. ac.at/> [accessed 17 February 2017].

Kings as historical agents are first introduced in the prologue (*KC*, 19), along with popes, as the protagonists of the 'crônicâ' (*KC*, 17). Rulers — be they kings or emperors — only become the structuring feature of the text with the death of Caesar and his succession by Augustus, when the *Kaiserchronik* for the first time utilizes its characteristic closing and opening formulas (*KC*, 597–605). Before Caesar's coronation, kings are only referenced in passing as the nebulous authority behind the prehistorical pagan worship of the Romans (*KC*, 48). Caesar himself is never called *kunic*, but at one point, before he returns to Rome, conquers the city, and becomes its sole ruler, he is referred to as 'chaiser' (*KC*, 426). Otherwise, he is normally called either Julius (*KC*, 402, 406, 421, 434, 435) or *Cêsar* (*KC*, 417, 437). Augustus is the first named ruler of the *Kaiserchronik* on whom the title of *kunic* is conferred (*KC*, 614). After Caesar, the title *kaiser* is used for the first time for Tiberius (*KC*, 741).

This overview of the early usage of the two terms shows that the *Kaiserchronik* assumes the presence of kings in Rome as a historical constant and permanent certainty. While structurally Caesar becomes the first ruler and Augustus is referred to as the first king, kingship as a political institution is imagined to have been always present, without need of narrative introduction or aetiological treatment, and largely identical with emperorship.

To form a clearer impression of the usage of the two congruent terms, a qualitative examination will follow in order to distinguish which of the chronicle's rulers are titled either *kunic* or *kaiser* or both. With regard to all rulers, it will be of special interest whether there are tendencies in whether a ruler is presented as a positive or a negative figure. For the German kings, it will be particularly interesting to see whether the terminology switches with their imperial coronation where that is included in the text.

The *Kaiserchronik* knows two states of political modification with regard to the office of the emperor: papal consecration and *sede vacante*. The only ancient emperor who is consecrated is Constantine (*KC*, 8128). After him, there is of course the prominent consecration of Charlemagne (*KC*, 14,751), but also of the emperors Henry III (*KC*, 16,485), Henry IV (*KC*, 16,915–21), and Lothair II (*KC*, 17,083). Interestingly, with regard to consecration, there seems to be a coherent application of the emperor title, or at least a very clear tendency: Constantine and Lothair II are never referred to as emperors before they are consecrated, and Charlemagne is called *kaiser* only four times before Pope Leo consecrates him, but overwhelmingly so after the event. Henry IV is twice called *kaiser* before receiving papal consecration, but concurrently with the title *kunic*; he is exclusively *kaiser* for the short remainder of his reign afterward.

The state of *sede vacante* occurs several times in the text: before Titus ('Daz rîche was duo lære'; *KC*, 5364), Lucius Accommodus ('si sprâchen, daz des rîches stuol | stuonde ubel lære'; *KC*, 7848), Constantine ('Diu rîche stuonden lære'; *KC*, 7806), and Charlemagne (*KC*, 14,282) take over power. Before Charlemagne enters the stage, the Roman Empire is already conceived as something transpersonal that can be detached from previous incumbents (*KC*, 14,278–81), and the lacuna in rulership is presented rather prominently in this instance: 'Daz rîche stuont do lære' (*KC*,

14,282). Within the political imagination of the *Kaiserchronik*, the Empire clearly has an abstract transpersonal and transtemporal existence. It is also striking that all the emperors who come to power after such a situation are rather positive figures.

As far as the usage of the two titles *kunic* and *kaiser* for individual rulers of the *Kaiserchronik* is concerned, the text does not pursue a consistent strategy. Some episodes do adhere to a scheme in and of themselves, but as is so often the case in the *Kaiserchronik* it remains impossible to extrapolate more general conclusions for the entirety of the text. Two rulers are conspicuously only referred to as *kunic* and never as *kaiser*: Nero features as *kunic* eleven times and Tarquin twenty-five times. The case of Tarquin is easily explained by the relatively long nature of his episode and by the source tradition, which would have known Tarquin only as *rex* of the Roman royal period and never as *imperator*, a situation which doubtlessly informed the author of the *Kaiserchronik* when he compiled his version of the legend. This means the anonymous author does not think of Roman kings as constituting a distinct pre-Republic and pre-imperial phase of Roman history; *kunic* is just another form of manifestation of Roman rulers to him. One might be tempted to assume that Nero is denied the title of *kaiser* to deny him imperial honour and dignity, and this might well be true within the boundaries of the Nero episode, but it does not indicate a general trend of the chronicle as a whole. Claudius, who is certainly not a positive figure in the context of the *Kaiserchronik*, is referred to both as *kunic* and as *kaiser* (three times for each). Another excellent example of the interchangeable use of the two titles is the Trajan episode. Trajan is called *kaiser* thirteen times, on eight of those occasions even very emphatically 'kaiser Trajân'. But he is also called *kunic* six times, apparently without any difference in sense. When Trajan rectifies the injustice an old widow has suffered, she thanks him: 'ze dem kunige si sprach: | jâ dû, kaiser Trajân' (*KC*, 5982–83).

In the space of two lines, Trajan, an exemplary and universally virtuous ruler, can be both king and emperor. This configuration serves as the default setting, at least for the Roman part of the chronicle. Nerva, however, whose wisdom as a ruler is universally praised (*KC*, 5832) and who at his death is lamented as a ruler 'tiure und mære' (*KC*, 5837), is consistently called *kunic*.

4.1.4. The Romans and the German Kings

It will not come as a surprise that the Romans are mentioned less and less as the chronicle crosses the threshold of Charlemagne. For the remainder of the text, they feature only nine more times, which marks a drastic decline.[23] The Romans of the medieval part of the *Kaiserchronik* usually appear as the opposite of the emperor, somehow relational to him but no longer identical with the Empire. They are needed to bestow legitimacy and authority, but are no longer assumed as the default public of the Empire's workings.

The antagonism between Romans and the Empire starts with Charlemagne, who has to defeat them (*KC*, 14,824) before he becomes the first emperor 'von

---

23   The German emperors comprise about 18 per cent of the *Kaiserchronik*, but only about 4 per cent of the references to *Rômære* can be found in these episodes.

Diutisken landen' (KC, 14,819). The Romans resurface again when King Arnold comes to Rome (KC, 15,548–54). The textual existence of the Romans depends on the emperor's presence in Rome. As soon as he leaves the city, they fade into the background. They are still an authority to assert the legitimacy and quality of an emperor's rule: his victory over the Huns marks him as a 'guot rihtâre' in the eyes of the Romans and ensures him their gratitude. This same relation is invoked when the pope approaches King Otto I during a diet in Aachen (KC, 15,858–61). The pope actualizes the king's title as 'Rômære voget unt des rîches rihtâre' (KC, 15,869) to compel him to intervene in Milan. Again, it is a projection of the city of Rome, the pope in this case, who brings up the Romans, and again they are used solely as a means of bestowing power and legitimacy on a German king.

When the Romans re-emerge in the episode of Otto II, this again happens in circumstances similar to Arnold's: the Romans are put back on the map to assure Otto II that they will help him to fight the Greeks in southern Italy (KC, 15,998), where he is poised to intervene on the side of a local noble called Regenwart who had been expelled by the Greeks from his holdings in Calabria (KC, 15,978–87). It is not entirely clear where Otto gathers his princes in council (KC, 15,996–97). Regenwart has to send letters to him to persuade him, but at the same time the entire setting of a conflict with the Greeks firmly situates the action in southern Italy. The pope tries to hold the emperor and his princes off from intervening on behalf of Regenwart (KC, 16,002–04), but they nevertheless march on Apulia to do just that (KC, 16,005). Both the presence of the pope and the fact that Otto and his entourage are able to move immediately to Apulia suggest that they are already in Italy, albeit somewhat removed from Regenwart's position in Apulia; hence, it seems not entirely unlikely that the text is implicitly locating them in Rome. This is further corroborated by the fact that when Otto's army returns from battle, badly defeated by the Greeks and Roman treachery, the pope addresses the Senate to argue that the traitors should be put to death (KC, 16,040–47). Here again, Rome is not explicitly mentioned as destination — the Germans simply 'kômen wider an daz lant' — but the presence of pope and Senate strongly suggests that they have returned to the city of Rome.

This would turn the Romans who initially assure Otto of their allegiance into citizens of the city of Rome once more and not a general term for the people of his empire. In accordance with the wider historiographical tradition of the time, the Romans are associated with treacherousness:[24] as soon as 'Rômære sumelîche' (KC,

---

24   The presentation of the Romans in Otto of Freising's *Chronica* is of course complex. But for a good example of the set of negative traits associated with the Romans — like unreliability, avarice, cowardice, and treachery — see the *Gesta Friderici*. Fearing a trap as he approaches Rome, Frederick I asks Pope Hadrian for counsel. The pope responds: 'My son, you will learn more about the guile of the Roman rabble as time goes on. For you will discover that in treachery they came and in treachery they have departed. But aided by the clemency of God, Who says "I shall take the wise in their own craftiness", we shall be able to circumvent their shrewd schemes' (Otto of Freising and Rahewin, *The Deeds of Frederick Barbarossa*, trans. by Charles Christopher Mierow (Columbia, 1966), p. 140). The entire episode does not shed a favourable light on the Romans: Otto of Freising and Rahewin, *Gesta Friderici I. Imperatoris*, ed. by Georg Waitz and Bernhard de Simson, MGH SS Rer. Germ., 46 (Hanover, 1912), II. 31–33, pp. 139–41.

16,006) have the opportunity, they change their allegiance and turn to the Greeks to help them in the fight against Otto (*KC*, 16,006–10). This leads to his humiliating defeat, the death of many a German (*KC*, 16,063), and ultimately the king's death (*KC*, 16,058–63).

After Otto's II defeat, the Romans only feature in two more episodes, both under the Salians. The first instance happens in a very clearly papal and urban context, when Henry III has to resolve a papal schism (*KC*, 16,455–57). This situation is not only closely tied to the city of Rome but also again set up as an antagonistic scenario, which Henry resolves by deposing all three competing Roman popes and installing Bishop Suitger of Bamberg in the papal see (*KC*, 16,476–84). The text enhances the Roman context of this episode further by moving the historical 1046 Synod of Sutri from Sutri in the province of Viterbo, fifty kilometres south of Rome, to Rome directly (*KC*, 16,466, 16,476, 16,489). The second instance marks the last task the Romans have to perform in the *Kaiserchronik*, which is to provide the ceremonial frame for Henry V's imperial consecration by the pope (*KC*, 16,916–20).

As soon as the German kings appropriate the Empire, the position of the Romans within the text radically changes. They are pushed out of the role of default public and supporting power behind the emperor or king, and mutate into a closely circumscribed entity inseparable from the city of Rome and from political and religious contexts closely tied to it: the papacy, the consecration of emperors, the Senate, or more general Italian concerns like the crisis in Milan or the military conflict with the Greeks in Apulia and Calabria. This shift is mirrored by the emerging *Diutiscen*, who now take over the default role hitherto fulfilled by the Romans. Charlemagne is 'von Diutisken landen' (*KC*, 14,819), and King Arnold returns 'in Diutisk lant' (*KC*, 15,554), as does Henry IV (*KC*, 16,916), after being consecrated, which suggests that the Empire's core is now considered detached from Rome. This becomes even more evident after the disappearance of Henry IV, who is erroneously believed to be dead (*KC*, 16,804–06). Only after the news reaches Germany are political consequences triggered. The generative centre for the succession of power has clearly moved to Germany. Rome's only function in this remains to bestow the additional dignity of the imperial consecration and provide a legitimizing framework of authority.

Finally, in Otto II's devastating defeat in southern Italy, it is the Germans who have formed the bulk of his army and whose losses are greatly emphasized by the *Kaiserchronik*:

> welch wunder daz was,
> daz ie dehain Diutisker genas!
> [...]
> der Diutisken wart dô vil reslagen. (*KC*, 16,038–63)

Similarly, when Henry V finds himself in dire straits in Rome, he is assailed by the Romans, while the group surrounding him and fighting their way out of Rome are the Germans (*KC*, 16,895–16,902).

In religious terms, the Romans of the first part of the *Kaiserchronik* are clearly presented as polytheists. But they also subscribe to a courtly canon of values and interests, as evidenced again in the Tarquin episode. During the protracted siege of

Viterbo, they while away the time by indulging in a discussion of their favourite topics: they begin by commenting on the performance of their fellow knights and their conduct in battle. From there, the debate moves on to other courtly pastimes like beautiful horses, good dogs, trained falcons, and finally — last, but hopefully not least — noble women, whom they dearly miss and who display no sign of imperfection (*KC*, 4415–30). Drawing up this catalogue of courtly preoccupations is essential for the Tarquin episode in order to root the upcoming conflict between Tarquin and his (nameless) wife and Conlatinus and his wife, Lucretia, in a competition about the appropriate conduct of women, which ultimately leads to Tarquin's wife inciting Tarquin to rape Lucretia, Lucretia's subsequent demonstrative suicide, and Conlatinus's slaying of Tarquin in revenge. But it also goes to show that it was perfectly conceivable to present ancient Romans as preoccupied with the same interests and pastimes as contemporary German nobles of the twelfth century, who presumably constituted a sizeable part of the *Kaiserchronik*'s audience. The literary discourse on courtly norms, communality, and chivalric conduct is already present in the *Kaiserchronik*.[25] So, despite being devout polytheists, the Romans are also knights and courtiers, or, as the text frames it: 'Rômære hêten grôze rîterscaft' (*KC*, 4565). This reduces the qualitative difference between the narrated figures and the audience significantly.

4.2 Shifting Perspectives on the Empire

Over the course of the *Kaiserchronik*, the office of king or emperor is foregrounded in many crucial passages, two of which will be examined in the following section: first, Caesar's conquest of the German peoples north of the Alps and his subsequent military return to Rome (*KC*, 247–602), together with the amalgamated version of Daniel's prophetic dreams, which is inserted after Caesar's victory in Rome (*KC*, 526–90); second, the rule of Charlemagne, the first king the text presents as 'German' (*KC*, 14,282–15,091). These two episodes are the crucial thresholds on the *Kaiserchronik*'s teleological trajectory approximating the ancient Empire with its current medieval form.

4.2.1. Daniel, Caesar, and the Germans

When approaching the Caesar episode of the *Kaiserchronik*, which is crucial for the text's political modulation of the Empire, it is important to consider first the situation of the *Annolied*. Only one complete version of it survives, in a print by Martin Opitz from 1639.[26] About 225 of the lines transmitted in this print can also be found in the *Kaiserchronik*,[27] mainly in the episodes on Caesar and Augustus. Among them is also the Daniel passage, sometimes following the model of the *Annolied* to the letter, sometimes, however, significantly altering it. The Daniel passages in the *Annolied*

---

25   See Joachim Bumke, *Höfische Kultur: Literatur und Gesellschaft im hohen Mittelalter* (Munich, 2002), pp. 576–77. Bumke mentions the Totila episode in the context of an incipient culture of courtly *Minnegeselligkeit* in Germany.

26   On the transmission of the *Annolied*, see Eberhard Nellmann, 'Annolied', in *Verfasserlexikon*, 14 vols (Berlin, 1978–2008), I, ed. by Kurt Ruh (1978), cols 366–71.

27   See Müller, p. 1.

(11. 1–17. 14) and the *Kaiserchronik* (526–90) are loose adaptations and conflations of the Old Testament dream interpretations from Daniel 2, where the prophet expounds a dream of the Babylonian King Nebuchadnezzar, and Daniel 7, where Daniel is himself the dreamer. The canonical interpretation of these two dreams is mainly informed by Jerome's commentary on Daniel, which offers an in-depth reading and interpretation of Daniel's visions that would later become a cornerstone of Christian theology, especially Christology.

Annegret Fiebig has demonstrated conclusively that the changes made by the *Kaiserchronik* should not be considered a corruption of an already canonical tradition of interpretations of the dreams. Rather, they ought to be seen as yielding an original version with its own narrative purpose.[28]

The idiosyncrasy of the *Kaiserchronik*'s version is especially striking when compared to the *Annolied*. The latter largely takes its cue from Jerome's interpretation of Daniel 7. Of special interest is the fourth animal emerging, the one characterized by its iron teeth. It is not identified in Daniel 7, but Jerome, referring to Psalm 79, specifies it as a boar with ten horns and sees it as a symbol of the Roman Empire.[29] When an eleventh horn with an eye and a mouth uttering overweening boasts sprouts from its forehead (Daniel 7. 8), Jerome writes, this marks the destruction of the fourth beast, and hence the empire represented by it, and its transformation into something else. Jerome argues against the interpretation of the Neoplatonic philosopher Porphyry, who argued that the beast symbolizes the Seleucid King Antiochos IV Epiphanes — a contemporary to the writing of the Book of Daniel and antagonist of the Hebrews — and tried to convince his readers that it in fact represented a human being in whom Satan would assume bodily form at the end of days.[30] Jerome aims to synchronize Daniel's vision from chapter 7 more explicitly with Nebuchadnezzar's dream from chapter 2,[31] where a statue composed from four materials — or five if one considers that the feet are actually made out of two — is crushed by a huge boulder (Daniel 2. 31–45). The exegetical sum of Jerome's linked reading of both prophecies is that with the end of the fourth empire, the end of creation itself will arrive.[32] This eschatological dimension of the fourth empire, the

28   Fiebig, pp. 31–38.
29   Jerome, *In Danielem*: 'Romanum regnum nulli bestiae compararit: nisi forte ut formidolosam faceret bestiam, vocabulum facuit, ut quidquid ferocius cogitaverimus in bestiis, hec Romanos intelligamus. Iloc quod hic tacitum est, Hebraei in Psalmis dictum putant: Devastavit eam aper de silva; et singularis ferus depastus est eam (Psalms 79. 14)' (7, l. 4), and 'Quartum quod nunc urbem tenet terrarum, imperium Romanorum est, de quo in statua dicitur: Tibiae ejus ferrae: pedum quoedam pars ferrae, quoedam fictilis; et tamen ipsius ferri ex parte nunc meminit, dentes ejus ferreos, et magnos esse contestans' (7, l. 7).
30   Ibid.: 'Ergo dicamus quod omnes scriptores ecclesiastici tradiderunt: in consummatione mundi, quando regnum destruendum est Romanorum [...] Ne eum putemus juxta quorumdam opinionem, vel diabolum esse, vel daemonum; sed unum de hominibus, in quo totus satanas habitaturus sit corporaliter' (7, l. 8).
31   e.g. 'Bestia secunda urso similis, ipsa est de qua in visione statuae legimus (Supra II,32): Pectus ejus et brachia de argento, haec ob duritiam, et ferocitatem urso comparatur' (ibid., 7, l. 5).
32   Most explicitly: 'In uno Romano imperio propter Anitchristum blasphemantem, omnia simul regna delenda sunt, et nequaquam terrenum imperium erit, sed sanctorum conversatio, et adventus Filii Dei triumphantis [...]' (ibid., 7, l. 11).

Roman Empire, is also present in the *Annolied*'s version. Here, the boar is clearly identified with the Romans (*AL*, 16. 1–2), who have subjugated all their enemies (*AL*, 16. 10) and now rule 'diu werlt al' (*AL*, 16. 12). The boar's ten horns are explained as 'cîn kuninge, | dî mit Rômêrin rittint ce sturme' (*AL*, 17. 1–2). The eleventh horn signifies the Antichrist (*AL*, 17. 9), 'der noch in diese werlt kunftig ist' (*AL*, 17. 10). It clearly points to an eschatological future yet to come. But, as Fiebig has pointed out, the main function of the Daniel passage in the *Annolied* is not eschatological or to comment on and interpret history, but simply to bridge the gap in the historical narrative between Semiramis (*AL*, 10. 16) and the Romans (from *AL*, 18).[33]

The *Kaiserchronik* offers a distinctly modified version of the Daniel material. The 'lewin' (*KC*, 579), which takes up the first position and stands for Babylon in Jerome and the *Annolied*, has moved to the final, fourth position and is immediately identified as the 'Antichrist' (*KC*, 585). Thus, the lioness pushes the 'fraislich eber' (*KC*, 571) and with it 'den tiurlîchen Julijum' (*KC*, 572) and 'daz rîche ze Rôme' (*KC*, 578), to which the boar is linked, into the third position. Here, one would more conventionally expect the 'liebarte' (*KC*, 536) representing the Greek Empire, or more specifically 'den Chrîchisken Alexandrum' (*KC*, 538), but it is not only shunted to the second position but all the way to the first one, where the lioness used to be. This leaves the second position free for the mysterious 'pere wilde' (*KC*, 565), which supposedly illustrates 'driu kunincrîche, | diu wider aim solten grîfen' (*KC*, 567–68). Most notably, the horn remains with the fourth beast and thus now adorns the lioness (*KC*, 583). The other markers of the Antichrist, too — 'mennisclîchen sin' (*KC*, 580) and 'mennisken ougen unt munt' (*KC*, 581) — are transplanted to the lioness. While 'mennisclîchen sin' corresponds to *AL*, 12. 2, where it is an attribute of the lioness, the 'mennisken ougen unt munt' are closest to *AL*, 17. 5, where they are clearly attributed to the eleventh horn and not the animal itself.[34] The mirroring of the adjective *mennisken*, which does not feature in *AL*, 17. 5, aims at an increased synchronization of the two traits as defining qualities of the beast standing for the Antichrist.

This unique arrangement of the Daniel passage in the *Kaiserchronik* caught the attention of editors and scholars early on and attracted mostly scornful commentary when, for example, Schröder characterized the sequence as 'sehr ungeschickt hier eingereiht und umgestellt'.[35] Ohly offered a more helpful approach, in that he tried to make narrative sense of the idiosyncratic presentation of Daniel's vision in the *Kaiserchronik*. For him, the key is the altered point of insertion when compared to the *Annolied*. In the *Kaiserchronik*, the Daniel passage is inserted close to the end of the Caesar episode. Only the remuneration of the Germans and Caesar's death at the hands of the Romans follow in the *Kaiserchronik* after Daniel's prophecies. For Ohly, the purpose of the exegesis is to present Caesar's rule and his inauguration

33   See Fiebig, p. 40.
34   For Ohly, *Sage und Legende*, p. 48, the resemblance between *KC*, 581 and *AL*, 17. 5 is not sufficiently close. He claims that this line does not have any equivalent in the *Annolied* and thus proves the conscious and deliberate adaptation choices made by the author of the *Kaiserchronik*.
35   Schröder, p. 90, n. 1.

of the Roman Empire in the light of prophetic Providence. For him, this explains the changes the *Kaiserchronik* makes, apparently consciously, to the template it takes from the *Annolied*. Ohly places great emphasis on the fact that in the *Kaiserchronik*, the four beasts are not supposed to signify four empires but are personalized as four 'chunige rîche' (*KC*, 534), 'powerful kings'.[36] In the Book of Daniel, they are unambiguously identified as 'quattuor regna' (Daniel 7. 17), and the *Annolied* sees them as representatives of four 'künincrîche' (*AL*, 11. 11).

Since the *Kaiserchronik* needs Caesar as a positive founding figure for the Empire, Ohly argues that the text strives to exonerate him from the close association of the Roman Empire with the eschatological fourth beast as presented in Jerome and the *Annolied*.[37] For that reason, the *Kaiserchronik* pushes the boar and the Romans from the fourth back to the third position and moves the Babylonian lioness from the first to the now vacated last position to have her stand for the Antichrist — not a surprising decision given the significance of Babylon in Revelation 17. Eschatology and the Antichrist now have one specific and exclusive representative, while Caesar and the Roman Empire, as represented by the boar, have been disencumbered of this symbolic burden.

And indeed, comparing the presentations of Caesar in both the *Annolied* and the *Kaiserchronik*, his more positive portrayal in the latter soon becomes evident. In the *Annolied*, he is introduced as the 'edelin Cêsarem' (*AL*, 18. 9), but after this not much effort is devoted to developing him. Most mentions of him remain neutral: he is simply *Cêsar* or represented by a simple pronoun.[38] Only his adversaries level the accusation against him that because of his 'geile' (*AL*, 24. 3) he lost too many men on his campaigns. On one occasion, he is referred to as the 'iunge man' (*AL*, 28. 1), but that is the limit of the ornamental epithets the *Annolied* can muster for Caesar. Of course, it can be argued that this might simply be a trait of the sober language of the *Annolied*, but the sheer quantity of apparently deliberate changes in the *Kaiserchronik* is nonetheless remarkable. Ohly sees in this the text's effort to complete Caesar 'nach seiner ethischen Seite hin'.[39]

This semantically enhanced Caesar of the *Kaiserchronik* is now connected to the four German *gentes* of the Swabians, the Saxons, the Bavarians, and the Franks.[40] Caesar is commissioned by the Roman Senate, which has been alerted by the *salvatio Romae* (*KC*, 235–46), to subjugate the Germans as they rise in rebellion against Rome. Generally, the *Kaiserchronik*'s account follows the *Annolied*, but some

36   Ohly, *Sage und Legende*, p. 48.

37   Ibid., p. 50. More generally on Caesar, see Almut Suerbaum, 'Caesar als Integrationsfigur im Mittelalter?', in *Praktiken europäischer Traditionsbildung im Mittelalter: Wissen — Literatur — Mythos*, ed. by Manfred Eikelmann and Udo Friedrich (Berlin, 2013), pp. 229–43.

38   *AL*, 18. 11, 12, 13, 15, 17, 18; 19. 2, 14; 20. 1, 2, 3, 25, 26; 21. 2, 3, 4; 22. 1; 23. 25; 24. 1, 3, 5, 7, 9, 11, 13, 14, 15, 16; 25. 9, 10, 19; 26. 2, 8; 27. 14; 28. 2, 3, 4, 8, 9, 11, 13, 14, 15; 29. 1.

39   Ohly, *Sage und Legende*, p. 45.

40   On the problem of 'tribes' and *gentes*, see Joachim Ehlers, 'Erfundene Traditionen? Zum Verhältnis von Nationsbildung und Ethnogenese im deutschen und französischen Mittelalter', in *Geschichte der Gleichung 'germanisch-deutsch'*, ed. by Beck and others, pp. 131–62. See also Jörg Jarnut, 'Die Entstehung des mittelalterlichen deutschen Reiches als Forschungsproblem', in *Geschichte der Gleichung 'germanisch-deutsch'*, ed. by Beck and others, pp. 255–64.

significant details are added or changed; for example, in the *Annolied* the German peoples remain leaderless, whereas in the *Kaiserchronik* the Swabians are commanded by Prenne, who is a 'helt vil vermezzen' (*KC*, 274–75), and the Bavarians are ruled by Duke Boimunt and his brother Ingram (*KC*, 300–01). The addition of these named opponents Caesar has to face — the Swabian hero Prenne apparently even in direct combat (*KC*, 273–79) — has been read as the *Kaiserchronik*'s attempt to distinguish not only the German peoples but also Caesar by establishing daunting adversaries for him to overcome.[41] In addition to this, each of the *origines gentium* of the four German *gentes* in the *Kaiserchronik* is slightly shortened, reorganized, or adapted in comparison to the *Annolied*. Of these, the Swabians and the Franks are of particular interest here.

When Caesar advances against the Swabians, they first 'werten wol ir land' (*KC*, 282), before they finally and only after a 'teidinge' (*KC*, 284) yield to him. The *Kaiserchronik* almost completely does away with their *origo gentis*. The *Annolied* knows that they 'dari cumin wârin ubir meri' (*AL*, 19. 4), which is a necessary trait for the ancestors of the German *gens* in the *Annolied* because only if they at some point migrated into the German lands is it possible to connect them genealogically to people of historical significance and importance. They, of course, are to be rooted in the legitimizing sphere of traditional historiography, ancient legend, and biblical record, and not in the German outback of history. Anneliese Grau argues that the *Annolied*'s presentation of the *origines* of the four *gentes* is influenced by Fredegar's origin legends, and that according to these each of the four German peoples descends from a historical *gens* of classical or biblical provenance.[42] The *Annolied* explicates this only in three cases: the Bavarians descend from 'Armenie' (*AL*, 20. 16), the Saxons hail from the lands ruled by the heirs of Alexander the Great (*AL*, 21. 5–11), and the Franks can trace their genealogy all the way back to 'Troie der altin' (*AL*, 22. 5). Apart from the fact that they came from beyond the sea, no further information is provided concerning the genealogy of the Swabians, but following Grau's parallel reading with Fredegar they would have to descend from the Babylonians. The *Kaiserchronik*, however, does not take over the Swabians' migrative origins and only picks up the naming of the Swabian *gens* after the mountain 'Suêvo' (*AL*, 19. 7), which now becomes 'Swêro' (*KC*, 288). This prompted Fiebig to assume that the *Kaiserchronik* presents the Swabians as an indigenous people who can give Caesar 'ir lant' (*KC*, 285).[43]

After the Swabians, Caesar deals with the Saxons and the Bavarians before he confronts the fourth and final German *gens*: the 'vil edelen' (*KC*, 345) Franks. Initially, they are introduced as his 'alten mâgen' (*KC*, 344) whose ancestor Franko settled on the Rhine and himself hailed from the 'Trôjâni' (*KC*, 361). This passage clearly implies a shared Trojan heritage of Caesar and the Franks, even though it is never explicitly mentioned in the *Kaiserchronik*. By and large, their *origo* is taken

---

41   Ohly, *Sage und Legende*, p. 44.
42   Anneliese Grau, *Der Gedanke der Herkunft in der deutschen Geschichtsschreibung des Mittelalters: Trojasage und Verwandtes* (Leipzig, 1938), pp. 17–21.
43   Fiebig, p. 43.

over from the *Annolied* with only slight abridgement. It is the rearrangement of the Cyclops episode that seems particularly jarring. In the *Annolied*, it appears as one in a sequence of episodes illustrating the fate of the Greek survivors of the Trojan War; basically, it is employed to exemplify Ulysses and his travails (*AL*, 22. 16). After the Greeks, the various groups of Trojan survivors are named,[44] culminating with Franko (*AL*, 23. 16), who builds a 'luzzele Troie' (*AL*, 23. 20) on the Rhine and becomes the forefather of the Frankish *gens*. The *Kaiserchronik*, on the other hand, reduces the Greek context around the Cyclops episode, mainly by omitting Agamemnon, whose ignoble fate precedes the Ulysses episode in the *Annolied* (22. 11–16). Without this context, the Cyclops–Ulysses passage no longer appears as an illustrative passage to show what happened to the individual combatants of the Trojan War after the city's fall. The *Annolied* advances its version of the tales about the several survivors with the assessment that in them God's 'urteil' (*AL*, 22. 7) over the warring parties was manifested (*AL*, 22. 7–10). Again, the *Kaiserchronik* does not provide this explanatory contextualization. Instead, the episode begins with an almost defiant 'Ob ir iz glouben wellent, | daz ih iu wil rehte zellen' (*KC*, 349–50), perhaps best translated with an explicating negation as 'Whether you believe it or not | this I will tell you truthfully'.[45] After the episode, the text moves without any further transition to the Trojans and their fate, again narrated in much closer conformity to the *Annolied* (*KC*, 361–75). The Greeks are only mentioned in passing as the ones who destroyed Troy (*KC*, 348). As it stands, the Ulysses and the Cyclops of the *Kaiserchronik* are surrounded on both sides by Trojans. The chronicle may have been trying to turn this episode from the *Annolied*'s exemplary illustration of a Greek fate following the Trojan War into a part of the Frankish *origo*. This would fit in with a tendency of the *Kaiserchronik* to very loosely and rather occasionally associate elements of German history with famous historical events or personalities.

Having defeated all the rebellious German peoples, Caesar consolidates his victories by founding a string of cities and fortresses to defend them (Deutz and Boppard, Andernach and Ingelheim, Mainz and Oppenheim; *KC*, 381–86). This passage does not correspond to any from the *Annolied*, and supposedly aims to tie Caesar as a founding figure more closely to the German peoples and territories.[46]

After his victory, Caesar remains with the Germans 'unz im alle Dûtiske hêrren | willic wâren ze sînen êren' (*KC*, 453–54). He manages to obtain the fealty of the German *gentes* and is now, just as in the *Annolied* (24), able to summon them to his aid against Rome. The Senate refuses to receive him back in the city, accusing him of waging war 'in Dûtisken landen' (*KC*, 459) without its permission and having lost too many men while doing so (*KC*, 455–79). As Goerlitz has pointed out, this army consisting of discrete German *gentes* becomes a unified German army as soon as it

---

44   All old acquaintances from the *Aeneid*: Elenus (*AL*, 23. 3), Antenor (*AL*, 23. 9), Eneas (*AL*, 23. 13).
45   Even though there is no negating particle in the verse. Chinca and Young's unpublished translation: 'Believe it if you will | but I am going to tell you truthfully'; Herweg offers: 'Wenn ihr es glauben wollt, werde ich euch wahrheitsgemäß erzählen' (*Kaiserchronik*, trans. by Herweg, p. 33).
46   See Ohly, *Sage und Legende*, p. 44.

crosses the Alps to the south.[47] With this German army, Caesar advances against Rome 'als ain fluot' (*KC*, 476) and puts the Senate — namely Cato and Pompey — to flight (*KC*, 479–87). He follows them and finally defeats Pompey in a great battle (*KC*, 499–510) not specifically identified as, but corresponding to, the Battle of Pharsalus, which ended the Roman Civil War in 48 BCE.

In two instances, the *Kaiserchronik*'s version of the events of the Roman Civil War differs from the *Annolied*. Both texts emphasize that Caesar advances against Pompey with a much smaller army (*AL*, 26. 7; *KC*, 496) and that the ensuing battle is the largest in written history (*AL*, 26. 10; *KC*, 500). However, only in the *Kaiserchronik* is it explicitly 'durh der Dûtiscen trôst' (*KC*, 497) that Caesar prevails in the end. The second substantial change concerns Pompey. In the *Annolied*, he simply disappears after the defeat (*AL*, 28. 13–14). But the *Kaiserchronik* takes an interest in his further fate and follows him to 'Egipten lant' (*KC*, 511), where he is ultimately killed (*KC*, 513). This gives the author an opportunity to tell briefly of Caesar's revenge for Pompey's death (*KC*, 514), thus alluding to the deeper personal bonds between the two men, which are again not part of the text but certainly part of the cultural and historical background knowledge of author and audience.

The *Annolied*'s account of the Roman Civil War is mainly informed by Lucan's *De Bello Civili*, which was an important part of the Latin school curriculum in the eleventh and twelfth centuries and thus certainly widely read and known. Caesar's own works were not widely read in the Middle Ages, and when they were, they were often wrongly attributed to other authors like Suetonius.[48]

In both the *Annolied* and the *Kaiserchronik*, Caesar can only now, after he has defeated Pompey and consolidated his rule over the Roman Empire, return to Rome and celebrate his triumph (*AL*, 28; *KC*, 519–23). To honour him, the Romans create a new custom: 'si begunden irrizen den hêrren' (*KC*, 520). Caesar orders that this new honorary style should be taught to 'alle Dûtisce man' (*KC*, 524–25). This marks the transfer of a Roman 'site' (*KC*, 524) to the Germans without, however, implying the implementation of a deeper political conduit of *translatio* or even the planting of a political kernel into the German *gentes* that will later, with the German emperors, come into its inevitable blossoming. But the episode does certainly mark a hiatus within the historical logic of the text. For the first time, the 'gewalt | der ê was getailet sô manicvalt' (*KC*, 522–23) is now concentrated in one person: Caesar. Before him, the text spun only a very vague web of pagan authorities: the founding myth of Romulus and Remus (*KC*, 49–54), the three hundred wise men of the Senate (*KC*, 57–61), and the review of the pagan week with its ceremonies for the pagan gods (*KC*, 75–208). Caesar's function in the text is now to usher in the sequence of kings and emperors that serves as the structural backbone of the text. This corresponds to the textual marking of his episode as discussed earlier: the episode centred on him grows organically out of the review of the pagan week and the *salvatio Romae* passage, but he is treated to the full closing formula reporting on

47   Goerlitz, *Identität*, pp. 134–35.
48   See Franz Brunhölzl, 'Caesar im Mittelalter, A: Allgemeines', in *Lexikon des Mittelalters*, ed. by Bautier, Avella-Widhalm, and Auty, II (Munich, 1983), cols 1352–53.

his death and quantifying the duration of his rule. Again form carries content. After the instruction of the Germans in Roman 'site' (*KC*, 524), the *Kaiserchronik* finally comes to the vision of Daniel and its singular interpretation of it (*KC*, 526–90), while the *Annolied*'s version, of course, is positioned before the Romans, let alone Caesar, even figure in the text.

The comparison of the Caesar episode from the *Kaiserchronik* with the older one from the *Annolied* sheds light on what appear to be deliberate changes by means of which the younger text aims first to embellish and idealize Caesar; second, to turn the Germans into more distinctly profiled adversaries, and subsequent allies, of the Romans; and third, to associate or perhaps even causally link the inception of a unified Roman Empire with the martial prowess of the German peoples. At the same time, it maintains the *Annolied*'s strategy of connecting the Germans to historical peoples who hail back to a prehistory not narrated, or only implied and alluded to, in the *Kaiserchronik*. The text's upgrading of Caesar not only distinguishes it from the *Annolied* but also from other important sources like Frutolf or Orosius, who all at least acknowledge the problematic nature of Caesar's bid for power and his subsequent sole reign in the Roman Empire.

The connection of Caesar and Daniel in a single episode is of crucial importance for Ohly. He reads it as a programmatic foil for understanding the internal typological references of the text. For him, the Daniel excursus marks the beginning of a teleologically unfolding historical process of the Roman Empire that finds its providential conclusion in the shaping of an increasingly perfect Christian empire. This empire might be contested by the trappings of the Antichrist, but can never be thoroughly corrupted to eventually turn into his empire of evil, as the more conventional Daniel exegesis would have it.[49]

Ohly's ideas have dominated scholarly discourse into the present day but also created several problems. As Annegret Fiebig demonstrated, there was, at least at the time of the composition of the *Kaiserchronik*, no fixed form of exegesis of Daniel's dreams and the conception of the four empires tied to them. Rather, the interpretation only assumed its canonical form over the course of the twelfth century. Hence, the *Kaiserchronik*'s version should not be regarded as an aberration from an established exegesis but rather as a late example of a long line of alternative interpretations of the Daniel tradition. Accordingly, Fiebig reads the Daniel passage of the *Kaiserchronik* quite differently from Ohly: not as a basic scheme of history, but merely as an image that illustrates the causes for the *translatio* of power and thus can be seen as the foil for *translatio imperii* in the *Kaiserchronik*.

Another problem of Ohly's emphasis on the Daniel passage is that his argument hinges on the differentiation of 'künincriche' in the *Annolied* (11. 11) from 'chunige rîche' in the *Kaiserchronik* (534), the allegedly intentional shift from 'kingdoms' in the older text to 'mighty kings' in the more recent one. The third animal is interpreted as personifying Caesar, thus raising the historical unfolding of the Empire to a salvation-historical level. This conclusion, however, is largely based on Schröder's edition and unfounded in the manuscripts. In his apparatus, Schröder offers two

---

49   See Ohly, *Sage und Legende*, p. 50.

variants, 'kuninc riche' (Vorau, Stiftsarchiv, Ms 276, fol. 3va) and 'chunig reich' (Wolfenbüttel, Herzog August Bibliothek, Cod. Guelf. 15.2 Aug. 2°, fol. 27ra), to underpin the text of his edition. He mainly bases his decision on context, arguing that the animals, because of their rearrangement, cannot signify the empires but point to the individual kings. But even looking at Vorau 276 requires caution, as only a few lines later 'kŭnincriche' (fol. 3rb) can be found when the text tells about the three rows of teeth in the mouth of the bear, the second animal. Save for the superscript on the first vowel and the clear compound spelling of the word, the form is identical to its earlier appearance on fol. 3va. Looking at other manuscripts of recension A, like Munich, Bayerische Staatsbibliothek, Cgm 37 or Heidelberg, Universitätsbibliothek, Cpg 361, complicates matters further. The Heidelberg manuscript does not contain the Daniel passage at all, and the Munich manuscript has 'chvnichriche' (fol. 4vb), where it is quite difficult to ascertain whether the two words are supposed to be connected or not. For the bear, the Munich manuscript offers 'chvnriche' (fol. 5^r), clearly written as one word.

From the manuscripts of recension B, Vienna, Österreichische Nationalbibliothek, Codex 2693 presents quite clearly 'kunicriche' and 'kvnich riche' (fol. 3^r); Codex 2770, however, offers 'chûnig reich' and later 'chûnigreiche' (fol. 3^v). The fragment Prague, Národní Knihovna, Codex 23 G. 43 provides the same reading in both cases: 'kvni(n)griche', with the g and r clearly connected (fols 5^{r-v}).

Finally, in the C recension, to which most of the complete manuscripts of the *Kaiserchronik* belong, the Daniel passage is not transmitted at all. This indicates that the Daniel passage might never have had the crucial importance for the whole of the chronicle that scholarship has assigned to it (or that, at least in the middle of the thirteenth century — at the height of *Kaiserchronik* reception and copying — its compilers and audiences did not consider it significant enough any more).

And even if we only consider recensions A and B, the unclear variance of readings has to be acknowledged. This makes it increasingly dubious whether the passage actually has the importance Ohly saw in it and whether there really was a planned shift from 'kingdom' to 'powerful king' from the *Annolied* to the *Kaiserchronik*, resulting in a purposeful personalization of the Empire in Caesar.

The presentation of Caesar in the *Annolied* prompted the historian Heinz Thomas to speculate about the possibility of a retroactive construction of Caesar as a specifically German founding figure. His stylization as such would have closed a gap for the *gens Teutonica*.[50] What Arthur became for the British, Charlemagne for the French, Piast for the Polish, and Přemysl for the Czechs, Caesar would have become for the Germans. Thomas himself dismisses this notion as 'abwegig', and all things considered he is probably right to do so. He is, however, mainly looking at the *Annolied*. He only passes over the *Kaiserchronik* quickly when summarizing the success of the *Annolied*'s German *origo gentis*, without further considering what the *Kaiserchronik* actually makes of it.[51] It is very tempting to bring Thomas's idea together with the results of the comparison between the Caesar of the *Annolied*

---

50   See Thomas, p. 254.
51   Ibid., pp. 250–56.

and the *Kaiserchronik* made above. This would, of course, by no means imply the deliberate modelling of Caesar into a German King Arthur. Rather, the *Kaiserchronik* picks up the basic function of Caesar in the *Annolied* and shapes his character into the idealized founding figure that it needs for its own purposes. This is facilitated by weaving the Daniel passage into the Caesar episode. Ironically, this would mean that the *Kaiserchronik* is much closer to the 'mythisch-sagenhaft-national[]' texts Ohly calls 'Historien' than to the 'biblisch-heilsgeschichtlich-imperial[]' ones he refers to as 'Chroniken'.[52] All of a sudden, the *Kaiserchronik* seems to be closer to Grundmann's twelfth-century Latin *origines gentium*[53] than to the — likewise Latin — texts Ohly wants to associate it with because only the latter draw their meaning from the 'Gesamtraum göttlicher Heilsgeschichte'[54] and are therefore accessible for interpretation according to his salvation-historical extra-biblical typologies.

To conclude, I would like to suggest that we no longer consider the Caesar–Daniel episode as the text's matrix for a typological and salvation-historical reading of events but rather as an example of the *Kaiserchronik*'s tendency to foreground German presence in history. The text achieves this by pointing out, every now and then, the anecdotal presence of Germans in famous and easily recognizable historical situations and occurrences. The *Kaiserchronik*'s approach to this strategy regarding the source material is far from systematic, and at times almost opportunistic, but it does represent one of the main strands that run through the Roman part of the text in particular. It often vanishes for a considerable number of lines, or even episodes, behind other material, but it remains continuously available for narrative exploitation. In case of the Daniel–Caesar episode, the Germans are prominently inserted to powerfully associate them with the inception of the Empire and to emphasize the continuity of the German association with imperial power to the chronicle's twelfth-century German audience.

4.2.2. Charlemagne and the Romans: Clash of Cultures

The figure of Charlemagne in the *Kaiserchronik* has attracted a great deal of scholarly attention, not only because of the historical importance of *Carolus Magnus* but also because in the fabric of the *Kaiserchronik*, the process of *translatio imperii* is perceived to hinge on the episode centred on him. After all, the text explicitly states that he 'der êrste kaiser wart ze Rôme | von Diutisken landen' (*KC*, 14,818–19). Several other markers single out his importance. First, Ohly pointed out that thanks to the modified length of the reigns of several of the chronicle's emperors, Charlemagne ends up in the middle of the regnal years that the *Kaiserchronik* encompasses.[55] Second, his episode concludes with an anaphoric doxology extolling his virtues, which is unique in this form within the *Kaiserchronik* (*KC*, 15,073–87). Third,

---

52   Ohly, *Sage und Legende*, pp. 15–16.
53   Herbert Grundmann, *Geschichtsschreibung im Mittelalter* (Göttingen, 1965), pp. 12–14.
54   Ohly, *Sage und Legende*, p. 12.
55   Ibid., p. 18: 'Die Regierungszeiten von Caesar bis zu Kaiser Karl ergeben also in ihrer Summe genau die gleiche Zahl von Jahren wie die Zeit von Karl dem Großen bis zum Abbruch der Dichtung.' This argument, however, does not take into account that the *Kaiserchronik* is open-ended and extendable, like any chronicle; hence, this state of affairs could be purely coincidental.

Charlemagne's episode is preceded by the rather puzzling Constantius/Constantine VI episode, which — as Pézsa has argued — only makes sense if read as a mirroring prefiguration of the events of the Charlemagne episode.[56] This is amplified by the fact that the two episodes are separated not by the formulaic framework that usually concludes and opens emperor episodes, but by a vacancy in the rule of the Empire. Neudeck might be slightly overstating this connection when he claims that the Constantius/Constantine VI and the Charlemagne episode form a unity, but he is correct to point out that the 'überhöhende Variation' of the passage structurally marks its importance for the chronicle as a whole.[57]

Geith characterized the Charlemagne episode mainly as a 'Wunderbericht' focused on the person of the emperor and not on the historical plot.[58] He casts doubt on the idea that this passage marks a decisive turning point in the Kaiserchronik's conception of history.[59] Neudeck, however, stresses this pivotal element very much, singling the Charlemagne episode out as a 'zentrale[r] Wendepunkt[]'.[60] He also elaborates on the parallels between Charlemagne and preceding episodes, not only Constantius/Constantine VI but also Constantine the Great.[61] Rubel ventured to continue Ohly's work when he set out to examine the typological connection between Caesar and Charlemagne. He too sees in Charlemagne's rule a 'heils-geschichtlich bedeutsamen Wendepunkt' that marks the translatio imperii ad Francos, which is in turn prefigured by Caesar's rise to power at the beginning of the Kaiser-chronik. Thus, the relationship between the two is one of 'gesteigerter Spiegelung'.[62]

Most recently, Uta Goerlitz has tried to show that Charlemagne is not profiled as an explicitly German ruler, as he oscillates between a Carolingian and a German background, and that his descent is never quite clarified. Furthermore, she argues that, contrary to most of the preceding scholarly literature, the text does not support a straightforward reading of the Charlemagne episode as a document of translatio imperii, as this concept was still being formed in the twelfth century and the Kaiserchronik itself is much closer to the idea of renovatio imperii.[63] While some of her observations are certainly true, the case cannot be considered closed just yet, and the question remains as to whether the doubling of Charlemagne's coming to Rome could not also have a significance of its own, beyond the merely compositional, with regard to the political changes happening in the Empire within this episode.[64]

The task of this section will be to examine whether the rule of Charlemagne indicates a qualitative change in the trajectory of the Kaiserchronik's emperor

56   Pézsa, pp. 116–17.
57   Neudeck, pp. 281–82.
58   Karl-Ernst Geith, *Carolus Magnus: Studien zur Darstellung Karls des Großen in der deutschen Literatur des 12. und 13. Jahrhunderts*, Bibliotheca Germanica, 19 (Berne, 1977), pp. 80–81.
59   Ibid., p. 53.
60   Neudeck, p. 279.
61   Ibid., pp. 283–87.
62   Alexander Rubel, 'Caesar und Karl der Große in der "Kaiserchronik": Typologische Struktur und die translatio imperii ad Francos', *Antike und Abendland*, 47 (2001), 146–63.
63   Goerlitz, *Identität*, pp. 183–86.
64   Robert Folz, for example, did not rely too much on typological and compositional arguments (*Le Souvenir et la légende de Charlemagne dans l'Empire germanique médiéval* (Paris, 1950), pp. 160–70).

episodes. In this regard, not the portrayal of the person of Charlemagne himself but much more how he and his rule reorganize Romanness and Germanness are of interest. This should provide insights into how interested the *Kaiserchronik* actually is in notions of *translatio imperii* and how deep the conceptual divide between the Roman and the German emperors of the chronicle is conceived to be.

When Charlemagne first travels to Rome, prompted by an incorporeal voice, which informs him that his brother — Pope Leo in the *Kaiserchronik*'s account — needs his help (*KC*, 14,316), Rome is characterized as the 'houbetstete' (*KC*, 14,327). This springs from a mechanism introduced earlier in the episode, which ties the various lands ruled by Rome closer to the capital: the system of sending young noblemen to Rome to receive a knightly upbringing before returning to their native lands causally underpins the disposition of those lands to serve Rome as their 'houbetstete'. So, initially, the hierarchy within the Empire seems to be coherent with what the narrative of the *Kaiserchronik* has developed so far: Rome is the capital and centre, and countries like 'Karlingen' (*KC*, 14,309), where Charlemagne's father, Pippin, rules as 'chunich rîche' (*KC*, 14,310), are subordinate satellites.

There is still the question of why Charlemagne does not deal with Leo's vulnerable situation in Rome when he is in the city for the first time (*KC*, 14,346–14,412). It has been argued that his two 'steigernd wiederholten Romzüge[]'[65] are mainly motivated to mirror the configuration of Caesar conquering the Germans and returning to Rome to subdue the Senate.[66] The difference is that this time it is a German who, after a first visit, returns to Rome to conquer the city. Pézsa contrasts the visits to Rome as follows: the first is undertaken by Charlemagne as a pilgrim, the second as a warlord.[67]

Similarly, Charlemagne's clash with the Romans unfolds on different levels: on the level of religious practice and the level of legal culture. Both areas set the new 'voget und rihtære' (*KC*, 14,358) of Rome apart from the inhabitants of what has until now been the centre of the Empire.

To start with, Charlemagne's first coming to Rome sees a voluntary and publicly acclaimed bestowal of the imperial crown and dignity by the Romans upon him (*KC*, 14,376–80). This is connected to the idea that, after the crisis of the Greek rulers, the Romans express a wish to elect an absent king who would 'entwîchen' (*KC*, 14,295) from them. Hence, they give the imperial crown to Charlemagne because they have reason to believe he will go away once his primary interest in Rome — visiting the tombs of the saints (*KC*, 14,334–38) — has been satisfied.

Instead, he comes back, slaughters many Romans, and imposes his new legislation, which happens to be a restoration of Constantine's law. But equally important is that the legislation is forced on the Romans by an outsider. The text needs to mark the seizing of the Roman power by force to indicate a clear break: a foreign — transalpine, Carolingian, German — ruler comes in and restores the Empire, but this time on his terms. The renewal of the Empire is entirely imposed and thus marks a qualitative change of who is in charge and who gets to determine

65   Pézsa, p. 117.
66   Rubel, pp. 158–60.
67   Pézsa, p. 117, n. 249.

the political structure of the Empire, meaning that the changeover can indeed be read as a *translatio imperii* and not only as a *renovatio imperii*.[68]

Another reason why the chronicle splits the coronations of Charlemagne from his consecration might be more structural: the format of the emperor episodes requires the rulers to become Roman rulers as soon as possible. For Charlemagne, the *Kaiserchronik* reorganizes the entire sequence of his life and rule to first solve the question of this succession (up to *KC*, 14,826) and only then to expound his achievements as a warlord and conqueror and the miracles connected to his rule (*KC*, 14,827–15,091).

Charlemagne's status as a foreigner in Rome is corroborated by the creation of a cultural gap between him and the Romans. The geographical opposition between 'Karlingen'/'Kerlingen' and later the 'Riflan[t]' on the one hand and Rome and Italy on the other is complemented by a clash of opposing legal cultures. After having besieged Rome and forced the gates of the city open, Charlemagne sits in judgement over the Romans who mutilated Leo, 'di sculdigen | nâch rehter urtaile' (*KC*, 14,642–43). Charlemagne's demand for a trial by combat to punish the Romans, who assaulted his brother and closed the city to him, scandalizes the Romans; Charlemagne's idea of which legal procedure would be appropriate to resolve the issue clashes sharply with the customary 'reht' (*KC*, 14,654) of the Romans, and sets an extraordinary precedent in their relationship to the imperial authority: 'sie getwungens kaiser ê nie nehain; | si solten rihten mit ir vingeren zwain' (*KC*, 14,655–56). Charlemagne's imported transalpine law is a law in which legal issues can be resolved by combat with the implication that God will know his own. The Romans conceive of the issue as being solvable by simply swearing an oath. The Romans' defence that 'sie getwungens kaiser ê nie nehain' connects the episode back to the past of the Roman Empire where the Romans were ruled by an emperor of their own and a clash like this would have been unimaginable. Charlemagne is clearly singled out as the outsider whose foreign idea of legal practice clashes with the established Roman culture. But the *Kaiserchronik*'s negotiation of the relationship between the new emperor to be and the Romans is more nuanced than this seemingly stark opposition. This becomes evident when we look at the way Charlemagne resolves the situation. He acknowledges Roman legal custom: 'von iwerem rehte netrîbe ich iuh niht mêre' (*KC*, 14,664). Subsequently, he even goes so far as to appropriate it so that he can dictate the conditions of the oath. His condition, that the oath should be sworn in the church of St Pancras in the name of that saint, fills the Romans with dread (*KC*, 14,671–82), as if they already know that they will not be able to sustain their oath in the presence of the saint, who functions like a polygraph and would immediately make their deceit obvious. And, sure enough, Charlemagne can rely on divine support, because as the Romans congregate at the church of St Pancras, one of them collapses and another one takes flight without being able to take the oath. Charlemagne, who deftly set this trap, can now regard the legal matter as judged in his sense, with all Romans guilty, and

68   I am very grateful to Mark Chinca for sharing with me his interpretation of the Charlemagne episode, which has greatly shaped the reading presented here.

he can pursue and massacre them for three days even after they flee into St Peter's Church (*KC*, 14,683–87).

Charlemagne is able on the one hand to respect the Romans' legal custom and on the other hand to turn it into a trap, with the result that the matter is finally resolved in a way that is probably very close to the outcome that would have been produced by the legal procedure of trial by combat initially suggested by him. But he is not only an outsider who outwits the Romans on their own turf and in their own legal practices; he is also a restorer who rectifies changes made to the constitution of the Empire. This emerges in his exhortative prayer to Christ, after he has cleared the rebellious Romans out of the Vatican (*KC*, 14,697–14,707). After his words are initially unsuccessful, Charlemagne has to resort to threatening the saint in his second address to St Peter. Only now is the requested miracle granted, and his brother Pope Leo regains his eyesight. Upon this, Charlemagne and 'daz volc uber al' (*KC*, 14,748) prostrate themselves in the form of a cross and Charlemagne is subsequently consecrated as the new emperor (*KC*, 14,751–56). Charlemagne's prayer has restored the pope's eyesight and his office, to which he was elected by the Romans and from which he was ignominiously removed by the Romans. But his work as a restorer of Romanness is not done. His first legislative measure as the new emperor, which reinstates the authority of priests and bishops, is explicitly linked back to the earlier Roman Emperor Constantine (*KC*, 14,779–83). The Romans' negligence has allowed Constantine's legislation, to which the *Kaiserchronik* devoted a lot of time and space, putting it at the heart of Rome's Christianization (*KC*, 7958–8199), to be all but forgotten. Charlemagne's role is not only to introduce the rule of the transalpine emperors but also to restore Christian religious practice, which had become quintessentially Roman since the time of Constantine. Where Charlemagne's second coming to Rome, his massacre of the Romans, and his ascent to the throne marked him as a disruption to the political constitution of the Empire, his renewal of Constantinian legislation aims to foreground the continuity of his rule within the Romanness of the Empire. The emperor, with his ambiguously shifting Carolingian and German background, acts within both the premises of a *renovatio imperii* and a *translatio*. Finding its own way without feeling the need to pick a side between the two concepts, the *Kaiserchronik* not only allows for breaks and ellipses in the chronology of its account, but manages at the same time to maintain the 'vollkommene politisch-ideelle Kontinuität' evidenced by the chronicle's strict emperor episode framework.[69]

The way the *Kaiserchronik* presents the political genesis of the Roman Empire is not so much a *translatio imperii* from the Romans to the Germans as it is a change of perspective on the same imperial entity. The chronicle's point of view shifts from a Roman cisalpine perspective to a Carolingian and German transalpine one, which, however, shares a lot of the underpinnings that have hitherto informed the cisalpine Roman Empire. This is hardly surprising considering how eager the *Kaiserchronik* is to consistently emphasize the continuing presence of the Germans in relation to this empire from its beginnings.

69   Goerlitz, *Identität*, p. 176.

CONCLUSION

❖

Over the *Kaiserchronik*'s course, the Roman Empire emerges as its actual protagonist. Its coherence is maintained throughout. The episodic framework allows for the employment of various narrative strategies to translate what could become jarring historical differences between narrated past and medieval present into a simple countable distance. Years of rules and imperial lifetimes are easier to present as the backbone of history than the structural changes that qualitatively alienate the past from the present. Where the quantitative axial paradigm encounters its limitations — especially regarding the transitions within the political and religious identity of the Empire — neither the Empire's turn from a pagan into a Christian, nor from a cisalpine into a transalpine Empire endangers the paradigm's continual Romanness. The pivotal stations of both processes show a purposeful and highly reflected implementation, with passages explicitly referencing and repeating each other and reverberating meaningfully.

The transformation of the Roman Empire from a pagan into a Christian one follows the gradual substitution of the polytheistic worship of demons disguised as gods with Christian monotheism. This is the driving motivator behind the selection of much of the narrative material up to Constantine and Theodosius. The aim here is not to devise a teleological salvation-historical trajectory but to negotiate the qualitative change of religious identity in the conceptually unchanged Roman Empire. This means that Christianity, even after its establishment, always remains vulnerable.

While the Roman Empire always remains Roman, the perspective on it and its rulers changes significantly. Even when the Roman Empire is ruled by Roman emperors, the chronicle opportunistically latches onto several opportunities to emphasize the historical closeness of the Germans or of discrete German peoples to the body and history of the Roman Empire. This is especially striking during the Caesar episode, which sees the inauguration of the Empire as an imperial genealogy, and in the Charlemagne episode, which marks the switch of perspective from an internally and essentially Roman one to a transalpine one that, however, never fully asserts a fully conceptualized Germanness.

This sheds a new light on one of the questions most frequently posed about the text. Why are the Roman and the German, the ancient and the medieval, parts so different? Petersen explained the differences by ascribing to the Roman part a negative meaning: the history of the Empire has been semanticized retrospectively from the perspective of the twelfth century, and through this lens the ancient Roman part can only be read as an 'Aufschub des im Anfang der Geschichte schon angelegten Zieles'. The ancient history of the Empire has to be artificially injected with meaning, through narrativization and mythopoiesis, while the history of the Empire since Charlemagne shares a 'konzeptuelles Kontinuum' with the twelfth-century present and therefore does not require such treatment. In Petersen's view, this turns the Roman part of the *Kaiserchronik* into the account of a 'Vorzeit' that is categorically different from everything that happens with and after Charlemagne. But Petersen remains vague about what characterizes this 'konzeptuelles Kontinuum' that the German part shares with the present.[1] His suggestions — the temporal axis or the institution of the German-Roman Empire — are present throughout the text and extend back prior to the Charlemagne episode instead of originating in it. Charlemagne's rule does not affect the quantitative framework of the chronicle's time axis, and it does not indicate any qualitative change in the Empire either. It is merely a change of perspective on the always contingent, self-contained, and freely retrievable concepts that organize the history of the *Kaiserchronik*'s Empire. It is not the ancient part of the chronicle that suffers from a lack of meaning, but the German part, for the very reason Petersen cites. Thus the conclusion should be the other way round: after Charlemagne, the text has caught up with the two columns of the conceptual continuum that the chronicle's content shares with the present: Christianity and Germanness. Having thus happily achieved its aetiological mission, the *Kaiserchronik* can dutifully complete its linear account of the Empire's history by adding the German emperors in a highly unified account until the chronicle catches up with its own present day. Because of their conceptual unity with the present, the episodes centred on the Carolingian and German emperors lack any potential for narrative semanticization of history, which is the chronicle's main objective. The *Kaiserchronik* wants to narrate 'Vorzeit'. It does not provide an embarrassed compensation for an inherent lack of meaning in the past, but utilizes the semantic openness of the past to establish an aetiological connection to the present. Over the course of the chronicle's own narrative, the distance between narrated time and medieval present necessarily collapses. Once the present day of the twelfth century is reached by the text's narrative progression, it is treated as categorically different, as 'Nachzeit', so to speak, that holds very little in which the chronicle's author is interested.

Yet, to pursue its narrative interests, the text does not develop a coherent programme or inscribe into itself a hermeneutical metastructure in need of unlocking. The importance of salvation-historical thought and patterns, in particular, has traditionally been considerably overestimated in this regard. Instead, the chronicle parcels out its complex and unwieldy object — the continual unfolding of imperial time and rule — in an encyclopedia of diverse stories presented in all the possible modes of narration that German vernacular storytelling in the middle of the twelfth century was able to muster. Thus, the *Kaiserchronik*'s past is not a foreign country but is turned into a space where a contemporary audience can negotiate their historical origins and role. As the past comes up to meet the audience on their own terms, they can themselves project back the questions they have about their identity

---

1   Petersen, pp. 352–53.

and history and find their answers arranged as historical truths. Their ancestors' presence and role in the history and continuity of the political entity they inhabited touch on contemporary points of bewilderment and excitement.

Andrew Marbot would probably not have approved of the *Kaiserchronik*'s use of the Roman past. Like the ruins of Rome he commented on, the *Kaiserchronik* allows its audience to live in an era of their own choosing. But the present the chronicle speaks to understands itself very much as a prolonged past sharing the Romanness that is the qualitative backbone of the Empire with all stages of its earlier life. Just like the droves of visitors Marbot describes being drawn to the ruins of Rome, the author of the *Kaiserchronik* strives to appropriate the past and turn it into present. For those writing, reading, and listening to the *Kaiserchronik* in the second half of the twelfth century, the past was present all along.

REFERENCES

❖

Primary Texts

Annolied, in *Deutsche Dichtung des Mittelalters*, ed. by Michael Curschmann and Ingeborg Glier (Munich, 1980–81), I: *Von den Anfängen bis zum hohen Mittelalter* (1980), pp. 92–147

ARISTOTLE, *Opera Omnia: Volumen Alterum*, ed. by Immanuel Bekker and Georg Reimer (Berlin, 1831)

——*Rhetoric*, trans. by William Rhys (New York, 1954)

DER ARME HARTMANN, *Rede vom Glauben*, in *Die religiösen Dichtungen des 11. und 12. Jahrhunderts*, ed. by Friedrich Maurer, 3 vols (Tübingen, 1964–70), II (1965), 568–628

AUGUSTINE, *De Civitate Dei*, ed. by B. Dombart and A. Kalb, Corpus Christianorum: Series Latina, 47–48, 2 vols (Turnhout, 1955)

——*Confessions*, ed. by James O'Donnell, 3 vols (Oxford, 1992)

BEDE, *The Complete Works of Venerable Bede*, ed. by J. A. Giles, 8 vols (London, 1843–44), II–III: *Historia Ecclesiastica Gentis Anglorum* (1843)

——*The Ecclesiastical History of the English Nation*, trans. by L. C. Jane (New York, 2007)

Biblia Sacra Latina: Ex Biblia Sacra Vulgatae Editionis (London, 1970)

BODEL, JEHAN, *La Chanson des Saisnes*, ed. by Annette Brasseur, Textes littéraires français, 369, 2 vols (Geneva, 1989)

'Briefe Meinhards von Bamberg', in *Briefsammlungen der Zeit Heinrichs IV.*, ed. by Carl Erdmann and Norbert Fickermann, MGH Briefe der deutschen Kaiserzeit, 5 (Weimar, 1950), pp. 107–31

CASSIODORUS SENATOR, *Historia Ecclesiastica Tripartita*, ed. by Walter Jakob and Rudolf Hanslik, Corpus Scriptorum Ecclesiasticorum Latinorum, 71 (Vienna, 1952)

The Central Franconian Rhyming Bible ('Mittelfränkische Reimbibel'): An Early Twelfth-Century German Verse Homiliary: A Thematic and Exegetical Commentary with the Text and a Translation into English, ed. and trans. by David Wells, Amsterdamer Publikationen zur Sprache und Literatur, 155 (Amsterdam, 2004)

CHRÉTIEN DE TROYES, *Erec und Enide*, trans. by Ingrid Kasten, Klassische Texte des Romanischen Mittelalters, 17 (Munich, 1971)

——*Erec and Enide*, trans. by Dorothy Gilbert (Los Angeles, 1992)

CICERO, *De Inventione*, in *On Invention, Best Kind of Orator, Topics*, trans. by H. M. Hubbell, Loeb Classical Library, 386 (Cambridge, MA, 1949), pp. 1–348

——*Rhetorica*, ed. by A. S. Wilkins, 2 vols (Oxford, 1963), I: *De Oratore*

——*Über die Weissagung: De Divinatione*, ed. and trans. by Christoph Schäublin (Berlin, 2013)

Codice topografico della città di Roma: Saec. XII–XIV, ed. by Roberto Valentini and Giuseppe Zucchetti, 4 vols (Rome, 1940–53)

The Conferences of John Cassian, trans. by Edgar C. S. Gibson, Select Library of Nicene and Post-Nicene Fathers of the Christian Church, 2nd ser., 11 (New York, 1894)

EKKEHARD OF AURA, *Chronica*, ed. by Georg Waitz, in MGH SS, 6 (Hanover, 1844), pp. 1–267

The Etymologies of Isidore of Seville, trans. by Stephen Barney and others (Cambridge, 2006)

EUSEBIUS OF CAESAREA, *Historiae Ecclesiasticae Libri X*, ed. by Friedrich Adolf Heinichen, 3 vols (Leipzig, 1827)

—— *The History of the Church*, trans. by G. A. Williamson, ed. by Andrew Louth (London, 1989)

—— *De Vita Constantini: Über das Leben Konstantins*, ed. by Bruno Bleckmann, trans. by Horst Schneider, Fontes Christiani, 83 (Turnhout, 2007)

Ezzolied, in *Die kleinen Denkmäler der Vorauer Handschrift*, ed. by Erich Henschel and Ulrich Pretzel (Tübingen, 1963), pp. 2–27

FLAVIUS JOSEPHUS, *The Jewish War*, trans. by G. A. Williamson, ed. by Mary Smallwood (London, 1959; repr. 1981)

Frivolities of Courtiers and Footprints of Philosophers: Being a Translation of the First, Second, and Third Books and Selections from the Seventh and Eighth Books of the Policraticus of John of Salisbury, trans. by Joseph Pike (New York, 1972)

GODFREY OF VITERBO, *Pantheon; sive, Vniuersitatis Libri*, ed. by Johannes Herold (Basle, 1559)

—— *Memoria Seculorum*, ed. by Georg Waitz, in MGH SS, 22 (Hanover, 1872), pp. 94–106

—— *Speculum Regnum*, ed. by Georg Waitz, in MGH SS, 22 (Hanover, 1872), pp. 21–93

HEGEL, GEORG WILHELM FRIEDRICH, *Lectures on the Philosophy of History*, trans. by J. Sibree (New York, 1956)

HEINRICH VON VELDEKE, *Eneasroman: Mittelhochdeutsch/Neuhochdeutsch*, ed. by Ludwig Ettmüller, trans. by Dieter Kartschoke, RUB, 8303 (Stuttgart, 2004)

HERODOTUS, *The Histories*, trans. by Robin Waterfield (Oxford, 1998)

Das himmlische Jerusalem, in *Kleinere deutsche Gedichte des 11. und 12. Jahrhunderts*, ed. by Werner Schröder (Tübingen, 1972), pp. 189–201

IRENAEUS, *Libros Quinque adversus Haereses*, ed. by William Wigan Harvey, 2 vols (Cambridge, 1857)

ISIDORE OF SEVILLE, *Etymologiarum sive Originum Libri XX*, ed. by W. M. Lindsay, 2 vols (Oxford, 1911; repr. 1957)

JEROME, *Epistolae*, ed. by J.-P. Migne, Patrologiae Cursus Completus: Series Latina, 22 (Paris, 1845)

—— *Commentariorum in Danielem Libri III*, ed. by F. Glorie, Corpus Christianorum: Series Latina, 75a (Turnhout, 1964)

JOHN CASSIAN, *Conlationes XXIIII*, ed. by Michael Petschenig (Vienna, 1886)

JOHN OF SALISBURY, *Policraticus*, ed. by Clement Webb (London, 1909)

—— *Historia Pontificalis*, ed. by Reginald Poole (Oxford, 1927)

HEINRICH VON VELDEKE, *Eneasroman: Mittelhochdeutsch/Neuhochdeutsch*, ed. by Ludwig Ettmüller, trans. by Dieter Kartschoke (Stuttgart, 2004)

Herzog Ernst: Mittelhochdeutsch/Neuhochdeutsch, ed. and trans. by Mathias Herweg, RUB, 19,606 (Stuttgart, 2019)

Die Hochzeit, in *Frühe Deutsche Literatur und Lateinische Literatur in Deutschland 800–1150*, ed. by Walter Haug and Benedikt Konrad Vollmann, Bibliothek des Mittelalters, 1 (Frankfurt a. M., 1991), pp. 784–847

Die Kaiserchronik: Mittelhochdeutsch/Neuhochdeutsch, trans. by Mathias Herweg, RUB, 19,270 (Stuttgart, 2014)

Die Kaiserchronik eines Regensburger Geistlichen, ed. by Edward Schröder, MGH Dt. Chron., I.1 (Hanover, 1895)

König Rother: Mittelhochdeutsch/Neuhochdeutsch, ed. and trans. by Peter Stein, ed. by Ingrid Bennewitz, RUB, 18,047 (Stuttgart, 2000)

The Letters of John of Salisbury, ed. and trans. by H. E. Butler and W. J. Millor, rev. by Christopher Brooke, 2 vols (Oxford, 1979)

Liber Pontificalis, ed. by Theodor Mommsen, MGH Gesta Pontificum Romanorum, 1 (Berlin, 1895)

LIVY, *Ab Urbe Condita*, ed. by Robert Seymour Conway and Charles Flamstead Walters (Oxford, 1914)

Das Lob Solomons, in *Frühe Deutsche Literatur und Lateinische Literatur in Deutschland 800–1150*, ed. by Walter Haug and Benedikt Konrad Vollmann, Bibliothek des Mittelalters, 1 (Frankfurt a. M., 1991), pp. 702–17

OROSIUS, *Historiarum adversum Paganos Libri VII*, ed. by Karl Zangmeister (Vienna, 1882)

——— *Seven Books of History against the Pagans*, trans. by Andrew T. Fear, Translated Texts for Historians, 54 (Liverpool, 2015)

OTFRID VON WEISSENBURG, *Evangelienbuch: Auswahl*, ed. by Gisela Vollmann-Profe, RUB, 8384 (Stuttgart, 1987)

——— 'Ad Liutbertum', in *Frühe Deutsche Literatur und Lateinische Literatur in Deutschland 800–1150*, ed. by Walter Haug and Benedikt Konrad Vollmann, Bibliothek des Mittelalters, 1 (Frankfurt a. M., 1991), pp. 72–83

OTTO OF FREISING, *Chronica; sive, Historia de Duabus Civitatibus*, ed. by Adolf Hofmeister, MGH SS Rer. Germ., 45 (Hanover, 1912)

——— *The Deeds of Frederick Barbarossa*, trans. by Charles Christopher Mierow (Columbia, 1966)

——— *Chronica; sive, Historia de Duabus Civitatibus*, ed. by Adolf Schmidt and Walther Lammers, Freiherr vom Stein-Gedächtnisausgabe, 16 (Darmstadt, 1990)

——— *The Two Cities: A Chronicle of Universal History to the Year 1146 A.D.*, trans. by Charles Christopher Mierow (New York, 2002)

——— AND RAHEWIN, *Gesta Friderici I. Imperatoris*, ed. by Georg Waitz and Bernhard de Simson, MGH SS Rer. Germ., 46 (Hanover, 1912)

Ortnit und die Wolfdietriche, ed. by Arthur Amelung and Oscar Jänicke, Deutsches Heldenbuch, 3.1 (Berlin, 1971)

Ovid's Fasti, ed. by Sir James Frazer (London, 1931)

PFAFFE KONRAD, *Rolandslied: Mittelhochdeutsch/Neuhochdeutsch*, ed. and trans. by Dieter Kartschoke, RUB, 2745 (Stuttgart, 1993)

PFAFFE LAMPRECHT, *Alexanderroman: Mittelhochdeutsch/Neuhochdeutsch*, ed. by Elisabeth Lienert, RUB, 18,508 (Stuttgart, 2007)

POLYBIUS, *The Histories: Books 9–15*, trans. by W. R. Paton, Loeb Classical Library, 159, 6 vols (Cambridge, MA, 2011)

Porphyry's Against the Christians: The Literary Remains, ed. and trans. by Joseph Hoffmann (Amherst, 1994)

QUINTILIAN, *Institutio Oratoria: Books I–III*, trans. by H. E. Butler, Loeb Classical Library, 124, 5 vols (Cambridge, MA, 1920; repr. 1963)

RUDOLF VON EMS, *Alexander: Ein höfischer Versroman des 13. Jahrhunderts*, ed. by Victor Junk (Darmstadt, 1928; repr. 1970)

SUETONIUS, *De Vita Caesarum Libri VIII*, ed. by Robert A. Kaster (Oxford, 2016)

Trierer Silvester, ed. by Carl Kraus, in MGH Dt. Chron., 1.2 (Hanover, 1895), pp. 1–45

ULRICH VON ETZENBACH, *Alexander*, ed. by Wendelin Toischer, Bibliothek des Litterarischen Vereins in Stuttgart, 183 (Tübingen, 1888)

Vindicta Salvatoris, in *Two Old English Apocrypha and their Manuscript Source: The Gospel of Nichodemus and the Avenging of the Saviour*, ed. by E. J. Cross, Cambridge Studies in Anglo-Saxon England, 19 (Cambridge, 1996), pp. 248–93

VIRGIL, *Aeneis*, ed. by George Long, 3 vols (London, 1883)

Vita Sadalbergae, ed. by B. Krusch and W. Levison, in MGH SS Rer. Merov., 5 (Hanover, 1810), pp. 40–66

Die Wahrheit, in *Die kleinen Denkmäler der Vorauer Handschrift*, ed. by Erich Henschel and Ulrich Pretzel (Tübingen, 1963), pp. 50–61

Secondary Literature

ALEXANDER, PHILIP, 'The Parting of the Ways from the Perspective of Rabbinic Judaism', in *Jews and Christians: The Parting of the Ways, A.D. 70 to 135: The Second Durham–Tübingen Research Symposium on Earliest Christianity and Judaism*, ed. by James Dunn (Tübingen, 1992), pp. 1–26

AMSLER, MARK, *Etymology and Grammatical Discourse in Late Antiquity and the Early Middle Ages*, Studies in the History of the Language Sciences, 44 (Amsterdam, 1989)

APEL, KARL-OTTO, *Transformation der Philosophie*, 2 vols (Berlin, 1994–99), II: *Das Apriori der Kommunikationsgemeinschaft* (1999)

AUERBACH, ERICH, 'Sermo Humilis', *Romanische Forschungen*, 64 (1952), 304–64

BAKHTIN, MIKHAIL, 'Forms of Time and of the Chronotope in the Novel: Notes toward a Historical Poetics', in *The Dialogic Imagination: Four Essays by M. M. Bakhtin*, ed. by Michael Holquist, trans. by Caryl Emerson and Michael Holquist (Austin, 1998), pp. 84–110

BERTAU, KARL, *Deutsche Literatur im europäischen Mittelalter*, 2 vols (Munich, 1972–73)

BIEDERMANN, HERMENGILD, 'Homoiousios, Homoiousianer', in *Lexikon des Mittelalters*, ed. by Robert-Henri Bautier, Gloria Avella-Widhalm, and Robert Auty, 10 vols (1980–99), V (Munich, 1991), col. 112

—— 'Homoousios', in *Lexikon des Mittelalters*, ed. by Robert-Henri Bautier, Gloria Avella-Widhalm, and Robert Auty, 10 vols (1980–99), V (Munich, 1991), cols 112–13

BINDING, GÜNTHER, 'Arius, Arianismus, Arianer', in *Lexikon des Mittelalters*, ed. by Robert-Henri Bautier, Gloria Avella-Widhalm, and Robert Auty, 10 vols (1980–99), I (Munich, 1980), cols 949–51

BLAMIRES, DAVID, *Herzog Ernst and the Otherworld Voyage: A Comparative Study* (Manchester, 1979)

BLOCH, HERBERT, 'Der Autor der "Graphia Aureae Urbis Romae"', *Deutsches Archiv für Erforschung des Mittelalters*, 40 (1984), 55–176

BLUMENBERG, HANS, *The Legitimacy of the Modern Age*, trans. by Robert Wallace (Cambridge, MA, 1983)

BLUMENKRANZ, BERNHARD, *Die Judenpredigt Augustins: Ein Beitrag zur Geschichte der jüdisch-christlichen Beziehungen in den ersten Jahrhunderten*, Basler Beiträge zur Geschichtswissenschaft, 25 (Basle, 1946)

BOWDEN, SARAH, 'Zur Poetik des mehrsinnigen Verstehens: Der allegorische Stil der Hochzeit', in *Literarischer Stil: Mittelalterliche Dichtung zwischen Konvention und Innovation*, ed. by Elizabeth Andersen and others (Berlin, 2015), pp. 305–21

BRANDT, HARTWIN, 'Historia magistra vitae? Orosius und die spätantike Historiographie', in *Jenseits der Grenzen: Beiträge zur spätantiken und frühmittelalterlichen Geschichtsschreibung*, ed. by Andreas Goltz, Millennium-Studien zu Kultur und Geschichte des ersten Jahrtausends n. Chr., 25 (Berlin, 2009), pp. 121–33

BRINKMANN, HENNING, 'Der Prolog im Mittelalter als literarische Erscheinung', in *Studien zur Geschichte der deutschen Sprache und Literatur*, 2 vols (Düsseldorf, 1955–66), II (1966), 79–105

BROOKE, CHRISTOPHER, *The Medieval Idea of Marriage* (Oxford, 1989; repr. 2002)

BRUNHÖLZL, FRANZ, 'Caesar im Mittelalter, A: Allgemeines', in *Lexikon des Mittelalters*, ed. by Robert-Henri Bautier, Gloria Avella-Widhalm, and Robert Auty, 10 vols (1980–99), II (Munich, 1983), cols 1352–53

—— 'Quintilianus', in *Lexikon des Mittelalters*, ed. by Robert-Henri Bautier, Gloria Avella-Widhalm, and Robert Auty, 10 vols (1980–99), VII (Munich, 1995), cols 123–30

BUTZER, GÜNTER, 'Das Gedächtnis des epischen Textes: Mündliches und schriftliches Erzählen im höfischen Roman des Mittelalters', *Euphorion*, 89 (1995), 151–88

CARROLL, JAMES, *Constantine's Sword: The Church and the Jews* (Boston, 2001)

CHINCA, MARK, *Studies in the Poetics of Gottfried's Tristan*, Modern Humanities Research Association Texts and Dissertations, 35 (London, 1993)

—— AND CHRISTOPHER YOUNG, 'Uses of the Past in Twelfth-Century Germany: The Case of the Middle High German "Kaiserchronik"', *Central European History*, 49 (2016), 1–20

COURTRAY, RÉGIS, 'Der Danielkommentar des Hieronymus', in *Die Geschichte der Daniel-Auslegung in Judentum, Christentum und Islam*, ed. by Katharina Bracht and David du Toit, Beihefte zur Zeitschrift für die alttestamentliche Wissenschaft, 371 (Berlin, 2007), pp. 123–50

CROSSLEY, RALPH GEORGE, *Die Kaiserchronik: Ein literarhistorisches Problem der altdeutschen Literaturgeschichte* (Munich, 1939)

CURTIUS, ERNST ROBERT, 'Zur Literaturästhetik des Mittelalters', *Zeitschrift für romanische Philologie*, 59 (1938), 1–50, 129–232, 433–79

—— *European Literature and the Latin Middle Ages* (Princeton, 1953; repr. 2013)

DERRIDA, JACQUES, *Of Grammatology*, trans. by Gayatri Chakravorty Spivak (Baltimore, 1967)

DEICHMANN, FRIEDRICH WILHELM, 'Frühchristliche Kirchen in antiken Heiligtümern', in *Rom, Ravenna, Konstantinopel, Naher Osten: Gesammelte Studien zur spätantiken Architektur, Kunst und Geschichte* (Wiesbaden, 1982), pp. 56–94

DICKHUT-BIELSKY, JOHANNES, *Auf der Suche nach der Wahrheit in Annolied und Kaiserchronik: Poetisch-historiographische Wahrheitssuche in frühmittelhochdeutschen Geschichtsdichtungen*, Beihefte zur Zeitschrift für deutsches Altertum und deutsche Literatur, 23 (Stuttgart, 2015)

DITTRICH, MARIE-LUISE, *Die Eneide Heinrichs von Veldeke: Quellenkritischer Vergleich mit dem Roman d'Eneas und Vergils Aeneis*, 2 vols (Wiesbaden, 1966)

DÖPP, HEINZ-MARTIN, *Die Deutung der Zerstörung Jerusalems und des Zweiten Tempels im Jahre 70 in den ersten drei Jahrhunderten n. Chr.*, Texte und Arbeiten zum neutestamentlichen Zeitalter, 24 (Tübingen, 2002)

DUBY, GEORGES, *The Knight, the Lady and the Priest: The Making of Modern Marriage in Medieval France* (London, 1984)

DUCHESNE, LOUIS, 'L'Auteur des Mirabilia', *Mélanges d'archéologie et d'histoire*, 24 (1904), 479–89

DUFFY, S. J., 'Parousia, 2: In Theology', in *New Catholic Encyclopedia*, 15 vols (Washington, 1967), x, cols 1037–40

EHLERS, JOACHIM, 'Erfundene Traditionen? Zum Verhältnis von Nationsbildung und Ethnogenese im deutschen und französischen Mittelalter', in *Zur Geschichte der Gleichung 'germanisch-deutsch': Sprache und Namen, Geschichte und Institutionen*, ed. by Heinrich Beck and others, Ergänzungsbände zum Reallexikon der Germanischen Altertumskunde, 34 (Berlin, 2004), pp. 131–62

ENGELS, O., 'Konrad III., dt. Kg.', in *Lexikon des Mittelalters*, ed. by Robert-Henri Bautier, Gloria Avella-Widhalm, and Robert Auty, 10 vols (1980–99), v (Munich, 1991), cols 1339–40

FERLUGA, J., 'Edessa, Stadt in der heut. sö. Türkei, II: Die Grafschaft Edessa', in *Lexikon des Mittelalters*, ed. by Robert-Henri Bautier, Gloria Avella-Widhalm, and Robert Auty, 10 vols (1980–99), VIII (Munich, 1996), cols 1568–69

FIEBIG, ANNEGRET, 'vier wilde tiere: Weltdeutung nach Daniel in der "Kaiserchronik"', in *Deutsche Literatur und Sprache von 1050–1200: Festschrift für Ursula Henning zum 65. Geburtstag*, ed. by Annegret Fiebig and Hans-Jochen Schiewer (Berlin, 1995), pp. 27–49

FIX, ULLA, *Rhetorik und Stilistik: Ein internationales Handbuch historischer und systematischer Forschung* (Berlin, 2008)

FOERSTER, THOMAS, *Godfrey of Viterbo and his Readers: Imperial Tradition and Universal Historiography in Late Medieval Europe* (Abingdon, 2016)

FOLZ, ROBERT, *Le Souvenir et la légende de Charlemagne dans l'Empire germanique médiéval* (Paris, 1950)

FRAPPIER, JEAN, *Chrétien de Troyes: The Man and his Work*, trans. by Raymond Cormier (Athens, OH, 1982)

FREDRIKSEN, PAULA, *Augustine and the Jews: A Christian Defense of Jews and Judaism* (New York, 2008)

FRIED, JOHANNES, *Geschichte und Gehirn: Irritationen der Geschichtswissenschaft durch Gedächtniskritik*, Akademie der Wissenschaften und der Literatur: Abhandlungen der Geistes- und Sozialwissenschaftlichen Klasse, 7 (Mainz, 2003)

FRIEDRICH, UDO, 'Topik und Narration: Zur rhetorischen und poetischen Funktion exemplarischen Erzählens in der "Kaiserchronik"', *Poetica*, 47.1–2 (2016), 1–24

FROMM, HANS, 'Die Disputationen in der Faustinianlegende der "Kaiserchronik": Zum literarischen Dialog im 12. Jahrhundert', in *Deutsche Literatur und Sprache von 1050–1200: Festschrift für Ursula Henning zum 65. Geburtstag*, ed. by Annegret Fiebig and Hans-Jochen Schiewer (Berlin, 1995), pp. 51–69

FUKUYAMA, FRANCIS, *The End of History and the Last Man* (London, 1992)

GARDT, ANDREAS, *Geschichte der Sprachwissenschaft in Deutschland: Vom Mittelalter bis ins 20. Jahrhundert* (Berlin, 1999)

GEHRKE, HANS-JOACHIM, 'Die Bedeutung der (antiken) Historiographie für die Entwicklung des Geschichtsbewußtseins', in *Die antike Historiographie und die Anfänge der christlichen Geschichtsschreibung*, ed. by Eve-Marie Becker (Berlin, 2005), pp. 29–51

GEITH, KARL-ERNST, *Carolus Magnus: Studien zur Darstellung Karls des Großen in der deutschen Literatur des 12. und 13. Jahrhunderts*, Bibliotheca Germanica, 19 (Berne, 1977)

GELLINEK, CHRISTIAN, 'The German Emperors' Chronicle: An Epic Fiction?', *Colloquia Germanica*, 5 (1971), 230–36

——— *Die Kaiserchronik: Erzähltechnik und Kritik* (Frankfurt a. M., 1972)

GERTZ, SUNHEE KIM, *Poetic Prologues: Medieval Conversations with the Literary Past*, Analecta Romanica, 56 (Frankfurt a. M., 1996)

GOERLITZ, UTA, *Literarische Konstruktion (vor-)nationaler Identität seit dem Annolied: Analysen und Interpretationen zur deutschen Literatur des Mittelalters (11.–16. Jahrhundert)*, Quellen und Forschungen zur Literatur- und Kulturgeschichte, 45 (Berlin, 2007)

——— '(Un-)Wahrheit und (Nicht-)Erinnern: Erzählen ze diute in der frühmittelhochdeutschen "Kaiserchronik"', in *Damnatio in Memoria: Deformation und Gegenkonstruktionen in der Geschichte*, ed. by Sebastian Scholz, Gerald Schwedler, and Kai-Michael Sprenger, Zürcher Beiträge zur Geschichtswissenschaft, 4 (Berlin, 2014), pp. 225–42

GOETZ, HANS-WERNER, *Das Geschichtsbild Ottos von Freising*, Beihefte zum Archiv für Kulturgeschichte, 19 (Cologne, 1984)

GRAU, ANNELIESE, *Der Gedanke der Herkunft in der deutschen Geschichtsschreibung des Mittelalters: Trojasage und Verwandtes* (Leipzig, 1938)

GRAZIOSI, BARBARA, *Inventing Homer: The Early Reception of Epic* (Cambridge, 2002)

GREEN, DENNIS HOWARD, *Medieval Listening and Reading: The Primary Reception of German Literature 800–1300* (Cambridge, 1994)

GRÉGOIRE, R., 'Bernhard von Clairvaux, Leben und Wirken', in *Lexikon des Mittelalters*, ed. by Robert-Henri Bautier, Gloria Avella-Widhalm, and Robert Auty, 10 vols (1980–99), I (Munich, 1980), cols 1992–94

GRUNDMANN, HERBERT, *Geschichtsschreibung im Mittelalter* (Göttingen, 1965)

HASKINS, CHARLES HOMER, *The Renaissance of the Twelfth Century* (Cleveland, 1967)

HAUBRICHS, WOLFGANG, 'Theodiscus, Deutsch und Germanisch — drei Ethnonyme, drei

Forschungsbegriffe: Zur Frage der Instrumentalisierung und Wertbesetzung deutscher Sprach- und Volksbezeichnungen', in *Zur Geschichte der Gleichung 'germanisch-deutsch': Sprache und Namen, Geschichte und Institutionen*, ed. by Heinrich Beck and others, Ergänzungsbände zum Reallexikon der Germanischen Altertumskunde, 34 (Berlin, 2004), pp. 199–228

HAUG, WALTER, *Literaturtheorie im deutschen Mittelalter: Von den Anfängen bis zum Ende des 13. Jahrhunderts* (Darmstadt, 1992)

HELLGARDT, ERNST, 'Dietrich von Bern in der deutschen "Kaiserchronik": Zur Begegnung mündlicher und schriftlicher Traditionen', in *Deutsche Literatur und Sprache von 1050–1200: Festschrift für Ursula Henning zum 65. Geburtstag*, ed. by Annegret Fiebig and Hans-Jochen Schiewer (Berlin, 1995), pp. 93–110

HENGEL, MARTIN, 'Heilsgeschichte', in *Heil und Geschichte: Die Geschichtsbezogenheit des Heils und das Problem der Heilsgeschichte in der biblischen Tradition und in der theologischen Deutung*, ed. by Jörg Frey, Stefan Krauter, and Hermann Lichtenberger, Wissenschaftliche Untersuchungen zum Neuen Testament, 248 (Tübingen, 2009), pp. 3–36

HERWEG, MATHIAS, 'Kohärenzstiftung auf vielen Ebenen: Narratologie und Genrefragen in der "Kaiserchronik"', *Zeitschrift für Literaturwissenschaft und Linguistik*, 47.2 (2017), 281–302

HEYSE, ELISABETH, 'Homer, I: Lateinisches Mittelalter', in *Lexikon des Mittelalters*, ed. by Robert-Henri Bautier, Gloria Avella-Widhalm, and Robert Auty, 10 vols (1980–99), v (Munich, 1991), cols 109–10

HILDESHEIMER, WOLFGANG, *Marbot: Eine Biographie* (Frankfurt a. M., 1981)

HIRT, JENS, *Literarisch-politische Funktionalisierungen: Eine Untersuchung mittelhochdeutscher Kreuzzugsdarstellungen: 'Wilhelm von Wenden', 'Die Kreuzfahrt des Landgrafen von Thüringen', 'Wilhelm von Österreich' und 'Das Buch von Akkon'*, Göppinger Arbeiten zur Germanistik, 766 (Göppingen, 2012)

HORN, HANS-JÜRGEN, 'Origenes, Cassian, der vierfache Schriftsinn und seine Beziehung zu ontologischen Vorstellungen des Platonismus', in *Platonismus im Orient und Okzident*, ed. by Ralf Georges Khoury and Jens Halfwassen (Heidelberg, 2005), pp. 49–60

HYDE, JOHN KENNETH, 'Medieval Descriptions of Cities', *Bulletin of the John Rylands Library*, 48 (1966), 308–40

JANOWSKI, BERND, 'Vergegenwärtigung und Wiederholung: Anmerkungen zu G. von Rads Konzept der Heilsgeschichte', in *Heil und Geschichte: Die Geschichtsbezogenheit des Heils und das Problem der Heilsgeschichte in der biblischen Tradition und in der theologischen Deutung*, ed. by Jörg Frey, Stefan Krauter, and Hermann Lichtenberger, Wissenschaftliche Untersuchungen zum Neuen Testament, 248 (Tübingen, 2009), pp. 37–62

JANTSCH, HEINZ, *Studien zum Symbolischen in frühmittelhochdeutscher Literatur* (Tübingen, 1959)

JARNUT, JÖRG, 'Die Entstehung des mittelalterlichen deutschen Reiches als Forschungsproblem', in *Zur Geschichte der Gleichung 'germanisch-deutsch': Sprache und Namen, Geschichte und Institutionen*, ed. by Heinrich Beck and others, Ergänzungsbände zum Reallexikon der Germanischen Altertumskunde, 34 (Berlin, 2004), pp. 255–64

JENTZMIK, PETER, *Zu Möglichkeiten und Grenzen typologischer Exegese in mittelalterlicher Predigt und Dichtung* (Göppingen, 1973)

KARTSCHOKE, DIETER, *Geschichte der deutschen Literatur im frühen Mittelalter* (Munich, 2000)

KERN, MANFRED, 'Titus', in *Lexikon der antiken Gestalten in den deutschen Texten des Mittelalters*, ed. by Manfred Kern and Alfred Ebenbauer (Berlin, 2003), p. 620

——— 'Vespasian', in *Lexikon der antiken Gestalten in den deutschen Texten des Mittelalters*, ed. by Manfred Kern and Alfred Ebenbauer (Berlin, 2003), pp. 669–71

KESSLER, ECKHARD, 'Das rhetorische Modell der Historiographie', in *Formen der Geschichtsschreibung*, ed. by Reinhart Koselleck, Heinrich Lutz, and Jörn Rüsen, Beiträge zur Historik, 4 (Munich, 1982), pp. 37–85

KINNEY, DALE, 'Fact and Fiction in the "Mirabilia Urbis Romae"', in *Roma Felix —* *Formation and Reflections of Medieval Rome*, ed. by Carol Neuman de Vegvar and Éamonn Ó Carragáin (Abingdon, 2008), pp. 235–52

—— 'The Discourse of Columns', in *Rome Across Time and Space: Cultural Transmission and the Exchange of Ideas c. 500–1400*, ed. by Claudia Borgia and others (Cambridge, 2011), pp. 182–99

KLOPSCH, PAUL, *Einführung in die Dichtungslehren des lateinischen Mittelalters* (Darmstadt, 1980)

—— 'Vergil im Mittelalter, I: Lateinische Literatur', in *Lexikon des Mittelalters*, ed. by Robert-Henri Bautier, Gloria Avella-Widhalm, and Robert Auty, 10 vols (1980–99), VIII (Munich, 1997), cols 1522–26

Kluge: Etymologisches Wörterbuch der deutschen Sprache, 25th edn, ed. by Elmar Seebold (Berlin, 2011)

KOCH, KLAUS, 'Das aramäisch-hebräische Danielbuch: Konfrontation zwischen Weltmacht und monotheistischer Religionsgemeinschaft in universalgeschichtlicher Perspektive', in *Die Geschichte der Daniel-Auslegung in Judentum, Christentum und Islam*, ed. by Katharina Bracht and David du Toit, Beihefte zur Zeitschrift für die alttestamentliche Wissenschaft, 371 (Berlin, 2007), pp. 3–30

KOCH, W., 'Invocatio', in *Lexikon des Mittelalters*, ed. by Robert-Henri Bautier, Gloria Avella-Widhalm, and Robert Auty, 10 vols (1980–99), V (Munich, 1991), cols 483–84

KOSELLECK, REINHART, *Futures Past: On the Semantics of Historical Time* (Cambridge, MA, 1985)

KRAUTHEIMER, RICHARD, *Rome: Profile of a City, 312–1308* (Princeton, 1980)

LAMMERS, WALTHER, *Weltgeschichte und Zeitgeschichte bei Otto von Freising*, Sitzungsberichte der wissenschaftlichen Gesellschaft an der Johann Wolfgang Goethe-Universität Frankfurt am Main, 14.3 (Wiesbaden, 1977)

LASKER, DANIEL, *Jewish Philosophical Polemics against Christianity in the Middle Ages* (New York, 1977)

LAUSBERG, HEINRICH, *Handbuch der literarischen Rhetorik: Eine Grundlegung der Literaturwissenschaft* (Munich, 1960)

LEXER, MATTHIAS, *Mittelhochdeutsches Handwörterbuch*, 3 vols (Leipzig, 1872–78)

LIENERT, ELISABETH, *Die historische Dietrichepik: Untersuchungen zu 'Dietrichs Flucht', 'Rabenschlacht' und 'Alpharts Tod'* (Berlin, 2010)

LIEU, SAM, 'Constantine's "Pagan Vision": The Anonymous Panegyric on Constantine (310): Pan. Lat. VII(6): Introduction', in *From Constantine to Julian: Pagan and Byzantine Views*, ed. by Samuel Lieu and Dominic Montserrat (London, 1996), pp. 63–76

LONG, BURKE, *The Problem of Etiological Narrative in the Old Testament*, Beihefte zur Zeitschrift für die alttestamentliche Wissenschaft, 108 (Berlin, 1968)

LORENZ, CHRIS, 'Kann Geschichte wahr sein? Zu den narrativen Geschichtsphilosophien von Hayden White und Frank Ankersmit', in *Konstruktion von Wirklichkeit: Beiträge aus geschichtstheoretischer, philosophischer und theologischer Perspektive*, ed. by Jens Schröter and Antje Eddelbüttel (Berlin, 2004), pp. 33–63

LOTMAN, JURIJ MICHAILOWITSCH, 'Vorwort zur deutschen Ausgabe', in *Kunst als Sprache: Untersuchungen zum Zeichencharakter von Literatur und Kunst*, ed. by Klaus Städtke (Leipzig, 1981), pp. 7–19

LUTZ, ECKART CONRAD, *Rhetorica Divina: Mittelhochdeutsche Prologgebete und die rhetorische Kultur des Mittelalters* (Berlin, 1984)

MACMULLEN, RAMSAY, *Christianizing the Roman Empire: A.D. 100–400* (New Haven, 1984)

MALECZECK, W., 'Eugen III., Papst', in *Lexikon des Mittelalters*, ed. by Robert-Henri Bautier, Gloria Avella-Widhalm, and Robert Auty, 10 vols (1980–99), IV (Munich, 1989), cols 78–80

MATTHEWS, ALASTAIR, *The Kaiserchronik: A Medieval Narrative* (Oxford, 2012)

MCAFEE MOSS, CHARLENE, *The Zechariah Tradition and the Gospel of Matthew*, Beihefte zur Zeitschrift für die neutestamentliche Wissenschaft und die Kunde der älteren Kirche, 156 (Berlin, 2009)

MEIJER, FIK, *Emperors Don't Die in Bed*, trans. by S. J. Leinbach (London, 2004)

MELVILLE, GERT, 'Durch Fiktionen von der Wirklichkeit zur Wahrheit: Zum mittelalterlichen Umgang mit Widersprüchen zwischen Empirie und kultureller Axiomatik', in *Fiktion und Fiktionalität in den Literaturen des Mittelalters: Jan-Dirk Müller zum 65. Geburtstag*, ed. by Ursula Peters and Rainer Warning (Paderborn, 2009), pp. 83–104

MIEDEMA, NINE, *Die Mirabilia Romae: Untersuchungen zu ihrer Überlieferung mit Edition der deutschen und niederländischen Texte*, Münchener Texte und Untersuchungen zur deutschen Literatur des Mittelalters, 108 (Tübingen, 1996)

MILDE, VERA, 'si entrunnen alle scentlîchen dannen: Christlich-jüdischer Disput in der Silvesterlegende der "Kaiserchronik"', in *Juden in der deutschen Literatur des Mittelalters: Religiöse Konzepte — Feindbilder — Rechtfertigungen*, ed. by Ursula Schulze (Tübingen, 2002), pp. 13–34

MILLET, VICTOR, 'Das 12. Jahrhundert und die Heldensage', in *Aspekte des 12. Jahrhunderts: Freisinger Kolloquium 1998*, ed. by Wolfgang Haubrichs, Eckart Conrad Lutz, and Gisela Vollmann-Profe, Wolfram-Studien, 16 (Berlin, 2000), pp. 256–81

Mittelhochdeutsche Begriffsdatenbank, ed. by Universität Salzburg (1992–2017) <http://www.mhdbdb.sbg.ac.at/> [multiple accesses]

MULDER-BAKKER, ANNEKE, 'A Pantheon Full of Examples: The World Chronicle of Godfrey of Viterbo', in *Exemplum et Similitudo: Alexander the Great and Other Heroes as Points of Reference in Medieval Literature*, ed. by W. J. Aerts and M. Gosman, Mediaevalia Groningana, 8 (Gröningen, 1988), pp. 85–98

MÜLLER, STEPHAN, *Vom Annolied zur Kaiserchronik: Zu Text- und Forschungsgeschichte einer verlorenen deutschen Reimchronik* (Heidelberg, 1999)

MÜLLENBURG, MARCEL, BRITTA MÜLLER-SCHAUENBURG, and HENRIK WELS, 'Und warum glaubst du dann nicht? Zur ambivalenten Funktion der Vernunft in Religionsdialogen des 12. Jahrhunderts', in *Integration und Desintegration der Kulturen im europäischen Mittelalter*, ed. by Michael Borgolte and others, Europa im Mittelalter, 18 (Berlin, 2011), pp. 261–324

MURPHY, JAMES, *Rhetoric in the Middle Ages: A History of Rhetorical Theory from Saint Augustine to the Renaissance* (Berkeley, 1974)

NAUMANN, BERND, 'Ein- und Ausgänge: Frühmittelhochdeutsche Gedichte und die Predigt des 12. Jahrhunderts', in *Studien zur Frühmittelhochdeutschen Literatur: Cambridger Colloquium 1971*, ed. by Leslie Peter Johnson and others (Berlin, 1974), pp. 37–57

NELLMANN, EBERHARD, *Die Reichsidee in deutschen Dichtungen der Salier- und frühen Stauferzeit*, Philologische Studien und Quellen, 16 (Berlin, 1963)

—— 'Annolied', in *Verfasserlexikon*, 14 vols (Berlin, 1978–2008), I, ed. by Kurt Ruh (1978), cols 366–71

NEUDECK, OTTO, 'Karl der Große — Der beste aller werltkunige: Zur Verbindung von exegetischen Deutungsmustern und heldenepischem Erzählen in der "Kaiserchronik"', *Germanisch-Romanische Monatsschrift*, 53 (2003), 273–94

NEWALD, RICHARD, *Nachleben des antiken Geistes im Abendland bis zum Beginn des Humanismus: Eine Überschau* (Tübingen, 1960)

NEWMAN, BARCLAY, and PHILIP STINE, *A Handbook on the Gospel of Matthew* (Stuttgart, 1988)

NOLLAND, JOHN, *The Gospel of Matthew: A Commentary on the Greek Text* (Milton Keynes, 2005)

NOTH, MARTIN, 'Der Beitrag der Archäologie zur Geschichte Israels', in *Congress Volume:*

Oxford 1959, ed. by G. W. Anderson and others, Vetus Testamentum: Supplements, 7 (Leiden, 1960), pp. 262–82

OHLY, ERNST FRIEDRICH, *Sage und Legende in der Kaiserchronik: Untersuchungen über Quellen und Aufbau der Dichtung* (Darmstadt, 1940; repr. 1968)

—— 'Wolframs Gebet an den Heiligen Geist im Eingang des Willehalm', *Zeitschrift für deutsches Altertum und deutsche Literatur*, 91 (1961–62), 1–37

—— 'Gebet an den Heiligen Geist', in *Wolfram von Eschenbach*, ed. by Heinz Wupp, Wege der Forschung, 62 (Darmstadt, 1966), pp. 455–518

—— 'Außerbiblisch Typologisches zwischen Cicero, Ambrosius und Aelred von Rievaulx', in *Schriften zur mittelalterlichen Bedeutungsforschung* (Darmstadt, 1983), pp. 336–60

—— 'Halbbiblische und außerbiblische Typologie', in *Schriften zur mittelalterlichen Bedeutungsforschung* (Darmstadt, 1983), pp. 361–99

—— 'Synagoge und Ecclesia: Typologisches in mittelalterlicher Dichtung', in *Schriften zur mittelalterlichen Bedeutungsforschung* (Darmstadt, 1983), pp. 312–38

—— 'Skizze zur Typologie im Mittelalter (1979)', in *Ernst Friedrich Ohly: Ausgewählte und neue Schriften zur Literaturgeschichte und zur Bedeutungsforschung*, ed. by Uwe Rüber and Dietmar Peil (Stuttgart, 1995), pp. 509–54

—— 'Typologie als Denkform der Geschichtsbetrachtung (1983)', in *Ernst Friedrich Ohly: Ausgewählte und neue Schriften zur Literaturgeschichte und zur Bedeutungsforschung*, ed. by Uwe Rüber and Dietmar Peil (Stuttgart, 1995), pp. 445–72

—— 'Typologische Figuren aus Natur und Mythus (1979)', in *Ernst Friedrich Ohly: Ausgewählte und neue Schriften zur Literaturgeschichte und zur Bedeutungsforschung*, ed. by Uwe Rüber and Dietmar Peil (Stuttgart, 1995), pp. 473–508

OPITZ, KAREN, *Geschichte im höfischen Roman: Historiographisches Erzählen im Eneas Heinrichs von Veldeke*, Beihefte zur Germanisch-Romanischen Monatsschrift, 14 (Heidelberg, 1996)

PARTNER, NANCY, *Serious Entertainments: The Writing of History in Twelfth-Century England* (Chicago, 1977)

PETERSEN, CHRISTOPH, 'Zeit, Vorzeit und Narrativierung von Geschichte in der "Kaiserchronik"', *Zeitschrift für deutsche Philologie*, 126 (2007), 321–53

PETERSOHN, JÜRGEN, *Kaisertum und Rom in spätsalischer und staufischer Zeit: Romidee und Rompolitik von Heinrich V. bis Friedrich II.*, MGH Schriften, 62 (Hanover, 2010)

PÉZSA, TIBOR FRIEDRICH, *Studien zu Erzähltechnik und Figurenzeichnung in der deutschen 'Kaiserchronik'*, Europäische Hochschulschriften: Reihe I, 1378 (Frankfurt a. M., 1993)

POHL, MONIKA, 'Untersuchungen zur Darstellung mittelalterlicher Herrscher in der deutschen "Kaiserchronik" des 12. Jahrhunderts: Ein Werk im Umbruch von mündlicher und schriftlicher Tradition' (unpublished doctoral dissertation, Ludwig-Maximilians-Universität München, 2004)

RADER, OLAF, *Friedrich II.: Der Sizilianer auf dem Kaiserthron: Eine Biographie* (Munich, 2010)

REUTER, TIMOTHY, 'Past, Present and No Future in the Twelfth-Century Regnum Teutonicum', in *The Perception of the Past in Twelfth-Century Europe*, ed. by Paul Magdalino (London, 1992), pp. 15–36

RUBEL, ALEXANDER, 'Caesar und Karl der Große in der "Kaiserchronik": Typologische Struktur und die translatio imperii ad Francos', *Antike und Abendland*, 47 (2001), 146–63

RÜSEN, JÖRN, 'Die vier Typen des historischen Erzählers', in *Formen der Geschichtsschreibung*, ed. by Reinhart Koselleck, Heinrich Lutz, and Jörn Rüsen, Beiträge zur Historik, 4 (Munich, 1982), pp. 514–605

SCHEUNEMANN, ERNST, 'Kaiserchronik', in *Verfasserlexikon*, ed. by Wolfgang Stammler and Karl Langosch, 5 vols (Berlin, 1933–55), II (1936), 732–46

SCHIMMELPFENNIG, BERNHARD, *Die Zeremonienbücher der römischen Kurie im Mittelalter* (Tübingen, 1973)

SCHMITT, CARL, *Political Theology: Four Chapters on the Concept of Sovereignty*, trans. by George Schwab (Cambridge, MA, 1985)

SCHNEIDMÜLLER, BERND, 'Ludwig VII., Kg. v. Frankreich', in *Lexikon des Mittelalters*, ed. by Robert-Henri Bautier, Gloria Avella-Widhalm, and Robert Auty, 10 vols (1980–99), v (Munich, 1991), cols 2183–84

SCHRAMM, ERNST PERCY, *Kaiser, Rom und Renovatio: Studien zur Geschichte des römischen Erneuerungsgedankens vom Ende des karolingischen Reiches bis zum Investiturstreit* (Darmstadt, 1957)

SCHRECKENBERG, HEINZ, *Die christlichen Adversus-Judaeos-Texte und ihr literarisches und historisches Umfeld*, Europäische Hochschulschriften: Reihe XXIII, 172 (Frankfurt a. M., 1990)

SCHRÖDER, EDWARD, ed., *Die Kaiserchronik eines Regensburger Geistlichen*, MGH Dt. Chron., 1.1 (Hanover, 1895)

SCHULZ, MARIE, *Die Lehre von der historischen Methode bei den Geschichtsschreibern des Mittelalters (VI.–XIII. Jahrhundert)*, Abhandlungen zur mittleren und neueren Geschichte, 12 (Berlin, 1909)

SCHWIETERING, JULIUS, 'Typologisches in mittelalterlichen Dichtungen', in *Philologische Schriften* (Berlin, 1925), pp. 40–55

——— *Die deutsche Dichtung des Mittelalters* (Potsdam, 1932)

SHAW, FRANK, ' "Kaiserchronik" and "Enide" ', *German Life and Letters*, 24.4 (1971), 295–303

——— 'Das historische Epos als Literaturgattung in frühmittelhochdeutscher Zeit', in *Studien zur frühmittelhochdeutschen Literatur: Cambridger Colloquium 1971*, ed. by Leslie Peter Johnson and others (Berlin, 1974), pp. 275–91

SMITS, KATHRYN, 'Zweimal Heraclius: Zu Sprache und Erzählstil der Heraclius-Episode in der "Kaiserchronik" und im "Buoch der künige niuwer ê" ', in *Deutsche Sprache: Geschichte und Gegenwart: Festschrift für Friedrich Maurer zum 80. Geburtstag*, ed. by Hugo Moser and Heinz Wupp (Berne, 1978), pp. 155–67

SPIEGEL, GABRIELLE, 'History, Historicism, and the Social Logic of the Text in the Middle Ages', *Speculum*, 65.1 (1990), 59–86

STACKMANN, KARL, 'Erzählstrategie und Sinnvermittlung in der Deutschen "Kaiserchronik" ', in *Erscheinungsformen kultureller Prozesse: Jahrbuch 1988 des Sonderforschungsbereiches 'Übergänge und Spannungsfelder zwischen Mündlichkeit und Schriftlichkeit'*, ed. by Wolfgang Raible (Tübingen, 1990), pp. 63–82

STENGEL, EDMUND, 'Die Entstehung der "Kaiserchronik" und der Aufgang der staufischen Zeit', in *Abhandlungen und Untersuchungen zur mittelalterlichen Geschichte* (Cologne, 1960), pp. 395–417

STERN, J. P., 'Sweet Sin', *London Review of Books*, 4.14 (1982), 3–6 <https://www.lrb.co.uk/v04/n14/jp-stern/sweet-sin> [accessed 25 October 17]

STOCK, MARKUS, *Kombinationssinn: Narrative Strukturexperimente im 'Straßburger Alexander', im 'Herzog Ernst B' und im 'König Rother'*, Münchener Texte und Untersuchungen zur deutschen Literatur des Mittelalters, 123 (Tübingen, 2002)

SUERBAUM, ALMUT, 'Erzählte Geschichte: Dialog und Dialogizität in der "Kaiserchronik" ', in *Aspekte des 12. Jahrhunderts: Freisinger Kolloquium 1998*, ed. by Wolfgang Haubrichs and others, Wolfram-Studien, 16 (Berlin, 2000), pp. 235–55

——— 'Caesar als Integrationsfigur im Mittelalter?', in *Praktiken europäischer Traditionsbildung im Mittelalter: Wissen — Literatur — Mythos*, ed. by Manfred Eikelmann and Udo Friedrich (Berlin, 2013), pp. 229–43

TAYLOR, JOAN, *The Essenes, the Scrolls, and the Dead Sea* (Oxford, 2012)

THOMAS, HEINZ, 'Julius Caesar und die Deutschen: Zu Ursprung und Gehalt eines deutschen Geschichtsbewußtseins in der Zeit Gregors VII. und Heinrichs IV.', in *Die*

Salier und das Reich: Gesellschaftlicher und ideengeschichtlicher Wandel im Reich der Salier, ed. by Stefan Weinfurter, 3 vols (Sigmaringen, 1991), III, 245–78

TROMPF, GARRY WINSTON, *Early Christian Historiography: Narratives of Retributive Justice* (London, 2000)

TULASIEWICZ, W. F., *Index Verborum zur deutschen Kaiserchronik* (Berlin, 1972)

URBANEK, FERDINAND, 'Zur Datierung der "Kaiserchronik": Entstehung — Auftraggeber — Chronologie', *Euphorion*, 53 (1959), 113–52

——— 'Herrscherzahl und Regierungszeiten in der "Kaiserchronik"', *Euphorion*, 66 (1972), 219–37

VAN EICKELS, KLAUS, 'Ehe und Familie im Mittelalter', in *Geisteswissenschaften im Profil: Reden zum Dies Academicus 2000–2007*, ed. by Godehard Ruppert, Schriften der Otto-Friedrich-Universität Bamberg, 1 (Bamberg, 2008), pp. 43–65

VOLLRATH, HANNA, 'Das Mittelalter in der Typik oraler Gesellschaft', *Historische Zeitschrift*, 233 (1981), 571–94

VON CAMPENHAUSEN, HANS FREIHERR, *Urchristliches und Altkirchliches* (Tübingen, 1979)

VON HOFMANN, JOHANN CHRISTIAN KONRAD, *Weissagung und Erfüllung im Alten und Neuen Testamente: Ein theologischer Versuch*, 2 vols (Nördlingen, 1841–44)

VON MOOS, PETER, 'Poeta und Historicus im Mittelalter: Zum Mimesis-Problem am Beispiel einiger Urteile über Lucan', *Beiträge zur Geschichte der deutschen Sprache und Literatur*, 98 (1973), 93–130

——— *Geschichte als Topik: Das rhetorische Exemplum von der Antike zur Neuzeit und die Historiae im 'Policraticus' Johanns von Salisbury* (Hildesheim, 1988)

WEHRLI, MAX, 'Antike Mythologie im christlichen Mittelalter', in *Max Wehrli: Gegenwart und Erinnerung: Gesammelte Aufsätze*, ed. by Fritz Wagner and Wolfgang Maas, Spolia Berolinensia, 12 (Hildesheim, 1998), pp. 90–104

WESLE, KARL, '"Kaiserchronik" und "Rolandslied"', *Beiträge zur Geschichte der deutschen Sprache und Literatur*, 48 (1924), 223–58

WESTERMANN, CLAUS, *Forschung am Alten Testament*, Theologische Bücherei, 24 (Munich, 1964)

WHITE, HAYDEN, *The Content of the Form* (Baltimore, 1987)

WISSMANN, WILHELM, *Skop*, Sitzungsberichte der deutschen Akademie der Wissenschaften zu Berlin, 2 (Berlin, 1955)

WITTHÖFT, CHRISTIANE, 'Zwischen Wahrheitssuche und Wunderglauben: Die christlich-jüdischen Disputationen der Silvesterlegende in der "Kaiserchronik"', in *Disputation 1200–1800: Form, Funktion und Wirkung eines Leitmediums universitärer Wissenskultur*, ed. by Marion Gindhart and Ursula Kundert, Trends in Medieval Philology, 20 (Berlin, 2010), pp. 291–310

ZUMTHOR, PAUL, *Essai de poétique médiévale* (Paris, 1972)

INDEX

❖